HERBERT HOOVER

Volume Two

Herbert Hoover, 1957 (*Photo by Tommy Weber*)

HERBERT HOOVER

The Postpresidential Years
1933–1964

Volume Two: 1946–1964

GARY DEAN BEST

HOOVER INSTITUTION PRESS
Stanford University, Stanford, California

Hoover Press Publication 275

Library of Congress Cataloging in Publication Data
Best, Gary Dean.
    Herbert Hoover, the postpresidential years, 1933–1964.

    (Hoover Press publication; 275)
    Includes bibliographical references and index.
    Contents: v. 1. 1933–1945—v. 2. 1946–1964.
    1. Hoover, Herbert, 1874–1964.
    2. Presidents—United States—Biography.   I. Title.
    E802.B46 1983   973.91′6′0924 [B]   82-23212
    ISBN 0-8179-7761-9 (set)
    ISBN 0-8179-7741-4 (v. 1)
    ISBN 0-8179-7751-1 (v. 2)

Manufactured in the United States of America

Design by P. Kelley Baker

Contents

Volume Two

9

Back in Harness

lthough the change of occupancy in the White House brought Herbert Hoover into cordial relations with the new administration, it did not alter his role as an evangelist of traditional Republicanism. Increasingly, the former president had come to use the word "conservative" to describe the philosophy he sought to re-establish in the United States. Late in September 1945, he responded to a request from Norman Chandler of the *Los Angeles Times* for an editorial by issuing a new manifesto for Republicans. In that editorial, Hoover argued that "one of the first necessities of successful democratic process is two major political parties." Where democratic government had failed in Europe, this failure was the result of an inability to coalesce into two such major parties. But the two parties, Hoover wrote, must also present real alternative programs and issues, and: "The natural division between men in private life and the natural division between old age and youth is conservatism and radicalism." He continued:

> Today the radicals on the "left" are organized and vigorous. The conservatives on the "right" are unorganized and impotent. The American people need and have a right to organized expression of conservative thought. Being a conservative is not a sin. It is not "fascism" or "reaction." It means today the conservation of representative government, of intellectual freedom and of economic free-

dom within the limits of what does not harm fellow men. It means the conservation of natural resources, of national health, education and employment. A conservative is not allergic to new ideas. He wants to try them slowly without destroying what is already good.[1]

Hoover insisted that the people of the United States deserved "an opportunity to express the conservative point of view" at the ballot box and that a conservative party might eventually "come into power against the radical excesses and the accumulation of errors and blunders which are the inevitable result of long continuance of one party in power." The GOP, therefore, should undertake to represent conservatism "and do it with pride in its principles and in the service it can perform for the country." It should not shrink from the smears that would emanate from the "left" at the use of the term conservative, because the American people would "see through the smears sooner or later." Republicans should disdain the use of the word "liberal," since it had been corrupted beyond utility and distorted to mean the reverse of its original ideals. The socialists and communists, Hoover argued, "have nested in this word until it stinks. Let them have the word. It no longer makes sense."[2]

Certainly Hoover was doing his bit to aid in the expression of conservative thought. Upon learning that a committee of House Republicans was working on a platform or declaration of principles for the party, Hoover sent Congressman Thomas Jenkins a six-point program that included: (1) support for an international organization to prevent future wars; (2) opposition to the collectivism and regimentation "imposed upon the American people by Franklin Roosevelt and its unnecessary enlargement during the war"; (3) the elimination of waste and corruption from the federal government, reduction of the federal work force, re-establishment of solid national finances, and independence of the judiciary; (4) encouragement of private enterprise and opposition to government competition with business, but regulation of business and the right of labor and business to organize; (5) aid to veterans and to "the ill, the aged and the unemployed, and to the constant building up of agriculture"; (6) the removal of trade barriers, except insofar as tariffs were needed to protect the livelihood of American farmers and workers.[3] He also continued his efforts to ensure that conservative ideas would be circulated through appropriate journals of opinion established for that purpose, by obtaining financial support for the magazine *Human Events*, as well as other conservative efforts.[4]

Peace brought new issues along with the continuance of old ones. One new issue was the Truman administration's call for universal military training during peacetime. Hoover was opposed. In April of 1945, the former president conducted a poll of congressmen concerning the issue and found nearly half of both the House and the Senate in favor of deferring the question until after the war had ended, with less than 20 percent in both houses favoring enactment before that time. Hoover was pleased with the sentiment.[5] Later, the unleashing of the atomic bomb upon Japan seemed to him to have destroyed whatever arguments there had been for any type of peacetime conscription. In writing to Senator Taft, Hoover argued for the deferment of college students, at least, under any conscription plan adopted, since the nation's defense in the future would, he said, "depend upon trained engineers, doctors and scientists and men who can undertake public service." However, he told Taft, he assumed "the atomic bomb has blown up the idea of conscription, and certainly it has at least proved the necessity of education for scientists as fast as we can give it."[6]

A harbinger of things to come was a letter from Ferdinand Eberstadt, a veteran of several wartime mobilization agencies, who wrote Hoover and others to solicit their views on reorganization of the military section of the executive branch of the government. The inquiry was at the request of Secretary of the Navy James Forrestal, and it solicited Hoover's views "concerning the essential elements of the military organization which will give promise of most effectively meeting our military responsibilities."[7] This opportunity to perform his initial service to the cause of reorganization of the government, however, was missed by Hoover, as he was away from New York fishing in the West and unable to answer the letter until nearly a month later, by which time Eberstadt had already submitted his report.[8]

In November Hoover took up another issue in a further editorial, which he mailed off to the *Los Angeles Times*. The war, he found, had brought "a new stimulant working among all nations to seek for more self-sufficiency for the future." An increasing number of countries were seeking to make themselves less dependent upon foreign trade. In their development of new industries for that purpose the countries must inevitably seek protective tariffs to encourage and sustain those industries. America would also "experience the stimulus to self-sufficiency." In addition, there would be the problem in the United States caused by the "impoverishment and lower standards of living and wages in many countries." In the event of a recession in the United States, American workers and farmers would oppose the importation of goods produced by the cheaper labor abroad. The war would thus furnish a "double impulse" in reviving "the age-old question of protection" just as had World War I. As president, Hoover had, he said, advocated international cooperation to reduce tariffs, and this had been one motive for calling the World Economic Conference for 1933. Roosevelt had chosen, instead, a policy of bilateral reciprocal trade agreements. But in comparing the Hoover administration with the four years of 1935–1938 under Roosevelt, he found that the average tariff rate in the latter period had been virtually the same as in his own administration, while the percentage of actual imports on which tariffs had applied grew substantially in the Roosevelt years. Hoover argued, therefore, that Roosevelt's promises to reduce tariffs had not been kept and that the reciprocal trade policy had neither increased American foreign trade nor had it preserved peace.[9] He furnished the tariff figures to Congressman Thomas Jenkins, who promised to take them up in a speech on the floor of the House.[10]

Hoover continued to be dissatisfied with the operations of the United Nations Relief and Rehabilitation Agency (UNRRA). In November of 1945, he suggested the creation of a distinctly American organization to handle America's charity in postwar Europe and found support for the idea in Congress.[11] Meeting with a UNRRA representative late in that month, he strongly recommended the strengthening of the organization, especially through the recruitment of experienced American personnel.[12] Early in December he expressed concern that UNRRA should do something to aid Finland, which the American Friends Service Committee had reported was among the critical spots in Europe. He wrote a UNRRA official that even if only $250,000 were sent to Finland "it would save much life and suffering."[13] UNRRA did allocate supplies in the amount of $2.5 million for that country.[14] But in Hoover's view UNRRA was still not operating up to the level of the American Relief Administration (ARA) under his leadership after World War I. As he wrote one correspondent: "U.N.R.R.A. scarcely parallels the A.R.A. We relieved 18 countries and coordinated the food supplies of 9 more with our work. U.N.R.R.A. up to date has given relief to only 5 countries plus the displaced persons. The A.R.A. looked after those also after the last war."[15]

At age seventy-one in late 1945, the former president seemed intent on cutting down his activities. He told John Bricker: "Just 'making a speech' is out of my life hereafter. When I am bursting to say *something*, I look around for a forum."[16] He was disappointed over the lack of interest that Republicans were showing in his proposed declaration of principles.[17] And too much of what was happening in Washington had a through-the-looking glass quality that defied understanding. When he learned of proposals that the United States share the secrets of the atomic bomb with the Soviet Union, he wrote: "Here we are building up a vast military establishment directed to Russia alone; there is no one else to harm us. And now we propose to give her [Russia] military power over us. Why not give her half our fleet?"[18] He derived, however, some satisfaction from the knowledge that a number of books were being written that were not kind to Roosevelt, and he was, himself, keeping three secretaries busy, seven days a week, at work on his own memoirs, which he expected to complete in the spring of 1946.[19]

But in late January, Hoover took time out to write a short piece for the Dutch Treat Club. He suggested, however, that Clarence Kelland put his own name on the piece, since as Hoover put it: "I would never be forgiven for such frivolity." Such "frivolity" deserves quoting:

> Now that we presumably have peace our diplomacy has a real job of converting its pre V-E day promises into the post V-J day realities. It

is doing this job of converting the war output of idealism fairly competently. It is done chiefly with words. The ammunition of diplomacy is words and naturally they have to be bent around difficult corners if they are to make a conversion in such a fashion that nobody will detect them. Some people have wistful notions that diplomatic words, phrases and slogans kept the same meaning for at least a year or two. But that is only the aspiration of iconoclasts or foolish people who don't like ideas all the time slipping from their intellectual grasp. However, it is the sign of a good diplomat to have a genius for changing meanings on us right in the middle of the game. This changing the meaning of words is one of the triumphs of the true art.

For instance, that word "appeasement." It is a term of vile reproach never to be used any more now that Hitler is buried. Moreover, we have to get over the hump of giving something to Joseph Stalin like a "sphere of influence" over 150,000,000 people in a dozen independent nations, all of which cynics might say was appeasement and that it was a violation of the Four Freedoms and the Atlantic Charter. But that is easy. We just call it (Yalta definition) "establishing a broad democratic basis."

We did start the war with a Pied Piper's tune called the Four Freedoms and the Atlantic Charter. It was especially charming to idealists and left wingers. All that was to be applied "everywhere" and was to be the glory of man right after V-E day. But the diplomats lost the charter somewhere on the road to Teheran and at once insisted with eloquence that, like the Ten Commandments and the Sermon on the Mount, it might take 2,000 years to get it over. When the dumb complained that this might be after World War X instead of World War II, diplomacy said, "We shall never recognize any government that did not conform." However, having put the Atlantic Charter and the Four Freedoms a long way off in this diplomatic way, then they decide to recognize various states provided they take two ministers into their Communist governments who "represent broad democratic interest" and who will be cooperative. They haven't yet mentioned that they will have to cooperate with 10 or 15 Communist ministers plus the secret police. However, that phrase fixes everything up beautifully except that these Communists have seized all American property "in the public interest." We will, no doubt, get over that hump by crediting it on Lend–Lease or something. Another example of preparing us for the worst with words was when our diplomats vested the Communists with the command of the underground in half a dozen nations. They did not like the sound the [word] Communist would make in the United States so they called them "partisans."

Also, when Soviet Russia annexed the economic and moral control of Manchuria, the same as she had done before the Japanese took it away from her forty years ago, the diplomats called it "re-establishing Chinese authority." When Dictator Vargas of Brazil proclaimed his Fascist government he was called "a democratic leader" by our diplomats who also said it was "the firm policy of the United States never to interfere in the domestic affairs of other nations." But when Dictator Peron appeared in Argentina, our Ambassador tried to upset him because he is a "fascist."

Perhaps some suggested definitions might help.

"Appeasement" — giving away something that belongs to somebody else.

"Cooperation" — giving away something that belongs to somebody else.

"Democracy" — now includes single-party government secret police to educate the voters.

"A Dictator" — depends on who he is.

"Open covenants openly arrived at"—when they are opened up later on.[20]

When President Truman appealed to the American people to save food in order that a surplus might be provided to meet the famine overseas, Hoover issued a statement on February 9, 1946 supporting the appeal and asking that it "be supported by the whole American people." Truman's statement, Hoover agreed, was "backed up by innumerable investigations and reports," and the shortages affected "the supplies available for import by Britain, France, Belgium, Holland and Norway as well as Central and Eastern Europe, India and China." Hoover called for the "organization of special food to undernourished children and mothers over the whole of Europe, including Germany," to combat the high infant mortality rate. "Peace and progress," he pointed out, "will not be restored if those who survive are to be infected by a generation of men and women stunted in body and distorted in mind." He expressed confidence that the need for increased food exports could be met entirely by "voluntary action to eliminate waste and unnecessary consumption and . . . without compulsory rationing," since the voluntary approach had worked during World War I.[21] Hoover's statement, his secretary confided, had resulted from the fact that Landon's release in support of Truman had been "pretty poor."[22]

The former president was also lending his support to Senator J. William Fulbright's effort to get the U.S. government to underwrite intellectual exchanges between the United States and other nations. Responding to a request from Fulbright for his views, Hoover wrote that he supported the proposal and went on to describe the work in that field of the Belgian–American Educational Foundation under his leadership, as well as his own efforts, as secretary of commerce and president, to establish such exchanges with ten countries, using war debts for financing.[23] Fulbright believed the former president's support would be "very helpful in the consideration of the bill" and he said he

hoped that "this time we have more success in persuading our own government to promote this program." He asked Hoover to testify in behalf of his bill
before the Senate committee considering it, but the former president was to be
in Florida on a fishing trip on the date of the hearings.[24] Meanwhile, Hoover
was continuing to promote the cause of international understanding in his own
way, by launching a major effort to collect documents in Europe for the
Hoover War Library.[25]

Before he left for his fishing trip, Hoover addressed Republicans at the
Lincoln Day dinner of the National Republican Club in New York City. In a
nationally broadcast speech, the former president declared:

> Today the great issue before the American people is free men against
> the tide of Statism which is sweeping three-quarters of the world—
> whether it be called Communism, Fascism, Socialism or the dis-
> guised American mixture of Fascism and Socialism called "Man-
> aged Economy" now being transformed into a further ambiguity,
> the "Welfare State." This growth of statism has been nourished by
> the confusion of a great war. And it can grow still more by continued
> excessive taxation and by creeping inflation.

The purpose of two-party government was not to gain office, Hoover said, but
to "give the people an opportunity to determine fundamental issues at the
ballot box rather than elsewhere." But the voters were not being given a
choice, since both parties had "straddled" on the issues. The Republican party
and the American people needed "a fundamental and constructive philosophy
of government with the principles which flow from it." That philosophy
"must reach far deeper than the froth of slogans or platform planks designed to
appease every pressure group." Since the writing of the Constitution and the
Declaration of Independence, the industrial revolution had profoundly affected American life, so that "the concept of freedom must include government
regulation of economic life." Government must always remain the "umpire
and mediator" and not the dictator or operator of the economy. The gigantic
growth in area and population since the time of the founding fathers, also
posed a thousand new problems that they had not anticipated. These problems, however, must be solved by a philosophy based on "the concept that man
can accomplish more by cooperation outside the government than by coercion
from the government." Hoover told his listeners:

> There are fields where cooperation can be properly aided by govern-
> ment, but government swollen with power and laden with burdens
> becomes something above and apart from the governed. It becomes
> the enemy of the governed, increasing its prerogatives with fanatical
> zeal.

> To delineate the appropriate boundaries of the government
> which preserve such a philosophy and principles is the task of the
> statemanship for which this country is waiting.

Government must stimulate the initiative of men and their moral rectitude, while statism, on the contrary, strangled and undermined these things.[26]

Hoover's fishing trip in the Florida Keys was not to last for very long. On February 25, 1946, Secretary of Agriculture Clinton Anderson phoned for the former president in New York City only to learn that Hoover was in Florida. Anderson left a message that he was anxious to meet with Hoover to discuss the civilian food conservation program and the problem of relief for Europe. The situation was considered so urgent that Anderson offered to send "a special plane—land or amphibious—to wherever he [Hoover] might be to take him to Washington and to return him to Florida." According to a memorandum of the phone conversation, Anderson said: "Mr. Hoover had always been very helpful to him, had given him the best advice he had ever received last July, and that everything Mr. H. had told him at that time had worked out as HH said it would." Anderson said that he did not want "to move in this problem without Mr. Hoover's knowledge and advice."[27]

Hoover responded the next day with a telegram advising against any committee organization outside of the government, such as Anderson seemed to be proposing, and argued that the secretary of agriculture should have all control over food consolidated under him. He had given similar advice in the past only to have it ignored; it should be followed now. In Hoover's view, "only an official of cabinet rank and an existing organization can organize and direct the quick campaign that is needed now because shipments from the United States after the end of June will be of no avail in this famine and it is thus already very late to start." He suggested immediate steps to combat hoarding and waste and unnecessary consumption, and gave measures to encourage substitution of foods as well as control over food exports and imports. The next step, Hoover advised, was to conduct a survey of the amounts and types of food that were in surplus in the world, and "how much of each kind you can and should export from the United States without injury to public health." He could not, he said, advise on this latter phase of the problem since "it would require me to do exhaustive investigations at home and abroad and I assume you already have such information." The former president then suggested that a national organization, modeled after his own World War I U.S. Food Administration, be formed, with state and county food administrators to encourage conservation and the use of substitute foods.[28]

Anderson arranged to have Hoover picked up by a Navy plane and brought from Florida to Washington. The former president arrived in Washington on February 28 looking "tanned and fit." He called for Americans to voluntarily eat less, eliminate waste, and use substitutes in order to help relieve the starving abroad.[29] Hoover then met with Truman, Anderson, and others. Hugh Gibson wrote to his wife:

> It is a pity this step was not taken at the time we went down [to Washington] last year. The Chief told him everything that was going to happen just as it has happened since, and made [Truman] a memorandum of suggestions as to what steps should be taken. Needless to say, none of them have been taken and the situation has got rather out of hand.[30]

The meeting resulted in the creation of the Famine Emergency Committee (FEC), with Herbert Hoover as the honorary chairman. The committee, composed initially of twelve civic leaders, called for a 25 percent reduction in the consumption of wheat and wheat products and all possible savings of food, oils, and fats. The committee was to work through hotels, restaurants, and industry groups to formulate conservation measures. President Truman called the meeting "the most important meeting, I think, we have held in the White House since I have been President." Hoover expressed confidence that the American people would respond to calls for voluntary conservation, describing the United States as "the last reservation from which starvation can be halted." The committee, he said, was calling for "a four-months sacrifice by the American people" in order to hold "together Western civilization against chaos." He insisted that Germany, Austria, and Japan would have to be included in the relief program, not only for humanitarian reasons but for the safety of American occupation troops in those countries.[31]

Things moved rapidly thereafter. Gibson did not at first derive much hope from the FEC, feeling that "none of them seem to have the wisdom that is needed to lay down a program and put it over to the people."[32] Hoover, too, did not believe that much would result, since he found Truman to be not very bright and seemingly incapable of grasping the points he had tried to make.[33] But soon there was talk in Washington that Hoover would be asked to journey to Europe to make a survey of the situation. On March 5, Gibson wrote his wife:

> What a day! This morning I was called out of bed by a telephone call from the Chief in Washington. He said that the President had just sent the Secretary of Agriculture to see him to ask if he would undertake to do a flying trip all over Europe and prepare a report on the food situation. He accepted on the spot. Of course the trip should have been made when he first suggested it last May, but he did not take the trouble to rub that in.[34]

A humorous sidelight on Hoover's renewed involvement in relief is furnished by Will Irwin's description of the reaction of the director of the New

York play *Lute Song*, to the former president's appearance in the audience after his trip to Europe was announced. According to Irwin:

> On the first New York night of Lute Song I stood in the back of the house waiting for the curtain to go up on the first act. The director stood beside me. "You see that bulky man on the center aisle, eighth row?" I asked. "That's Herbert Hoover." "Do you know if there are any of those aeroplane safety straps in the house?" he asked. "Why?" I asked. "Because I want to send an usher to strap him to his seat before the second act opens," said the director. "If I don't, he'll dive over the footlights and relieve that famine and there won't be any more show!"[35]

On the more serious side, Hoover's contacts with the president in connection with the FEC led him to conclude that Truman was a mediocrity such as had never previously occupied the White House. Hoover despaired that anything constructive could be accomplished by such a man in either foreign or domestic affairs.[36]

By mid-March it had become clear that the Hoover itinerary would not be limited to Europe, but would be broadened to circle the globe, since as Gibson put it: "The food problem is global and . . . it ought to be attacked on a world scale."[37] Hoover was recommending to Anderson that "aside from anything we can do in the United States in conserving food by human beings and animals, the greatest possibility of further covering the gap in supplies lies in mobilizing the Latin American states to join with us in conservation, reduction of imports, and expansion of their exports where they have such."[38] On the eve of his departure for Europe, the former president received a warm telegram from labor leader John L. Lewis:

> On the eve of your departure to aid the suffering peoples of other lands I extend the greetings of an old friend with earnest wishes for your complete success and a safe return to your own country. You are undertaking a task which no other citizen has the wisdom or ability to perform, yet I am sure you will succeed and will be followed by the blessings of the millions whom you succor. As a duty to your fellow citizens and as a favor to your friends, please conserve your strength and safeguard your health on your arduous journey.[39]

Hoover was 71 years old and already burdened with a cold he had caught in the course of his flight north from Florida.

The formation of the FEC, with Herbert Hoover as its head, was a clear repudiation by the Truman administration of UNRRA and Herbert Lehman. As one study has noted, Lehman had already grown disturbed over the lack of cooperation by the American government with UNRRA, and the formation of the FEC under Hoover "only confirmed Lehman's resolution to resign." According to the study's author, Milton Gustafson:

> He [Lehman] felt that the problem could not be solved by a committee, especially one headed by an old isolationist. When Truman asked Hoover to make a world-wide survey of food needs—including countries already expertly surveyed by UNRRA—Lehman correctly assumed that the United States was moving toward relief controlled strictly by the United States.[40]

It was certainly true that the international approach to relief symbolized by the UNRRA efforts was being rejected by the United States, but it was more than an issue of international versus national control of relief. Also at issue was the destination of American food supplies. In his meeting with President Truman on May 28, 1945, Hoover had argued that the parts of Europe under Soviet domination should be left to the USSR to feed, and he found Truman in agreement. Yet European food relief under UNRRA was going largely to countries within the Soviet zone of influence, and under the UNRRA agreement the Soviet Union was not only free from any responsibility for furnishing food supplies, but could, as an invaded country, ask for UNRRA aid.[41]

Lehman tendered his resignation as head of UNRRA at the meeting of the UNRRA council in Atlantic City in mid-March. Lehman called Hoover's plea for voluntary food conservation "most praiseworthy and sure to lead to substantial results," but felt that voluntary efforts would be insufficient and government controls would doubtless have to be instituted. Lehman also called for feeding the Allies first and the defeated enemies last, a stance that was at variance with Hoover's position. Meanwhile, the UNRRA officials showed their own concern for food relief and conservation by each breakfasting on three slices of toast, one corn muffin, one roll, cereal, fruit, bacon or ham and eggs, and coffee.[42] If all showed that level of cooperation with the food conservation effort, then Lehman's prediction of its insufficiency would doubtless be validated.

On March 16, Hoover appealed over nationwide radio for Americans to conserve food in order to avert famine for 500 million people. Congresswoman Clare Boothe Luce spoke on the same radio program and made a similar appeal.[43] Hoover then flew to Europe for the first leg of his around-the-world food survey. In Paris he again expressed opposition to food rationing, arguing that the American people would respond to a call for service. He told reporters: "This is the most prodigious call they have ever received in history, and I am sure they will answer it magnificently."[44] Herbert Lehman disagreed and called for rationing, but it was the former president whose views were now prevailing in food relief matters. On March 26, the FEC rejected rationing, and two days later President Truman expressed his opposition as well.[45]

In April, however, Truman seemed to become somewhat dubious that the food conservation program was taking hold in the United States. He asked Hoover to interrupt his world trip and return to the United States to make speeches to stir up support for food conservation; but Hoover refused to do so unless ordered.[46] While in Cairo the former president talked to Truman over the telephone and convinced him that the trip should go on.[47] Instead of returning to the United States to give speeches, Hoover broadcast a speech to the United States from Cairo as part of a joint program with President Truman, new UNRRA head Fiorello LaGuardia, and Secretary of Agriculture Clinton Anderson. In his speech, Hoover described the plight of the Europeans and outlined a program of international action for dealing with the problem. That program included a voluntary reduction in American consumption of bread to 200 grams per day as part of a general reduction in consumption of wheat products by 40 percent and of fats by 20 percent, and a reduction to 300 grams per day in European countries where there were fewer substitutes than in America for wheat products. He also proposed that the British release half of their breadstuff reserves, some 500,000 tons, for food relief, and that Latin American nations reduce their food imports by 40 percent during the next four months. The Soviet Union should also export 300,000 to 400,000 tons of grain during the four crisis months. He also called for priority in relief to the newly liberated countries, which had suffered the most and whose domestic resources were more limited than the other European countries. Hoover concluded:

> The burden will be heavy on the American people, but we cannot do more than this. Europe and other countries must look to other sources for the balance of their food. This present world crisis is unique among all crises of history. For this crisis has a definite terminal date. That date is the arrival of the next harvest. It is therefore a short pull. If every source of supply were scraped to the bottom of the barrel we can pull the world through this most dangerous crisis, and the saving of these human lives is far more than an economic necessity to the recovery of the world. It is more even than the path to order and to stability and to peace. Such action marks the return of the lamp of compassion to the world. And that is part of the moral and spiritual reconstruction of the earth.[48]

After stops in Asia, Hoover returned to the United States early in May, only to find the relief program faced with disruptions that would be created by a scheduled nationwide transportation strike. Reading a prepared statement at a press conference, the former president told reporters that if the proposed

railroad strike occurred it would "be a holocaust." He told the gathering that
the world was "faced with the greatest potential famine in all human hsitory"
and noted that there was only a 30- to 60-day supply of food in the 27-nation
famine area, while the next harvest was still five months away.[49]

On May 12, Hoover phoned Rickard in New York and communicated his
despair over the situation in Europe.[50] The next day Hoover and his team sent
their report to President Truman. They noted that

> We have traveled some 35,000 miles, visited twenty-two countries
> which have a deficiency of food, and informed ourselves of the situa-
> tion in several others . . . The dominant need of the world in this
> crisis is cereals, particularly wheat and rice. There is great need of
> fats and special food for children, but as cereals can furnish 85
> percent of an emergency diet, we considered cereal requirements
> were the first concern, and the best indicator. . . . At the time of our
> departure, the Combined Food Board's estimate of the available
> cereal supplies from surplus countries showed a deficit as compared
> with stated requirements of 11,000,000 tons, or 43 percent.

Hoover's team had found an estimated need of nearly 14.5 million tons. Their
estimate of the total probable supply was slightly less than 10.9 million tons,
leaving a gap of 3.6 million tons, rather than the 11 million tons that had
earlier been estimated. Furthermore, they believed there was a "possible"
supply of about 1.5 million tons more. They were, therefore, confident that
with rigorous conservation in surplus countries through the end of August,
and better cooperation between nations, the deficit would be overcome. "The
cooperation of Russia and the Latin American states," they suggested, "would
greatly aid in meeting the problem."[51] The former president obviously considered Latin America important to the success of the fight against famine, and
while in Europe he had discussed with the Pope the possibility of enlisting
Latin American support for that effort.[52]

For the next few days the press was filled with speculation about the
possibility of food rationing, with Hoover's opposition to rationing in favor of
voluntary conservation given prominent play.[53] On May 15, Truman responded to the Hoover mission and report by writing the former president that
he recognized "that the collection of the basic facts had been an arduous and
difficult task" and that Hoover and his group had "provided a great service to
your country and to humanity in making it possible for each of us to know
better the extent of world distress and to measure the magnitude of our
responsibilities."[54] He also asked the former president to go to South America
for a further survey, and Hoover consented.[55] The following day, Truman and
Hoover met, and Hoover suggested a telegram to Stalin encouraging the Soviet

Union to participate in the relief effort. According to Hoover's account of the conversation:

> In the course of conversation, the President mentioned his difficulties with the Russians. I told him that there was only one method of treating the present group of Russians and that was with a truculent spirit. They treated us that way and we should be truculent. Even if he were to present a gold watch, it should be presented in a truculent mood. It would be more highly appreciated.[56]

Rickard found the former president looking well and alert after his around-the-world trip and pleased with his success in having found food in unexpected places like Egypt and Iran.[57]

A few days later, Hoover left once again at the president's bidding, this time for the tour of Latin American countries. One newspaper wrote:

> His departure comes only a few days after he concluded an intensive round-the-world study of the food situation at the behest of the White House. Mr. Hoover's willingness to undertake these arduous assignments underscores both his deep patriotism and his high qualifications. The former President could not reasonably have been criticized had he politely refused. He is past 70 and the mere physical strain of an odyssey such as he recently completed would tax the strength of younger men not to mention the effort required to obtain and appraise the desired data. Few men in public life have been so shamefully abused and ruthlessly smeared for selfish ends, and Mr. Truman, whatever his merits in his own right, is the successor or political heir of the man who inspired the attacks. The fact that Mr. Hoover was requested to do the food survey job is the best testimony possible to his preeminence in this field. It emphasized again both the lack of qualified men in the present administration and the petty vindictiveness of the Roosevelt administration in failing to avail itself of his services throughout 12 years of real or fancied emergencies including the very real and tragic crisis of war.[58]

In late June, Hoover returned from a 25-day food survey of Latin America, which elicited promises from the countries there of over two million tons of food to help fight the world famine. Argentina had been especially cooperative.[59] This led Hoover to intervene with Truman concerning the low state of U.S. relations with Latin America, especially Argentina. The trip, however, had taken its toll on the former president. While in Caracas he had slipped in the bathtub, causing a contusion in his back.[60] A few days after his return, Hoover wrote to a friend: "Every molecule in my body yells at me that it is tired. I am just going away for a rest."[61]

From the time of his February press release supporting the president's plea for voluntary food conservation, Hoover had been active through press releases, speeches, and reports seeking to rally public support for the relief effort. In what he hoped would be his last effort in behalf of the food mission, he spoke in Ottawa, Canada, in a broadcast over the Canadian Broadcasting Company on June 28. It was, he told the Canadians, his "final report upon my food mission to 38 nations." He thanked the Canadians for their contribution to solving the world food problem, noting that four nations—Canada, the United States, Argentina, and Australia—had taken up 90 percent of the "overseas burden of relief to this, the greatest famine in all human history." He had "traveled some 50,000 miles visiting all of the important famine and food-deficit areas in the world and all of the major food-surplus areas except-ing South Africa and Australia" and had "discussed crops, animals, calories, rations, stocks, ships, railroads, supplies and hunger with the Presidents, the Prime Ministers, the food officials of each of these nations." His function, Hoover said, had "been mostly advisory—or perhaps persuasive would be a better word," and he was "deeply indebted for the most extraordinary wel-come and cooperation accorded to me and my associates."[62]

As a result of that cooperation, he concluded that the danger of mass starvation had been averted everywhere but in China, "where transportation to the interior and inadequate organization has rendered relief only partially successful." The problems elsewhere, however, were not over. He warned: "The war-devastated areas will not have fully recovered their ground crops nor have restored their flocks and herds during the next year," and the "food situation of the world in the next year will not be easy, but next year in my view will not be one of such dreadful crisis and drastic regimens as the one which we are now in." World food agencies were being consolidated under an International Emergency Food Council of the United Nations. He was con-cerned, however, especially with the food requirements of children, and he suggested that special efforts be made by the new agency to furnish a higher caloric intake to the young: "We cannot have recovery of civilization in nations with a legacy of stunted bodies or distorted and embittered minds."[63] This latter recommendation would lead to the creation of UNICEF.

Hoover's recommendations concerning the organization of the famine relief on the home front were now largely being followed under the direction of Chester Davis, operational head of the FEC. Under the FEC there were now local famine emergency committees and retail famine committees, housewife pledges, and even a youths' auxiliary famine emergency organization. The effort was designed to continue until at least the harvest in August.[64] A complication arose in July when President Truman, faced with a bill extend-ing the Office of Price Administration, which contained terms he would not accept, vetoed the bill and allowed the price controls of OPA to expire on July 1, 1946. Hoover was disappointed, for he had, he told Chester Davis, "secured substantial modifications" in Congress of the legislation in order to meet the president's objections.[65]

While the former president was performing distinguished service for the Truman administration in solving the famine problems of the world, he was opposed to much of the president's early foreign policy. On the last day of 1945, Hoover wrote O'Laughlin to describe the agreements reached by Secretary of State James Byrnes with the Soviet Union as "the last installment of appeasement." In Hoover's view, the United States had, in all of its dealings with the Russians "appeased every time at the expense of the liberty and freedom of more and more human beings."[66] The former president had tried to stiffen Truman's attitude toward the Soviet leaders, as in his meeting with the president after the European food survey, but apparently with little success. In the summer of 1946 he still regarded foreign relations as "half of our national problems," and as part of his effort to enhance Bricker's national stature he suggested that Bricker go to Europe after his election to the Senate, since "it would not only be most informative for you, but would be a great help to the country in handling these problems. It would place you in a position to speak authoritatively."[67]

As Hoover looked ahead to the 1948 presidential race, he was also looking back at the mistakes that he considered had been made in the past. Previous Republican candidates (the "Republican New Deal leaners" was Hoover's description of them) had won fewer total votes than local GOP candidates in 1940 and 1944, which to the former president meant that "people went to the ballot box, voted for the local Republican candidates, but believed that, as a choice of New Dealers, they preferred Roosevelt." In Hoover's view, the GOP needed in 1948 a "candidate who will stand up and fight the whole pack" of New Dealers and their communist and fellow-traveler allies. "I believe we could have won before on this line," he wrote a friend, "and I am even more sure of it now."[68] Hoover was also seeking to build General Douglas MacArthur as a potential candidate. In mid-October 1946, Hoover suggested to the general that he could perform "a service to this country comparable to that of John the Baptist when he came out of the wilderness," if he would make three speeches across the country.[69] MacArthur, however, felt that he could not do so as long as he was an active-duty army officer, and that his presence was required in Japan.[70]

Probably because of the relief effort, Hoover rarely took a partisan position in 1946 after being called to service by President Truman. But he remained on the attack where other issues were concerned. In his birthday statement in August, Hoover warned: "The dismemberment of the German state and the attempt to reduce the German people to a level of perpetual poverty will some day break into another world explosion." Reviewing the state of freedom in the world, he found: "Far from freedom having expanded from this war, it has shrunk to far fewer nations than a quarter of a century ago. And in addition there are at least 15,000,000 in concentration or forced-labor camps who are slaves in every sense of the word. Several scores of millions more are practically serfs." He warned of the depletion in American reserves and equipment as a result of the war and outlined three major policies that the United States should follow:

> In the economic field we must now conserve our resources, improve our equipment and reduce our spending. We must end our role of Santa Claus. Now that world famine No. 2 is about over we should announce that our economic relations with other nations are a two-way street. And balanced traffic at that.
> In national defense we should hold the atomic bomb until there is real cooperation for lasting peace, which must include general disarmament in the world—Allies as well as enemy countries. . . .
> We should devote ourselves to cooperation in the U.N. to maintain peace, and to do so appeasement must cease. To hold up the banner of the world we should at all times assert the principles of the Atlantic Charter for which we fought the war and to which all other nations pledged themselves. . . .[71]

Two weeks later, after a Yugoslav attack on American aircraft, Hoover observed that the attack seemed "like a pretty poor return" for the American assistance given to that nation through UNRRA, but added that the people of that nation should not be blamed since they were kept in ignorance by their communist government. He added that the United States should halt any further relief shipments to that country until free elections were held. He charged that the communists were eliminating dissidents in the areas under their control. In free elections they could gain only a small minority of the vote in those countries.[72] The Yugoslav official newspaper attacked Hoover for his statement, suggesting that he do his job better in relieving famine "and leave political questions alone."[73]

Yet, while the former president was unsympathetic to the Soviet Union's defensive aims in establishing control over the east European perimeter nations, he was quick to advocate a similar move by the United States in the Pacific. Late in August 1946, Hoover argued for American retention of the Pacific islands liberated from the Japanese by the U.S. forces "because we must extend our perimeter of defense." He argued that the United States could not be accused of imperialism since it was not economic interests that were sought. "We are simply looking after our own defense and the defense of the world."[74] Secretary of the Navy James Forrestal expressed public support for Hoover's position.[75]

Hoover took no role in the 1946 campaign, but predicted a GOP landslide. When Republicans swept into control of both houses of Congress for the first time since 1928, he told the press that it had "been much more than just another Congressional election." He explained:

> The whole world, including the United States, has been for years driving to the left on the totalitarian road of "planned economy." America is by this election the first country to repudiate this road.
>   And it defines that the Republican Party is the party of the right. We are again moving to the goal of free men. This decision of the United States will have a profound effect on nations which have been following along the road to the left.[76]

European newspapers were quick to see in the Republican victory and in Hoover's statement the possibility that American economic policy might now be used to strengthen conservative parties in Europe against leftists through the strategic use of credits and other devices.[77]

A short time later Hoover followed up his first reaction to the Republican victory by noting further that the election represented a demand by the country that "this creeping collectivism be swept into the sewer." Both political parties, he argued, now needed "to expel those who are so minded that they can take their title from the Moscow heaven instead of Yorktown." Hoover now laid down the legislative steps that he considered necessary to reverse the collectivist trend in America. To begin with, all the war powers and war agencies needed to be repealed and liquidated, thus ridding America of "half a million bureaucrats." Next, income taxes should be reduced by 20 percent, and twice that sum should be cut from expenditures. The third step must be "to relieve the people of labor tyrannies." The right to strike, Hoover asserted, was "no more unlimited a right than the right of free speech is unlimited—we must find a way of relieving our economy from the blight of [work] stoppages or we shall send ourselves again into the morass of depression that will end recovery from this war for years." The next step was to "dig out the Communist infiltration into our government and expose it to daylight." Finally, the misdeeds of government officials must be exposed. In foreign affairs, the problem was "communist imperialism," which had annexed 50 million people and put puppet governments over another 100 million, while being represented in the cabinets of countries totaling another 150 million. But there was a positive sign, Hoover noted. The American government "about six months ago abandoned appeasement and has put up some resistance. It should be stiffened even more, because it is only toughness that they understand." The United States must remain armed, "especially in the air," and keep the atomic bomb.[78]

Late in 1946, the food relief situation did not show the expected improvement. While America now had food to export, the difficulty lay with transportation. Maritime strikes had thrown shipments behind schedule, and a shortage of railroad boxcars was making it unlikely that shipments would reach the level sought. There were also difficulties with financing exports to certain countries that were under the jurisdiction of UNRRA. All of these difficulties were outside the scope of the FEC's responsibility. As Chester Davis wrote to Hoover, there was very little that the FEC could do about the labor situation and it was therefore in a "stand-by" status.[79] Hoover agreed that the responsibility of the FEC was to promote food conservation and that transportation difficulties were outside its jurisdiction. Therefore, he suggested that the committee "just ought to be moribund until something turned up." He added that there was one aspect of relief about which he had "strong feelings," and this was that the United States must never again "place control of its famine relief outside its own control as in UNRRA or any other international body. Whatever we do should be done directly by us—for humane reasons to avoid political use, and to get far more efficiency."[80]

Hoover reiterated this view in a letter to President Truman on December 3. The placing of American food relief under foreign control, he argued, could "only end in foreign control of American farmers' prices and production." He also repeated his belief that American food must be sold, even if on credit, rather than be given away: "However insecure the credit may be, the requirement ultimately to pay is the only real check on wasteful demands and wasteful distribution." Government charity ought to be ended, except for children, and government credits also ought to end except to prevent actual starvation.[81]

As Republicans prepared to take control of the House and Senate, the former president began to receive requests for his views on possible labor legislation.[82] On December 12 he met with congressional leaders to discuss the subject, and on December 21 he wrote to Senator Taft that he was glad Taft had taken the chairmanship of the Senate Labor Committee. He had, he told Taft, received requests from Congressman Charles Halleck and others for his views on labor legislation. He recalled for Taft his experience with attempts to settle labor problems as secretary of commerce, including the Railway Mediation Act of 1926. The central idea in that legislation had been a mediation commission to intervene if a strike were imminent:

> Upon failure of bargaining, mediation, conciliation and arbitration, an Emergency Commission of disinterested persons is appointed to investigate and declare a fair settlement with stay of strikes for 30 days for the Mediation Board to act, and an additional 30 days for the Emergency Commission to act. . . . This central idea appears in the Case bill to be applied to all public utilities. I have long thought, and there is in my opinion daily confirmation, that this is the right line in checking upon strikes.

He had added some new ideas on possible legislation, without absolutely prohibiting the right to strike, and had sent these to Congressman Christian Herter, who was having them drafted into legislative form. The ideas, however, had not originated with Hoover.[83]

Hoover expressed his general views, too, in a short article for *This Week* magazine at the end of the month. The American people, he wrote, must "work more efficiently than ever before and thus restore their lost wealth" if they hoped to recover from the war. They must also adopt new laborsaving devices and inventions and discoveries in order to "increase the productivity of each individual and of the nation." Strikes would only defeat the purpose and retard economic and social recovery. Hoover decried the new philosophy of striking, under which some labor leaders now seemed to believe "that this weapon [striking] can be employed for political and ideological purposes and that it can be used so as to injure and endanger the people at large that in their misery they or the government will be forced to do the strikers' bidding." A dozen men had risen to power in the labor movement through the use of this tactic, he charged, and now wielded "power over the lives and living of the people greater than the government." Such strikes must have prompt settlement, through the use of collective bargaining and mediation and, if those failed, "the judicial machinery of the country should be given power and penalties to end any strike which the President, through the Attorney General, declares constitutes a danger to large numbers of American people." The American people, Hoover wrote, now faced the responsibility of mastering "the difficult art of working together." Only if they succeeded could the country get on with the production through which America could recover from the war and remain "strong, prosperous and free."[84]

In mid-January the former president was again asked by the administration to make a foreign trip, this time to Germany. Hoover agreed to do so, provided he could make his findings public, but he did not believe that Truman would consent.[85] However, on January 18, 1947, President Truman asked him in writing to make the trip. The situation was better than in the previous year, the president admitted, but "a serious situation in food still exists in certain areas, particularly those in Europe occupied by our forces and for which we therefore have a direct responsibility."[86] Hoover responded the following day that he wished to be of service, but he thought that the purpose of the trip should be broadened beyond a mere survey of food needs. It would, he pointed out, "come as a great shock to our people that the American taxpayer for a second year must expend huge sums to provide money for the enemy peoples," and he believed that his mission should also inquire into what might be done in Germany to increase exports and thus enhance the German ability to become "self-supporting." Without some such report, indicating when American charity could be expected to end, "the Congress and the taxpayer are left without hope."[87] Three days later the former president traveled from New York to Washington for a talk with Truman. The two men agreed on the "formula" that made Hoover's trip an economic mission devoted to food and its collateral problems.[88]

The 1947 mission was of shorter duration and covered only Germany and Austria. But Hoover was approaching his seventy-third birthday, and flying in an unpressurized DC4 airplane he suffered a hearing impairment that would lead to the loss of his hearing and force him to wear a hearing aid.[89] Upon his return, he confided to Edgar Rickard that as a consequence of unheated hotels and conference rooms he had never been warm at any time during the three-week trip.[90] On March 18, Hoover submitted his report to President Truman, which contained his "conclusions upon the problem of reviving German industry and thus exports with which to relieve American and British taxpayers from their burden in preventing starvation in Germany." Hoover noted that American and British taxpayers were contributing nearly $600 million a year to fight famine in the American and British occupation zones and said that the "drain is likely to be even greater after peace unless the policies now in action are changed." There was, he argued, "only one path to recovery in Europe" and that was production. The European economy was so "interlinked" with that of Germany that "the productivity of Europe cannot be restored without the restoration of Germany as a contributor to that productivity."[91]

The Allied "level of industry" policy, adopted in March 1946, called for the reduction and removal of Germany's heavy industrial plants and the reduction of her industry to a level capable of maintaining in Germany the average European standard of living. Hoover argued that the policy was destructive of European economic recovery, for it not only slashed fertilizer production, which affected Germany's ability to produce food, but it also reduced her production of items she had previously exported to the point where she was now forced to import many of them. Germany needed heavy industry, since the light industries could never, in Hoover's view, "be expanded to a point where she will be able to pay for her imports." He suggested a "new economic concept in peace with New Germany." It consisted of four items:

> (1) We should free German industry, subject to a control commission, which will see that she does no evil in industry, just as we see that she does not move into militarism through armies and navies. The difference between this concept and the "level of industry" concept is the saving of several hundred millions of dollars a year to the American and British taxpayers. It is the difference between the regeneration and a further degeneration of Europe.
> (2) The removal and destruction of plants (except direct arms plants) should stop.

(3) A further obstacle to building Germany as an essential unit of European economy arises from the Russian Government's acquiring a large part of the key operating industries in their zone. Germany in peace must be free from ownership of industry by a foreign government. Such ownership can thwart every action of control or of up-building by joint action of other nations. German industry must be operated by Germans if any international control is to work, if she is to recover production and is to serve all nations equally.

(4) There can be no separation or different regime of the Ruhr or Rhineland from the New Germany. That is the heart of her industrial economy.

Hoover called for "a quick and sound" peace settlement in Germany, but if the Soviet Union (and perhaps France) would not cooperate, he advocated that "the Anglo–American zones should abandon the destruction of plants, the transfer of plants for reparations and the 'level of industry' concept, and start every plant, 'heavy' as well as 'light,' which can produce non-arms goods." This alone would relieve American and British taxpayers of the continued burden of feeding the Germans and would also "do infinitely more for Europe than American loans and charity." If the Soviet Union and France would not cooperate in the economic unification of the four zones, then a "self-sustaining economic community" should be built "out of the Anglo–American zones alone."[92] In August a new, higher "level of industry" was fixed for the Anglo–American zones, and the movement, already begun, for economic unity of the two zones was stepped up.[93]

Meanwhile, in late February, Hoover had testified before the House Committee on Foreign Affairs in behalf of Truman's request for $350 million to be used for relief assistance and had also conferred with Secretary of State George Marshall concerning forthcoming ministerial talks in Moscow.[94] He also told Senator Arthur Vandenberg that if the United States gave aid to Greece, it should forthrightly state that the assistance was being given to save that country from communism.[95] Again, in mid-March, Hoover spent three days in Washington, appearing behind closed doors before several committees dealing with the European economic and food problems.[96] The former president had suggested amendments to the $350 million relief appropriation, some of which had been adopted, but he continued to press for others, including the designation in the bill of the countries to be assisted, so that the bill would not be "blank-check legislation." He also sought provision in the bill that all or most of the supplies purchased with the appropriation be American-produced commodities; that purchase of goods be by U.S. government agencies rather than by the recipient governments; that the money received by the foreign governments from sale of the goods to their people be held in the countries on deposit for the United States; that any surpluses in these countries from the 1947 harvest be delivered to American representatives in exchange for the release of the equivalent funds on deposit to the account of the United States; limitations on shipment of relief supplies to Poland, Italy, China, and Hungary after the 1947 harvest, since these countries offered the prospect of self-sufficiency or surplus by that time; and he sought that "no relief shall be given to countries maintaining military establishments which, in the view of the President, are beyond the requirement to maintain public order."[97]

Hoover continued to support the appropriation, while simultaneously pressing for adoption of his amendments. In April Senator Vandenberg wrote the former president after his testimony before the Senate Foreign Relations Committee: "I shall submit your complete program of suggestions to the Committee. We shall collide with heavy opposition at certain points. On others the State Department (at my *urgent* request) has shown some disposition to approve your ideas." He was sure that with Hoover's amendments added it would be "a *better* Bill."[98] When the appropriation passed, Major General William H. Draper, Jr., Economic Advisor to the Headquarters, European Command, wrote Hoover: "There is no question in my mind that your report on food saved the day for our deficiency appropriation and I hope will prove equally effective with respect to the 1948 appropriation. Both Germany and all of those interested in the attainment of American objectives in Europe owe you a deep debt of gratitude."[99]

The following month, Hoover was consulted on the similar economic paralysis in Japan. Responding to a request for his views, the former president wrote to the secretary of war, Robert Patterson:

> At the outset I wish to say that when I think of the white crosses over tens of thousands of American boys in the Pacific and the millions of butchered Chinese, I sympathize emotionally with Draconian measures of punishment. But when we look to the real interest of the United States and the future peace of the world, we must confine punishment to the war leaders and realize that we must live with this 80,000,000 people.

Hoover's advice for Japan was similar to that he had given concerning Germany, namely, "that there must be a revolutionary change in the whole concept of 'levels of industry,' 'plant removals' for reparations and destruction of peace industry plants, if the Japanese people are to produce enough exports to pay for their food and other necessary imports, or become a stable and peaceable state." The policies in force, he suggested, were based partly upon inadequate data at the time they were made. Hoover made two suggestions: (1) allow as reparations only the machine tools and equipment from factories that could not be converted to peacetime production; assess the value of other plants and compel Japan to pay the value over a period of years as reparations while retaining the factories; (2) eliminate the concept of "levels of industry" entirely and replace it with "a few absolute prohibitions such as monopolies, arms manufacture, aircraft construction, speed (but not size) of ships, and install a general watch to see that industry is devoted to peace-time production." As with Germany, Hoover viewed the recovery of Japan as an aid to the recovery of her neighbors, and as the only way to get Japan "off the back of the American taxpayer." Hoover concluded:

> Finally, may I say that what the world needs today above all things is recovered peace-purpose productivity. The United States does not possess the strength to bear the deficient productivity which now dominates industry all over the world. Chains on any productive area are chains on the whole world. We need a larger vision of the primary basis of world peace which is productivity. Otherwise there will be a disintegration of Western Civilization everywhere.[100]

A few days later, the former president wrote Secretary of State George C. Marshall, enclosing a copy of the letter to Patterson. He could not, said Hoover, "too strongly express my anxiety over the situation in both Germany and Japan. In my view they are the major fronts of Western Civilization. If the ideologic front is lost in Germany all Western Europe and even the Near East is lost. The Japanese is [sic] the real ideologic dam against the march of Communism in Asia." He recommended that Germany and Japan have "priority over shipments of food to any other country." American occupation of those countries, he argued, imposed a special responsibility upon the United States, and the food levels were so low in these two countries that they could "only promote frustration at our efforts in democratization," as well as extend the burden upon the American taxpayer. He closed by assuring Marshall that he perhaps understood "the burdens upon you more fully than any other person."[101] Marshall responded that additional wheat supplies were being sent to Germany, which he believed met Hoover's suggestion regarding Germany, and that Japan was being considered, "but there appears to be a little more time for decision." He would, Marshall told the former president, keep him advised and "it may be that I will have to call on you for some assistance."[102]

The outlines for Hoover's next major contribution of public service were already beginning to develop. In September 1945, the former president offered to support President Truman's efforts to obtain authority from Congress for a reorganization of the executive branch of the government. To O'Laughlin, Hoover wrote that he was willing to send "a letter to somebody in the Senate or House" in support of the legislation that Truman sought if such action was considered desirable.[103] On October 1, 1945, he wired Congressman George Bender:

I have your request for my views on HR-4129 giving authority to President Truman to reorganize the executive departments. The bill provides a sensible procedure and makes the proper exceptions and I favor it. Six successive presidents over 35 years have recommended such reorganization. The overlap, waste, and conflict of policies between executive agencies have been a scandal for the whole 35 years.[104]

The president responded that he was grateful to Hoover for sending him, through O'Laughlin, a copy of his letter and telegram to Bender. "The fight for this measure," he told the former president, "has been long and futile," and he found it "heartening to know that you approve the bill in principle."[105]

The proposal, however, made little progress, and in January 1947 the Republicans, as majority party in Congress, proposed their own methods of governmental reorganization. Congressman Clarence J. Brown of Ohio introduced a reorganization bill in the House and wrote to Hoover requesting his view on the subject. Hoover responded:

I do not know how many dozen commissions have been invited by Congress and by every President since Taft to make recommendations for consolidation and improvement of the government and executive branches. The reason all these failed is because they had no real power. If a commission were set up with the power to issue orders, it might be worthwhile, but without the power to correct the matter it is just no use. Once during my administration I requested from the Congress authority to make these changes by executive order, provided there was no Congressional disapproval for a period of 30 days during which the order was to be tabled. Even this power was not granted. Where changes must be ratified by the Congress it has been impossible to reconcile the differences arising over new proposals of any kind—and that has been the sad state of affairs for 40 years. If you want to reorganize the government give the President the power to do it, or give a joint Congressional committee the power to do it, or some independent committee the power to do it, but you will never see any real changes if they are subject to ratification by Congress.[106]

Brown responded to Hoover's comments by writing that he had "had somewhat of the same thoughts on the subject as you have expressed and am mindful of the difficulty involved in getting such authority from Congress." He suggested as a first step that a study be made, which would then be followed by the granting of authority to "some individual or group to carry out the findings and recommendations of the commission."[107]

As Brown's bill began its desultory path through Congressional hearings, the problem of America's overseas economic commitments began to loom larger and larger in Hoover's thinking. Nearly two years earlier, with the war barely won in September 1945, the former president had addressed the Executives' Club of Chicago on the question of postwar foreign loans. He told the gathered executives that he favored "such financial assistance under safeguards and defined fiscal policies," but if the United States acted "without wisdom and without regard to experience, far from curing the ills of the world, we will make them worse." He reviewed for them the history of American financial assistance to Europe during and after World War I, and drew two great lessons from the experience: "The first is the moral and emotional coloring matter which infiltrates into these war and postwar financial transactions between governments; and second, there are certain economic phenomena which lie inherently in them." Under the first lesson, Hoover described the "coloring matter of the European view," which was "that they had saved us from destruction by Kaiser Wilhelm; that they had held the line alone for two years defending us; that our sacrifice of blood and treasure was much less than theirs; and that, therefore, we still owed them something," as contrasted with the American "coloring," which was that the United States had entered the war to save the democracies from defeat, that "we had made a great sacrifice to save the Allies and that we had continued these sacrifices in the debt settlements." The result was that the debt question became a political issue in Europe, with the "national visage" of the United States "changed from a great idealistic nation, crusading for the right, to that of Uncle Shylock." Such a situation, he said, must be avoided after this war.[108]

Under the second lesson, Hoover noted that except for "some proportionately small movement of gold and services, these sums [debts] must in the end be translated into movement of commodities." Large quantities of imports in payment of foreign debts would "tend to create unemployment in the United States by displacing our workmen ... Aside from the economic difficulties involved, they naturally consider any opposition by us to receiving unlimited goods from them in repayment as justification for ceasing payments." Moreover, such large-scale lending to other nations did not stimulate international goodwill. As Hoover pointed out: "Our greatest failure was Italy, where our government made over a billion [dollars] of war loans and 800 million [dollars] of postwar loans for reconstruction. She repaid less than four percent of even the reconstruction loans, and ultimately declared war on us."[109]

From this Hoover drew two conclusions:

> First: When our government makes postwar loans in excess of a few tens of millions, they are only going to be partly repaid at best.
> Second: Loaning money is a poor road to international friendship. Despite all this, there is the one over-riding necessity. We want

to aid our allies to recover, and we want within all of our capacities to help them.

The former president proposed a twelve-point program: (1) declare a world-wide moratorium on all intergovernmental war debts for five years, and then join with the Allies "in settling the disposition of all these debts," while insisting "that all weapons that we have sent on lend–lease should be destroyed"; (2) consider all further requests for assistance from the standpoint of "how much further burdens we can assume to aid others and still remain solvent"; (3) take the time to ascertain the actual needs of borrowing nations; (4) make loans only for specified productive purposes; (5) promote the exchange of surplus commodities among those nations that possessed them; (6) reduce all financial assistance to statements in terms of commodities that might be purchased in the United States, thus assuring the employment of Americans in producing the commodities; (7) require that in exchange for assistance the recipient nations impose "no quotas against us, no discriminatory tariffs against us, no dumping of goods upon us, no cartel operations against us," and promise "that no propaganda against the American system of life will be carried on." After listing the other points, Hoover concluded that while the United States must help, it must also keep its feet on the ground and "limit our help to what our taxpayers can afford. We should consider our own employment. We should organize our aid so as to minimize any ill will that might arise over these transactions."[110]

Much of Hoover's concern in his reports and recommendations to the Truman administration on Germany and Japan in 1946–47 had been with ways and means to liberate American taxpayers from the enormous load they were bearing in connection with the relief of those countries. Those worries were increased with the enunciation of the Truman Doctrine in early March of 1947 and with the president's request for a $400 million appropriation to assist Greece and Turkey. Increasingly, beginning in May 1947, the former president was consulted concerning the nation's capacity for undertaking the commitments that the Truman administration was asking of it.[111] In May, Congressman John Taber, chairman of the House Appropriations Committee, queried Hoover concerning the $725 million appropriation being sought by the War Department for relief of Germany, Japan, and Korea in the next fiscal year. Hoover replied on May 26 that the appropriation should be approved. "These enormous sums," he wrote Taber, "are inescapable for the next year unless millions of people under our flags are to die of starvation." But steps must be taken to "bring these burdens upon our taxpayers to an end." The difficulty lay, Hoover argued, in the "delay by Russia in making peace with Germany and Japan, together with the Allied policies of reparations and industrial demilitarization," which had "paralyzed the industrial productivity of these nations" so that they were "unable to make substantial exports and are not contributing, as they otherwise could, to their own support."[112]

Again Hoover suggested that if Russia and France would not implement with the United States and Britain the economic unification of Germany provided for under the Potsdam agreement, then the latter two countries should proceed alone to "set up the economy of the bizonal area so as to restore their industrial production and exports" and should insist that the French zone be incorporated into the bizonal area. Hoover also suggested the possibility of a separate peace treaty with a German government established over this bizonal area if "the next conference of Foreign Ministers does not succeed in more constructive policies." The reparations and demilitarization policies must be revised in both Germany and Japan, suspending the whole concept of "levels of industry," and placing restrictions only on "a few specified industries, such as shipping and aviation." He recommended summoning "at once" a "peace conference with Japan" to "make a peace with her by as many nations as wish to adhere." The whole world was suffering, Hoover insisted, because of the delay in the recovery of productivity in these two nations since "the whole world is an interlocked economy, and paralysis in two great centers of productivity is a world disaster." He added: "There has been announced an American policy of defending the frontiers of Western Civilization. The most vital of these frontiers are Germany and Japan. If they are lost, all Europe and the Far East are lost." The Soviet Union was obviously obstructing recovery for as long as it could in the hope that "the United States can be bled white by relief measures. We should wait no longer. Russia will not make war about it." Concluding, the former president called for "coordination of all aid which we are extending for relief and reconstruction abroad," since the "resources of the United States are not unlimited and we are carrying over 90% of these burdens." The United States could not get cooperation from abroad "unless there is coordination of our own organization at home so as to make American aid to other nations conditional upon their cooperation to the common end. I am talking about the American taxpayer, about mutual economic action and not about dollar diplomacy."[113]

Late in May, Hoover traveled to Washington for several days, during which time he met with GOP congressmen. When he returned to New York, Rickard found him pleased with the reception he had received in Washington and with the press comments on his letter to Taber.[114] The Truman administration, however, was not quite so appreciative of some of the former president's suggestions. While Secretary of State Marshall expressed gratitude for Hoover's support of the relief appropriations in Congress, he was not happy that Hoover had taken a position in favor of separate peace treaties without first consulting with the State Department. However, John Callan O'Laughlin, in passing along Marshall's sentiments to the former president, noted that "it is significant in view of the closeness of his relations with the Michigan Senator [Vandenberg] that the latter, in his remarks in the Senate today, advocated the proposal you had made in your letter to Mr. Taber. Which would seem to indicate that Marshall had come to the conclusion that it would be helpful for Vandenberg to support your view."[115] From Secretary of War Robert Patterson also came words of appreciation for Hoover's assistance in getting the relief appropriation through Congress. Patterson wrote that "in your recent testimony and press statement, supporting so effectively our request for the funds necessary to carry this work on through the fiscal year, you have done everything that one man can do, and more than any other living man would be able to do, in giving aid to the War Department toward the successful discharge of this responsibility."[116]

The secretary of state's enunciation of the Marshall Plan at the Harvard University commencement in early June led to new requests for Hoover's views concerning the "capacity of the United States to continue its aid to the world, and, at the same time, to effectively meet the continuing problems involved in achieving a sound domestic economy."[117] Hoover sent eight suggestions to Senator Styles Bridges in the middle of the month: (1) that all U.S. foreign economic relations must be under a single coordination; (2) that excessive exports must be prevented in order to avoid inflation; (3) if necessary to prevent famine, the United States should increase its export surplus of food by voluntary conservation and alteration of some trade practices; (4) the government should monitor the amounts of goods and services that could safely be exported and limit purchases of commodities by curbing gifts and loans; (5) the government should prepare to stockpile for defense certain surplus commodities from abroad, thereby aiding those nations economically by the purchases; (6) that countries receiving American aid should be required to cooperate with the United States in measures to reduce the relief burden, promote productivity, and bring about peace; (7) the United States should attach conditions to gifts and loans related to security and inspection of use; and (8) resources should be concentrated in areas where Western Civilization could be preserved.[118] Bridges wrote the former president a few days later that his office had received "a fine response" to the exchange of letters between them.[119] Senator Taft wrote that Hoover's letter "certainly expresses my views, and I hope we can follow it up."[120]

Hoover's response to the Marshall Plan was less than enthusiastic. As he expressed his views to O'Laughlin, his conduit to the State Department:

> Perhaps you can clear up a few mysteries for me. Why issue an invitation to Europe to gang up on the United States? Why ask Russia to join them in view of the Truman doctrine which was a flat declaration of a Western civilization bloc? Why this sudden switch? Do they realize that the first necessity of economic recovery is peace

in Europe? Will they demand (if Russia joins) that she sign a peace with Austria and Germany such as we demand? Are they believing that they can separate Russia into economic cooperation without political cooperation? Do they think we will aid Italy and the satellite states without suspension of reparations? Do they think any Republican Congress will give economic aid to Russia in view of all that has happened? Or to the satellite states? They set in train some bad moments. And if they want Republican cooperation (and many Democrats) why don't they consult somebody?[121]

Obviously, Hoover felt that he was the "somebody" who should have been consulted. Subsequently, the Truman administration appointed a special non-partisan committee of nineteen domestic leaders to determine the capabilities of the United States to assist Europe economically. Hoover was not invited to be a member, despite his obvious expertise. Clearly bitter at having been omitted from the committee, he wrote O'Laughlin that:

No one could be more relieved than I to read this morning's paper and find my name left off the list of the new fact-finding committee on our ability to pay Europe. Baruch telephones me of his relief also. Had we been on the list it would have been difficult enough to refuse. My advices are that Marshall resents my epistles to Taber and Bridges as intrusions on his exclusive field—the making of foreign policies. Vandenberg is also upset and poisons Marshall.

Marshall, he concluded, was out of his element in dealing with the "desperately selfish" politicians of Europe as if they were motivated "from the same altruism which animates this more comfortable land of our own." Hoover, however, considered that he had performed a constructive service in foreign relations. He regarded the letter to Taber as having accomplished two useful purposes. On the one hand, it had "shown the country that there is another foreign policy than the isolationism of [Col. Robert] McCormick and the appeasement of [Henry] Wallace," and it had helped to get the relief appropriation passed. On the other hand, it had shown Republicans "that there were constructive ideas besides those of the Republican crumb-eaters of the State Department," by which he clearly meant Vandenberg. Over four hundred newspapers, ranging from the *Chicago Tribune* to the *New York Times* and *Herald Tribune*, and including the Scripps-Howard and Hearst papers, had expressed editorial support for the letter to Taber, "it being the only time they have ever agreed on anything." The letter to Bridges, Hoover claimed, had also enjoyed "astonishing" press support and Marshall should have been "grateful" for it, for Hoover had made it clear that there were limits to what the United States could do. The former president predicted a gradual erosion of Republican support for Truman's foreign policies and an eventual awakening on the president's part to the fact that "the publicity crumb-eaters cannot deliver the Republicans."[122] It is apparent that Hoover was willing to support bipartisanship in foreign policy only so long as he had a hand in the formulation of those policies. Truman's failure to consult him before the launching of the Marshall Plan, and his omission from the advisory council, had cost the administration his support. By contrast, he viewed Vandenberg and the other "crumb-eaters," as he referred to them, as being willing to follow the administration in whatever it proposed.

Late in June, the former president began to develop his own plan for European reconstruction. On June 29 he sent to Bernard Baruch "A Suggestion by H.H." in which he expressed strong doubts about the ability of the United States alone to carry out the reconstruction of Europe and dealt with the long-term effects that were likely to flow from the granting of economic aid directly from the United States to recipient nations. The United States, he wrote, had only a limited ability to aid Europe, as reflected in the amount of the nation's favorable trade balance in recent years. Other nations, such as Argentina, Canada, and South Africa, also had favorable trade balances and should contribute their share to the reconstruction effort. Direct loans between governments created "a political liability," which did not exist in the case of loans through government-supported agencies. That political liability lay in the fact that direct government loans became a political issue when time came for repayment, as they had after World War I. Hoover argued that it was European opposition to repayment that had contributed to the rise of isolationism in the United States. Instead, he suggested that the World Bank be used as the device for financing and directing European reconstruction. The United States should subscribe to debentures of the World Bank in an amount "estimated on the basis of its 'favorable trade balance,' i.e., our surplus of goods available for exports in excess of our imports of goods and services"; and other nations with favorable trade balances should do likewise. This would remove the political character from the relationship between lenders and borrowers, it would broaden the effort to include other nations besides the United States, it would provide as security to the lenders the "portion of all assets of the World Bank to which their ration of debenture holdings entitle them." It would give the whole reconstruction program "the character of an international cooperative action, which this crisis needs, and," he continued, "it spreads the risks over the world, both as to loans and as to the assets created thereby," while it would also "tend greatly to establish the international money exchanges and thus promote private transactions."[123]

But when Hoover set forth his plan in greater detail for Baruch in a further memorandum of July 3, he gave American economic assistance a political character that was inconsistent with the internationalization of assistance that he had proposed in the first memorandum. As in his letter to

Congressman Taber, the former president now sought political concessions from recipient nations. All countries seeking American aid should be required to support the United States in making an immediate peace settlement with Japan. The French should get no aid unless they joined their zone of Germany with the American and British zones, and if the Soviet Union continued to obstruct a peace settlement with a unified Germany, then the United States, Great Britain, and France should make a separate peace with the unified western zone of Germany. Nations receiving aid from the United States should also be required to end the foolish policy of extracting reparations from the defeated enemy nations in the form of industrial plants, and the equally foolish policy of seeking "peace preservation" through the enforcement of "levels of industry," since these made it impossible for the defeated nations to "produce enough goods for export to pay even for their food." The Soviet Union and its satellites should be barred from receiving aid, and efforts should be concentrated on Britain, France, Italy, the western zone of Germany, Austria, Greece, Turkey, Holland, Belgium, Finland, China, and Japan.[124]

The west European nations should be required, as a *sine qua non* for American aid, to return to the prewar six-day workweek until their economic crisis was ended. If they were unwilling to do this, "then American sacrifice is unwarranted," since the recipient nations "cannot expect the American people to provide such supplies as they could make for themselves." The United States should also insist that the west European nations "form a customs and transportation union." Such a union would increase productivity and would be "a practical first step toward a United Nations of Europe." Hoover then set forth possible alternatives to direct American aid. One of these was "to stock-pile in the United States as part of national defense all the durable commodities of which we are or would be in short supply." He estimated that perhaps one-half billion dollars per year might be spent in the relief-seeking countries through such purchases. The other alternative was the use of the World Bank, as advocated in Hoover's June 29 note.[125] The memorandum, Hoover told Baruch, was "not for publication or circulation. These ideas would need a lot of sugar coating to take off resentment. My purpose was simply to give you personally my ideas as I will be away for two months or so."[126]

Meanwhile, the former president had been encouraged by the passage of the Taft-Hartley Labor Act, writing to Taft that the Ohio senator had "restored representative government to mastery in its own house." The continuance of powerful labor organizations, possessing more power even than the federal government, would have meant, he wrote, "disaster to every hope of free men." He was also glad, he told Taft, "to see the adoption of my favorite gadget of a secret ballot of the workers as the final stage of collective bargaining before a strike that jeopardizes widespread public interest."[127]

Hoover and Taft now began to consult on their response to the Marshall Plan. The Ohioan wrote to Hoover in July that he had intended to talk with him about the Marshall Plan during a visit to New York, but had found the former president absent from the city. He told Hoover:

> I read with great interest your letter to Senator Bridges, which is the best analysis of the subject anyone has offered. The chief characteristic of the Administration is the complete lack of analysis when they get down to figures. I felt that Arthur Vandenberg made a mistake in suggesting a special commission to be appointed by the President. Such a commission has now been appointed, but Harriman is its chairman, and the staff will presumably be selected by the Administration. . . . Neither do I like the implication that if we are capable of exporting more goods we should, therefore, do so, regardless of the wisdom, either from our standpoint or that of the countries of Europe.

Taft was, he told Hoover, "prepared to support some additional lending," but he thought it should be limited to food and to materials and supplies needed to get the European economy operating once again. He feared, however, "that European nations will agree on some global plan and global figure which Marshall may accept, and then we will be in the wrong if we try to cut it down to a reasonable plan."[128]

At this evidence of Taft's interest in the matter, Hoover sent him a copy of the memorandum he had mailed to Baruch two weeks earlier. He told the Senator that he was "really very much alarmed" that the Marshall Plan was "an invitation to gang up on the United States; it looks like committing the United States without authority of the Congress—until afterwards. Of course all of us want to do what we can, but we do not want to exhaust this country."[129] The broader implications of the Marshall Plan were, in Hoover's view, that Marshall had succeeded in dividing the world. But he was not sure that the present division along the Iron Curtain and Manchuria would remain, "for nations will remain within their present allotted places only so long as they can work the two now competitive Santa Clauses."[130] Of Hoover's memorandum, Taft wrote that, without having studied it completely, he fully agreed with the former president's position on the whole question. Like Hoover, he was concerned that the Marshall Plan had been presented in such a way that "invites the foreign nations to gang up and make unreasonable demands. Instead of making them come to us and imposing conditions on our assistance, we always seem to be begging them to let us help them as if it were to our financial or economic advantage to do so." The only advantage he could see to the United States was that the plan met the American "desire to see peace and prosperity in the world."[131]

Late in July, Congress passed and President Truman signed into law the act establishing a committee to study and make recommendations concerning the reorganization of the executive branch of the federal government. A new phase of Hoover's public service was launched when he accepted the chairmanship of the new Commission on Organization of the Executive Branch of the Government.[132] During the late summer and early fall of 1947, however, the former president was taken ill with a bad case of the shingles and was, for the most part, unable to work. As he described his bout with the disease, it had "developed into a rather unusual form of paralysis of the muscles in my right arm and therefore hangs on for a long time—although the total medical profession in New York seems confident that they can get rid of it in time."[133] Hoover was without any use of his right arm for several weeks.[134] But if the former president's pace was slowed, he refused to come to a full stop. On September 21 he spoke on the European food situation at Madison Square Garden.[135] And on September 29 he issued a statement on the new Commission on Organization of the Executive Branch of the Government.

Hoover described the new commission as "the most formidable attempt yet made for independent review and advice on the business methods of the Executive Branch of the Federal Government." It had been organized not only with the cooperation of both houses of Congress, but also that of the president and both political parties; and to keep it free of partisan politics the commission was not to make a report until after the 1948 election. The purpose of the commission, Hoover observed, was not to uncover wrongdoing—that was the responsibility of other agencies of the government—but rather to look for ways to secure "efficiency and economy," and thereby reduce the cost of government to the taxpayer. In his statement, Hoover reviewed the growth of the federal bureaucracy since before World War I, and noted that federal civilian employees now outnumbered those of all state and local governments combined. The commission also sought some way to relieve the president of the "intolerable labor and inadequate control imposed upon him by the multitude of independent establishments." It would especially concern itself with regulating agencies, which combined legislative, executive, and judicial powers, and with defining "Federal as against state and local responsibilities." Relations between the citizen and his government must also be streamlined. Hoover concluded: "There are a score of other areas which should be effectively explored. There is no hurry imposed upon this Commission, but the great responsibility involves the utmost thoroughness and the widest use of all the special abilities in the country."[136]

Involved with what would soon come to be known as the Hoover Commission, and with the effort to bring about modifications in the Marshall Plan, the former president had little time to devote to other matters. But in the summer and fall of 1947, he was already beginning to formulate a position on American military policy. For some time Hoover had carried on a correspondence with Bonner Fellers, a retired general and former MacArthur aide. In 1947 Fellers became director of public relations for the Veterans of Foreign Wars (VFW), and early in September he wrote Hoover that he had successfully convinced the organization to take up the advocacy of peace through air supremacy at their convention that year. If the convention accepted his plan, "the principal VFW objective for next year in the Congress and with the American people will be the creation of an American air force in being second to none." Fellers asked Hoover to pass along to Taft an article that he had written on "Our National Security."[137] The former president did so, and Taft responded that he entirely agreed with Fellers's position. "It seems to me," the senator wrote, "that common sense demands that we maintain a complete superiority in the air."[138] This emphasis on airpower for American defense would soon become a basic principle in the Hoover-Taft approach to American military policy.

Late in October, Hoover resumed his critical analysis of the Marshall Plan as it was unfolding. In a memorandum sent via Taft to Congressman Christian Herter, and in a letter sent direct to the Massachusetts congressman, Hoover continued to raise what he regarded as deficiencies in the Marshall proposal. In his memorandum Hoover raised ten familiar points. The United States should help needy nations to the fullest extent consistent with a healthy economy and adequate national defense, because the collapse of Western Europe would be detrimental to "our civilization" and to "the future progress of the United States and the Western Hemisphere." The "spiritual character of the American people" would not permit "hunger and cold" to exist so long as they had the ability to prevent it. While Europe and Asia were incapable of giving support to the United States in the event of a war with the Soviets, "their continued neutrality is of importance." But the United States should not pledge any long-term aid unless the recipient nations made "the necessary effort to restore their productivity," and the American people must recognize that the aid was a gift, whether it was called a loan or not. The recipient nations should understand that such aid was a privation for the United States and that the American ability to give aid was limited. Aid should be unified and should be administered more consistently than in the past.[139]

Aid should be divided into two categories. The first category, consisting of food, fertilizer, coal, and cotton, could be called "relief" goods. Hoover again insisted that any proceeds from the sale of these goods by the national governments to which they were consigned should be deposited to the account of the United States. The other category of goods the former president called "depletion" goods, which included those commodities that were a drain on American natural resources and that would have to be replaced by purchases from abroad at some time, as with oil and metals. These items should be paid for by the recipient governments in kind "to the full extent that exports of a given country to the United States permit." The balance should be secured by some form of collateral. There should be organized cooperation on the part of the Marshall Plan recipient countries to obtain oil from the Persian Gulf countries in order to supply their energy requirements. Finally, Hoover again insisted that Congress should "deny aid to any country which fails to cooperate with us in making immediate peace with Germany and Japan," and which did not cease to destroy industrial plants in former enemy countries. "The recovery of both the productivity of Europe and Asia will depend upon the restoration of industry in Germany and Japan," he wrote. "It is simply crazy for us to build up productivity in foreign countries out of American resources, and at the same time, to tear down productivity in these two areas."[140]

Early in November, Henry L. Stimson, now outside of the government, sought to enlist Hoover's membership on a Citizens' Committee for the Marshall Plan, which included, in addition to Stimson, such lights as Dean Acheson, Herbert Lehman, Robert Patterson, Winthrop Aldrich, and John Winant.[141] Hoover responded that he was "in favor of doing all that we can." He had, however, proposed "certain essential safeguards on any such operation," and he had, Hoover told Stimson, "the arrogance to believe that I have had more experience with these questions than any living person." If those safeguards were included in Marshall's plan he would be glad to support it, but if not, he wanted to be "free to state these safeguards in any support." Therefore, until the details of the plan were spelled out in full, Hoover preferred not to join such a committee.[142] Stimson responded that he was confident that Marshall's plan would "not permit indiscriminate giving or giving without proper safeguards," but he did not know if Marshall's safeguards would accord with Hoover's conditions. He therefore asked Hoover to let him know "what you regard as these essential safeguards" since it "would be a great help to me in many ways."[143] Whether the former president did so is not clear, but he did not join the committee.

If Hoover and his former secretary of state were at odds over the Marshall Plan, Hoover and Alf Landon were in agreement. Landon wrote Hoover in mid-November that he supported Hoover's position on the Marshall Plan and that he had scheduled a speech a few days hence for which he sought Hoover's views on the European situation and the policies of the Truman administration. Landon also told Hoover that he had suggested to Congressman Joseph Martin that "Congress should set up a board to administer whatever fund it provided, and you [Hoover] should be on it."[144] Hoover replied that he felt "great discontent with everything going on in connection with this program, but there seems to be no hope of much alteration at the present time due to the pressure now being exerted and the unwillingness of our people [the Republicans in Congress] to fight it." The United States had the responsibility to prevent hunger and cold, and it would be useful to "help these people return to productivity, but the methods of doing this I do not think have been adequately taken care of."[145] Landon was disappointed to learn from Hoover that congressional Republicans did not seem to be putting up much of a fight. He considered the president's message on aid to Europe "so general in its terms that it largely leaves the formulation of a program up to them." He planned to visit with Hoover within a few weeks to discuss the situation.[146]

To some it appeared that Hoover was already exerting too much influence on the foreign policies of the Truman administration. As early as April 1946, the executive board of the United Electrical, Radio and Machine Workers, a left-wing union within the Congress of Industrial Organizations (CIO), attacked Truman because of the influence of Hoover, Vandenberg, and other Republicans on his foreign policy.[147] More important, in September 1947 former vice-president Henry A. Wallace, now editor of *New Republic*, lashed out at the Truman administration in a speech in which he pointed out that, while there was no resemblance between the foreign policy views of Hoover and Roosevelt, within 46 days after Roosevelt's death, "Mr. Hoover was welcomed to the White House." Now, two years later, Wallace charged, "it is Hoover's thinking which guides our foreign policy." Specifically, Wallace pointed to Hoover's recommendations following his trip to Germany in which he had advocated the rebuilding of German industry. This policy, Wallace observed, had now become "the very core of our entire program for European construction."[148]

Wallace's speech to "progressives" was indicative that the nation was approaching a presidential election year. Hoover, too, was giving thought to the 1948 election. In late October 1947 he expressed the belief that, if nominated, Robert A. Taft could be elected president.[149] Both Dewey and Taft had been to see Hoover by the end of that month, both having concluded that the race for the nomination was between the two of them. According to Hoover's account of their visits, both Dewey and Taft wanted the former president to get them together at the proper moment and obtain a pledge from each to support whichever appeared to have a definite lead. This would mean that one of the two would gain the nomination, rather than a stalemate developing that could lead to the nomination of a dark horse. Hoover expressed a preference, privately, for Taft, but indicated that he could accept Dewey ahead of either Stassen or Eisenhower.[150] But as of mid-November 1947 Hoover believed that Truman was still sufficiently popular that he could win the election if it were held then.[151] He regarded the president as very adept at playing politics with national and international issues, and he warned the Republicans that if they were to have any success against him in 1948 they must learn to do the same.[152]

Generally, however, Hoover seems to have regained some optimism concerning the world by late 1947. In August, on the eve of his seventy-third birthday, he expressed a hopeful outlook for "continued Western Civilization" in an interview. He considered the situation better than a year earlier, despite the Soviet Union's "failure and unwillingness to cooperate in world restoration." He believed the Soviet Union was gradually being "isolated" and her "instrument of ideological penetration" was weakening outside of the USSR and her satellites. He continued to regard the retardation of productivity in Germany and Japan as the great obstacle to recovery, and again advanced the proposal for an immediate peace with Japan whether the Soviet Union joined in it or not. He added:

> Another year after the war's end finds the earth without peace, little recovery in production, increasing danger of starvation abroad and alarms of another world war. One nation alone, by refusal of cooperation and destructive acts is responsible. If we are to reverse this tide of disaster, then free nations have but one of two possibilities, first, cooperation from Russia, which is improbable, second, making peace among the peoples outside Russia and her satellites, together with subjugation of her international poison squads, which is possible. If neither is done then an armed United States can live in reasonable comfort, use our food surplus to stave off starvation and wait, even if it means isolation, which is most undesirable.

On the subject of the Marshall Plan, Hoover argued again that the most important thing for world economic recovery was immediate peace with Germany and Japan so that those two nations might be restored to productivity. With the $2.5 billion thus freed that the United States and Great Britain were being forced to spend on food relief there, the money could be spent to cover most of the rehabilitation needs of Western Europe. Again, the former president insisted that if the November foreign ministers' meeting did not produce Soviet cooperation over Germany, the United States, Britain, and France should organize a German government in their unified zones and make a separate peace with it. If other countries refused to cooperate with the United States in this, he said, then this country would "be driven into some degree of isolation." However, Hoover believed that "isolationism which contemplates the further degeneration of Western Civilization is no asset to American progress." He clearly hoped that European nations would cooperate.[153]

In November Hoover found in the reported purges behind the Iron Curtain grounds for hope that there was a growing opposition to the Soviet Union, and he expressed confidence that the "restiveness" there "ultimately would blossom into revolution." He could not but believe "that the Communist-ridden peoples will sooner or later throw off their chains." The greatest problem in Europe, both inside and outside of the Iron Curtain, was the lack of food and fuel, and free enterprise was "the only road to productivity." Pointing to the fact that the United States was supplying most of the food and fuel to free Europe, he pointedly observed that:

> Had we in this hemisphere yielded to the economic utopias of either Eastern or Western Europe, I venture to say that hardly a ton of food or fuel would be moving overseas. Sooner or later the utopia-seeking nations will notice these facts and their peoples will resume the only road to freedom from hunger and cold.[154]

Through the fall and winter of 1947 Hoover busied himself with organizing the "task forces" of the Commission on Organization of the Executive Branch of the Government and inaugurating the work of the commission. He had, Hoover told reporters, accepted service on the commission "with the distinct understanding" that it would be his last service to the nation.[155] In December he was asked by Senator Vandenberg to testify on the Marshall Plan before the Senate Foreign Relations Committee.[156] The former president responded that he was under orders from his doctor not to travel so much, and he suggested, instead, that he prepare a short memorandum for the committee and the press.[157] While Vandenberg preferred that he present any such statement in person before the committee, Hoover suggested that he send it to Vandenberg for public release and that he then perhaps testify before the committee at a later date.[158] Vandenberg accepted this proposal, suggesting that Hoover's statement be released and read into the committee's record shortly after it had finished hearing the government's witnesses in late January and then receive Hoover's personal testimony after he had returned from his Florida fishing vacation.[159]

Hoover then set to work on his statement concerning the Marshall Plan, revising it many times. On January 18, 1948, he mailed it off to the senator and released it to the press. In his memorandum, Hoover again expressed the conviction "that we should help to the full extent which does not weaken our own economy and thus defeat all world recovery." He found three dominant reasons why the United States should help: (1) because "the spiritual character of the American people" compelled them to "prevent hunger and cold to the full extent of their surplus, and even to the extent of personal self-denial"; (2) to bring about the defeat of communism in western Europe and the stimulation of the economic and political unity among the nations there; and (3) because "the project builds for peace in the world." But there were very great dangers in the project. On the one side was the possibility of failure in Western Europe, and on the other side was the danger that "the volume of exports and finance proposed may accelerate an already serious inflation; that it further delays our recuperation from the war; that it drains our natural resources and continues excessive taxation; all of which might bring depression and thus destroy the strength of the one remaining source of aid to a world in chaos." It was imperative, Hoover admitted, to take some risks. He would like to give unqualified endorsement of the Marshall Plan, but he was compelled, instead, "by conscience to say that the plan as presented should have certain constructive modifications and more safeguards."[160]

Hoover pointed out that the effects of the decisions made by those directing the plan would spill over into virtually every aspect of American economic and foreign policy. He suggested that the policies should be directed by a group that represented these many areas of its impact, "no doubt including department heads, but also including non-official citizens." He also suggested that the scope of the plan be broadened from the sixteen nations originally proposed to twenty, including China, Germany, Japan, and Korea, and perhaps more. "The food supply and reconstruction of industry in Germany, Japan, Korea and China," he argued, "are inseparable from the 16 countries." Alert for ways in which the drain on the American taxpayer might be decreased, Hoover suggested that conditions be imposed in return for American aid. If the recipient nations were required to abandon their restraints upon enterprise and economy, balance their budgets, and curb their inflation, American private capital would doubtless flow into those countries, and the demand for their exports would increase, "all of which would decrease the drains and strains upon the United States taxpayer." Once again he called for a requirement that the recipient nations be required to support the United States in making a separate peace with Japan and in establishing a trizonal union of Germany. The restoration of productivity in those two countries would, he declared, free $1.5 billion per year from food relief and make that amount available for reconstruction under the Marshall Plan without any additional demands upon the American taxpayer.[161]

Hoover also argued that the Marshall Plan appropriation should not be for a four-year period. It was impossible, he said, to forecast the course that the economies of the recipient nations would follow, or that of the United States, so far in advance. He also worried that the proposed commitment for the first fifteen months, when combined with the existing commitments for food relief, might be too great a strain on the American economy. Hoover then proposed some ways in which the burden might be lightened for American taxpayers and for the American economy. For one, Hoover noted that the program for industrial reconstruction of Europe implied "not alone a restoration of prewar productivity but a great increase in such production above prewar." "That," he said, "is indeed greatly to be desired, but whether Americans are able out of production and taxes at this time to provide more than a restoration to prewar levels is another question." He also suggested that the capital goods programs of the recipient nations might need to be extended over a longer term than planned in order to ensure that American industry could supply the steel and machinery and other capital goods without detriment to other exports or to

American industry. He suggested similar reductions in the amount of petroleum exports planned under the first fifteen months of the program. By these and a variety of other recommendations, Hoover sought to reduce the drain on the taxpayer, the economy, and America's natural resources.[162]

Hoover's letter to Vandenberg aroused harsh editorial criticism from the *New York Times* and *New York Herald Tribune*.[163] The former president turned to more research for the facts to back up his position. He was still angry that the dismantling of German industries was continuing despite his arguments against it.[164] Hoover had become convinced that Secretary of State Marshall was a poor administrator and found his policy of continuing the dismantling of German industry inexcusable.[165] Previously Hoover and Marshall had maintained fairly close relations. Those relations had apparently been disrupted by the pressure exerted upon Marshall by Democrats in Congress who, like Henry Wallace, complained that the impression was taking hold in the country that it was Republicans like Hoover and Under Secretary of State Robert Lovett who were actually formulating the administration's foreign policies. According to Drew Pearson's column, Marshall had, in fact, been called upon by seventeen Democratic members of the House to explain his close ties with Hoover and other Republicans. The meeting had been distorted by Pearson in his column, making relations between Hoover and Marshall very difficult. Now, in early March of 1948, John Callan O'Laughlin sought to bring the two men back together by furnishing Hoover with Marshall's explanation of the conference and seeking to arrange a meeting between the two men at his home. O'Laughlin told Hoover that the secretary of state was particularly anxious for such a meeting "as there is a number of matters he would like to talk over with you."[166] On March 3 Hoover wired O'Laughlin that he would be in Washington for a few days, beginning March 20, and would be glad to meet with Marshall.[167] That being satisfactory to both O'Laughlin and Marshall, the meeting was arranged for March 22.[168]

Whether the meeting with Marshall influenced his approach to the Marshall Plan or not, Hoover was more conciliatory towards the bill that was before the House of Representatives in another response that he wrote two days after the meeting, on March 24. In his letter to Congressman Joseph Martin, speaker of the House, the former president wrote that he had compared the bill as passed by the Senate and approved by the House Foreign Affairs Committee and found that many of his suggestions had been adopted. After reviewing those suggestions that he considered had been wholly or partially incorporated into the bill, Hoover turned to the recommendations he had made that he felt still ought to be added to it. Relief had not yet been provided for Germany, Korea, and Japan. He recommended that certain new provisions adopted in the House bill be included in the final bill. He suggested that the prohibition of trade by Marshall Plan countries with Iron Curtain countries be dropped except for munitions trade. He suggested changes in the legislation that would further encourage the participation of Latin American countries in the extension of aid to the Marshall Plan countries. Hoover concluded:

> I realize that many approach this gigantic experiment with great apprehension and a realization of the sacrifices it will mean to our people. All legislation must be the result of compromise. However, if it should produce economic, political and self-defense unity in Western Europe, and thus a major dam against Russian aggression, it would stem the tide now running so strongly against civilization and peace. The plan, if well devised and under a capable Administrator, stands a good chance of success. I believe it is worth taking the chance.[169]

Thus, whether from his conference with Marshall, or from his satisfaction with the changes that had been made in the original bill, or both, Hoover came to modestly support the bill in Congress. He wrote to Bernard Baruch:

> It is somewhat interesting to note that although the administration defamed all of my recommendations to Senator Vandenberg, a great many of them were essentially adopted and no doubt some of these others will be inserted. If these people would only send for us in advance, you and I could have shortened this whole legislation by at least two months.[170]

As the Hoover Commission proceeded with its investigations, Hoover was monitoring the political situation while the conventions drew nearer. It was a foregone conclusion that Truman would be nominated by the Democrats, but the Republican nomination was still very much undecided. In March there was an effort to promote Vandenberg for the nomination, but Rickard noted that Hoover disliked the Michigan senator, considering him to have been disloyal to the Hoover administration. On the Democratic side, Hoover believed that many Democrats would desert Truman because of the conviction that he could not win in November.[171] General Douglas MacArthur was a possible Republican standard-bearer, but Hoover thought he would have a difficult time if nominated, in part because the "left-wingers" would bring up his involvement in suppressing the bonus marchers in Washington during Hoover's presidency.[172] Taft was clearly Hoover's choice, and Hoover thought that the Ohioan should concentrate his campaign on Nebraska since he believed that a big win in that primary would assure Taft's nomination. But above all, Hoover was concerned that either Taft or Dewey should get the nomination rather than a compromise candidate. He was insistent that Taft and Dewey should agree that one or the other would be the nominee.[173]

Late in March 1948 the cold war was accelerated by the communist coup in Czechoslovakia, which led even Senator Taft to consider that it might now be necessary to reenact the draft as well as increase the airpower of the nation.[174] Hoover's response was more temperate, as set forth in a public letter to Paul Smith of the *San Francisco Chronicle*. The former president was convinced, he wrote, that the Truman administration was "putting on a fear and war blitz in order to intimidate the Congress into appropriations, etc., and possibly to create a sense of emergency which would be helpful in the forthcoming [political] campaign." But Hoover was convinced that the Soviet Union did not want war, nor would they be ready to wage war for five to twenty years. No victory was possible in such a war, and it could only result in the destruction of "American civilization." As for the coup in Czechoslovakia, it was, in Hoover's view, only a matter of the Soviet Union "consolidating areas conceded to them by Roosevelt and Churchill." The real danger from the USSR was not military attack, he argued, but the use of fifth columnists. The Marshall Plan was a weapon against fifth columnists, and that was why, Hoover said, he had supported the Marshall Plan. The United States ought to build up Western Europe as a buffer area against communism and pull its troops out as soon as possible. America "ought to keep at arms length from this whole Russian complex—indicating on the other hand, our impregnability and our ability for action." The United States should aid Western Europe in building up its self-defense capability, "but we should enter no military alliances or military guarantees" lest the European countries "lie down and do nothing for themselves." In closing, Hoover noted that he had expressed his objections over the years to American relations with the Soviet Union, and especially to the American alliance with them during World War II. He wrote: "I felt deeply at that time—and have ever since that we were aligning ourselves with wicked processes and that the old biblical injunction that 'the wages of sin are death' was still working. We see the consequences today."[175]

It was perhaps indicative of the former president's rise in stature that Republican candidates now not only sought meetings with him, but also wanted the meetings publicized. In June of 1947, Harold Stassen sought such a meeting and asked if Hoover had any objection to his answering in the affirmative if he were queried by reporters concerning any meetings with the former president. Hoover responded that he had "no objection to anyone knowing that I keep good company."[176] In April of 1948 Stassen again sought a meeting with Hoover.[177] When Robert Taft won the Ohio primary early in May, his campaigners felt that he was in the lead for the nomination. Congressman Clarence Brown, chairman of the national Taft-for-President committee wrote Hoover: "With your help victory seems certain." He pressed for a meeting with the former president.[178]

But Hoover did not come out for Taft's nomination. Adhering to a policy he had consistently maintained since leaving the White House in 1933,

Hoover refused to publicly support any of the candidates for the Republican nomination. Perhaps it was because of Taft's failure in 1948 that he would break with that policy in 1952 and endorse Taft against Eisenhower. But in the 1948 convention he limited his role to broker. He had earlier suggested to both Taft and Dewey that they each agree to withdraw in favor of the other if it appeared that the other's bid offered greater promise of success. As Hoover described it later, he had told the two men that "if there were a long struggle between them in the Convention, it would do great harm to the Party's chance of election; and a stalemate in the Convention would probably result in some third and less able man, such as had happened in the 1940 convention." Hoover had suggested, therefore, "that they agree with me that if I decide that either one of them could not make the grade that he should retire if I suggested it. Both agreed." When Taft's bid faltered, Hoover told the Ohioan that "for the good of the Party he should retire and support his rival."[179] As a result, Thomas Dewey was nominated for the second time. Republicans looked forward confidently to victory.

For the fourth successive time since he had left the White House, Hoover was called upon to address the Republican convention. On June 22, he spoke to the delegates on the grave crisis before America and the world:

> Liberty has been defeated in a score of nations. Those governments have revived slavery. They have revived mass guilt. They have revived government by hatred, by exile, by torture. Today the men in the Kremlin hold in their right hands the threat of military aggression against all civilization. With their left hands they work to weaken civilization by boring from within.
>
> These tyrants have created a situation new in all human experience. We saved them from Hitler but they refuse to cooperate with us to establish good will or peace on earth. Thus today a powerful nation, dominated by men without conscience, finds it useful to have neither peace nor war in the world.
>
> Whether some of us, who foresaw that danger and warned of it, were right or wrong, and whatever the terrible errors of American statesmanship that helped bring it about, we are today faced with a world situation in which there is little time for regrets.
>
> The only obstacle to the annihilation of freedom has been the United States of America. Only as long as America is free and strong will human liberty survive in the world.

It was in the interests of the United States that this nation aid in building strength and unity in Western Europe in order to "restore a balance of power in the world able to resist the hordes from the Eurasian steppes who would ruin Western Civilization." And the United States must take up the burden "of increased armament to assure that no hostile force will ever reach this hemisphere." But care must be taken that the American economy was not exhausted by all of these burdens "or the last hope of the world is lost." Those nations receiving American aid must recognize that it was "solely to aid their reconstruction," with "no room for non-essentials, for profligacy, or for inefficiency," and there must not be created "a perpetual dependence of Europe and Asia upon the United States." Moreover, the reconstruction of Europe must include Germany.

But Americans also faced the problem of restoring freedom at home from the infection of the "European intermittent fever of creeping totalitarianism," which had inserted "its tentacles into our labor unions, our universities, our intelligentsia, and our Government." The difficulty, Hoover asserted, lay not so much with communists, but with "fuzzy-minded people who think we can have totalitarian economics in the hands of bureaucracy, and at the same time have personal liberty for the people and representative government in the nation." Such "totalitarian liberals" had "provided the ladders upon which the Communist pirates have boarded the Ship of State" in every country where the communists had taken control. Hoover told the delegates:

> My fellow Republicans, from the inevitable passing of years, this is indicated as probably the last time I will meet with you in Convention. That does not mean I shall spend my days with less concern and less watchfulness of the deep currents which will determine the future of American life. But this does warrant my speaking from my heart of this great concern.

He called upon the delegates to "face the truth that we are in a critical battle to safeguard our nation and civilization which, under God, have brought to us a life of liberty," and to choose leaders "who seek not only victory but the opportunity to service in this fight."[180] It was the first of many farewells that the former president would make before Republican conventions.

Dewey's campaign manager, Herbert Brownell, wrote Hoover soon after the convention that he recalled the "fine help that you extended to me during the 1944 campaign," and hoped to see him soon to discuss the campaign plans for 1948.[181] Hoover agreed to meet with Brownell upon his return to New York.[182] The former president was certain that the 1948 campaign would not be very different from that in 1944, but "even so I don't see how it is possible to lose the election."[183] Hoover hoped that he would not be asked to help in the campaign because the reorganization commission and other obligations were taking all of his time. He concluded that he would only help if he felt his participation might mean the difference between victory and defeat for Dewey.[184] But a few days later, when both Truman and Congressman Sam

Rayburn had taken verbal potshots at him, Hoover wrote to Mark Sullivan: "I am wondering if they [the Democrats] intend to run me for President again. If so, I may have to change my mind about not making any speeches in this campaign."[185]

Despite his earlier optimism that the Soviet Union did not want war and would not be ready for war for a number of years, Hoover began to worry that the crisis over Berlin, which followed so closely after the coup in Czechoslovakia, would lead to war with the United States. In Hoover's view, it was imperative that the United States avoid a confrontation with the Soviet Union over Berlin and concentrate on organizing for defense of the western hemisphere. O'Laughlin transmitted the former president's concern to Secretary of State Marshall, who agreed with Hoover but insisted, in O'Laughlin's words, "that to give in on Berlin would be the signal for further aggressive advances by the Soviets."[186] Hoover was concerned, however, that if war did break out, the United States would be unable to prevent the occupation of France and Great Britain by the Soviet Union, which in his view clearly inclined these two nations toward neutrality in any showdown between the United States and the USSR.[187] O'Laughlin responded, however, that Marshall had assured him that the British and French were even more insistent about standing fast over Berlin than was the United States, and that their support could be relied upon should hostilities actually break out.[188]

In other foreign affairs matters, Hoover considered Truman's recognition of Israel to be purely a political act to enhance his reelection prospects, and he expected, wrongly as it turned out, that the Arab nations would eliminate the new Israeli state within ten days.[189] Among the few bits of advice he gave Dewey in the campaign was that Dewey take up the battle against "the destruction and removal of non-military manufacturing plants from Germany." Although the administration denied it, Hoover said that he had evidence that the process was still going on. The result was that German exports had been stifled to the point "where it costs us about $600,000,000 a year to keep Germans alive and in idleness and constant degeneration. Also, for lack of these exports, we are spending one-third more on E.R.P. [the Marshall Plan] than would be necessary."[190] Late in September, *Newsweek* magazine reported that Hoover and others were seeking to dissuade Dewey from selecting John Foster Dulles for the post of secretary of state if Dewey were elected. Hoover wrote to the magazine denying the charge and sent a copy to Dewey, who responded that: "I had not seen the canard in Newsweek but I would, of course, have known it would be false in any event."[191]

Hoover's relations with the Dewey campaign were congenial, and he phoned the campaign directors periodically with suggestions.[192] On September 30 the 74-year-old former president registered to vote in New York for the first time, having until that point been registered in California.[193] But beyond his advice to the candidate, Hoover took no active role in the campaign, being preoccupied with the work of the reorganization commission. There were some who sought to push the commission's work through to completion before the election, but Hoover held it back until afterward.[194] Still, as the former president confided to Rickard, the New Dealers had begun to realize that the report of the commission would be highly critical of the Roosevelt and Truman administrations, and they would try to prevent its publication, but they dared not attack the commission before the election.[195] Hoover clearly envisioned that the report would be issued after the election of Dewey to the presidency, and that with a friendly, GOP-dominated Congress the report could be used to roll back much of the New Deal.

However, the former president was to be disappointed. Truman was reelected in one of the great upsets of American political history. As usual, Hoover quickly submitted the election to analysis and concluded that the campaign had ignored two crucial issues—the positive accomplishments of the Eightieth Congress and of the Republican party. A number of speeches should have been delivered during the campaign, he wrote, defending the Republican record in the Eightieth Congress for (1) liberating the worker through the Taft-Hartley Act; (2) transforming emergency price supports into a fixed policy of the government—an action approved by all farm leaders, but not sufficiently publicized during the campaign; and (3) reducing taxes. Speeches should also have been made defending the GOP. In response to Truman's attacks on the party as representative of "big business and private interests," the Republican candidates, Hoover insisted, should have recounted the list of regulatory legislation enacted in the past by the GOP—legislation that in his view constituted "the most fundamental revolution in the economic history that the modern world has seen" by abandoning laissez faire and preventing monopoly in America. The Republican candidates should also have rebutted Truman's charge that the GOP was opposed to conservation and development of natural resources by pointing out that "every one of the great conservation services of the country today was created by the Republicans." Predictably, Hoover also argued that the GOP candidates should have attacked Roosevelt for his failure to cooperate with him in halting the bank panic of 1933 and should have pointed out that the rest of the world had recovered from the depression within two years, while New Deal policies had forced the United States "to wallow in depression until 1940." The candidates might also, he wrote, have attacked Roosevelt's foreign policies at Teheran and Yalta, and Truman's at Potsdam, which in Hoover's view had "wrecked peace in the world" and resulted in the enslavement of hundreds of millions of people. Had such speeches been made, Hoover believed, "it would have created pride and confidence in the Republican party" and would have resulted in more votes for the Republican ticket. He concluded:

One of the prime obligations of the presidential campaign is to put on an education of the people of the great public issues. It is the only time when the people listen and no one can convey this educational work except the Candidate for President. It was totally avoided and the Party was frustrated.[196]

In 1952 Hoover would take it upon himself to make such an educational campaign.

10

Final Years in an
Opposition Role

espite all of the portents for success in 1948, the Republican presidential candidate was again defeated. A Democratic president would govern for the next four years, but they would be the last four years that Herbert Hoover would be in an opposition role. The Truman victory was all the more disappointing to Hoover since he believed that it would now be very difficult to get the recommendations of the Hoover Commission put into effect.[1] The commission's report was now absorbing all of his time. As Hoover wrote Arch Shaw late in November, he had "just had to cut out everything for the present."[2] It is reasonable to assume that the unexpected victory of Truman meant that the report would take a somewhat different tone than if Dewey had been elected president. As the recommendations of the various task forces of the commission were submitted and circulated for comments among the commission members, some of the recommendations were leaked informally, in order to test public reaction before they were incorporated in the full report.[3] Still, Hoover doubted that Truman would give the recommendations his unqualified support, and even if he did there would be opposition from within the bureaucracy to any change.[4]

From early February until early March, the Hoover Commission sent a stream of reports to Congress. A total of 273 specific changes were recommended in the administrative structure of the executive branch of the government. In the first report, dealing with general management of the executive branch, the commission recommended the establishment of a clear line of responsibility and command, the reduction of the 65 agencies reporting to the president by two-thirds, the grouping of agencies and field services by function and purpose, the use of standard nomenclature, the creation of a presidential staff secretary post and an office of personnel, as well as other reforms. Turning to personnel management, the commission recommended that the Civil Service Commission concentrate on setting and enforcing personnel standards rather than hiring, and that hiring be turned over to departments and agencies, with each given its own personnel officer. In one of its most important recommendations, the commission suggested the creation of a new Office of General Services, directly responsible to the president, to supervise supply, records maintenance, and building management operations throughout the government, except for the Post Office and Defense Departments. The commission also recommended changes in the handling of inventories, rents, record maintenance and management, traffic management, and purchases.[5]

The commission also recommended that the Post Office Department place its operation on a business basis, that the postmaster general cease to be a party official, that the postal service be decentralized into fifteen regions under regional directors, that postmasters and top officials be named by the president without need for Senate confirmation, and other postal reforms. One of the areas involving the most sweeping recommendations for change was the State Department. The commission recommended reorganization to give the secretary of state a clear line of command over the State Department and the foreign service. It also recommended that the department concentrate solely on foreign affairs policymaking and coordination and that the department's Washington personnel be merged with the Foreign Service into a single Foreign Affairs Service to serve at home and abroad. The commission expressed its opposition to the use of the State Department for such purposes as the direction of occupied areas, granting of visas, munitions export control, and other nondiplomatic functions. Turning to agriculture, the commission recommended that overlapping responsibilities between the Agriculture and Interior departments be ended by locating all major land agencies in the Department of Agriculture; it also recommended that the department be organized into seven operating divisions, and other reforms.[6]

In making its recommendations for the Defense Department, the commission suggested reorganization to strengthen civilian control. It suggested greater authority for the secretary of defense, with the secretaries of the army, navy, and air force being demoted to under secretaries of defense. It also recommended that the chairman of the Joint Chiefs of Staff be named by the secretary of defense as his single link to his military advisers and that the secretary of defense be given authority over the preparation of the defense budget, among other reforms. Where the Veterans Administration (VA) was concerned, the commission suggested that VA insurance be handled by a separate corporation and recommended other reforms designed to streamline the administration's management and to correct bureaucratic defects. The commission recommended the adoption of performance budgets, under which funds were sought for specific functions, activities, and projects. It recommended groupings of kindred activities under the Departments of Labor and Commerce, including the transfer of some activities from other departments and agencies. Most transportation functions, for example, would be grouped under the Department of Commerce. Included was a recommendation that the Commerce, Agriculture, Interior, and State departments establish an interdepartmental committee to end overlapping between their functions. Turning to the Treasury Department, the commission recommended that it be reorganized along functional lines as the real government fiscal center, with the Reconstruction Finance Corporation, Federal Deposit Insurance Corporation, and Export-Import Bank transferred to its jurisdiction. It recommended that many nonfiscal functions, such as the Narcotics Bureau and the Coast Guard be transferred out of the Treasury Department, and that it serve as the central agency to examine lending agencies such as the Federal Farm Mortgage Corporation, the Home Owners Loan Corporation, and the Home Loan Bank Board.[7]

The commission recommended the liquidation of 30 government enterprises, the consolidation of others, and the incorporation of still more. It urged higher salaries for the members of regulatory commissions and criticized their inadequate planning. The commission suggested the conversion of the Interior Department into a public works agency that would have responsibility for flood control and river and harbor development work, which were presently under the Army Corps of Engineers. It urged that authority for all public works be consolidated under Interior Department control, except for grants-in-aid programs, and the removal of nonpublic works functions such as the Bureau of Land Management and the Fish and Wildlife Service. It recommended the transfer of the Selective Service System to the Labor Department, along with the Bureau of Employees' Compensation, the Employees' Compensation Appeals Board, and other labor-oriented agencies and activities.[8]

In another major recommendation, the commission proposed the creation of a new cabinet department to supervise welfare and educational programs; it also would take over such functions as those of the Federal Security Agency and the Bureau of Indian Affairs. It also suggested the creation of a United Medical Administration to oversee military and VA hospitals, the Public Health Service, and part of the Food and Drug Administration. Since the State Department would be limited to purely diplomatic functions, the commission recommended the creation of an administrator of overseas affairs, who would be responsible for occupied and dependent territories, the ECA, and other such activities. The commission also suggested the establishment of a National Science Foundation to regulate interdepartmental research.[9] In sum, the reports of the commission mirrored Hoover's opposition to waste and to duplication in the federal bureaucracy, as well as his general philosophy against a bloated central government and his preference for state and local responsibility. The recommendations were largely concerned with methods by which expenditures might be reduced and the activities of the executive branch might be curtailed and consolidated in the interest of efficiency and economy.[10]

Early in February 1949, President Truman phoned Hoover to express his appreciation and satisfaction with the commission's report. The two then began to cooperate to ensure that legislation would be forthcoming from Congress to implement the recommendations of the commission.[11] But the cooperation was not as close as Hoover would have liked. A few days after the report was released, Hoover met with the president to discuss the recommendations that had been made, as well as some recommendations that he felt strongly about but which the commission had been unable to agree upon.[12] Truman was not willing to commit himself to support of all of the recommendations, especially "those recommendations of the commission which involve the shifting of functions from one department to another," because it would be necessary, he told Hoover, to consider those carefully and to take into account the views of the responsible officials within the administration.[13] Hoover agreed with the president's desire to "keep a free hand," but he argued that some of the reforms could be carried through Congress if the two of them could agree to cooperate in supporting these reforms. Under this category Hoover included

> agreement upon the broad principles that the quasi-legislative and quasi-judicial functions are outside the executive arm; that there should be unification of public works and also of medical service and the grouping of certain lending agencies under the Secretary of the Treasury. All enable me to be of more service in holding this work in the nonpartisan field. Therefore, it has seemed to me that such personal understanding from time to time would forward our common purpose.[14]

Truman, however, refused to enter any joint harness with Hoover, even though he continued to express support for the commission's recommendations.[15] And whenever reorganization legislation that the president considered desirable was stalled in Congress, he was quick to call upon Hoover for assistance with the Republican members.[16]

Hoover early concluded that the commission's recommendations would need ample publicity and lobbying to overcome the resistance of bureaucrats and lobbyists for special interests, and he had assurances of financial support for a campaign in behalf of the commission's report.[17] As the commission's reports were sent to Congress, Hoover aided in the formation of the Citizens' Committee for the Hoover Commission, headed by Dr. Robert L. Johnson, president of Temple University. Some 2,000 telegrams were sent out to enlist members in March, and Hoover hoped to have it well organized by the end of the month. He expected that the organization would help enlist the support of some members of Congress who, until then, had been unwilling to go against the organized opposition to the commission's reforms.[18] While Hoover maintained close relations with the committee, he did not participate publicly in its efforts to mobilize public opinion.[19] He was, however, doing his own part to muster public support for the commission's report through speeches, radio talks, and testimony before congressional committees.

Meanwhile, Hoover was disturbed by the activities of some of his fellow Republicans. Dewey's Lincoln Day dinner speech in February had again sought to draw a distinction between the old guard and what Dewey seemed to regard as his "reform" group in the party. Hoover worried that the New Yorker was following Theodore Roosevelt's divisive tactics, which had cost the Republican party so dearly.[20] He was also shocked by Senator Robert Taft's support for public housing legislation in Congress, concluding that the Ohioan was following the path of outright political expediency in supporting what was, to Hoover, socialistic legislation.[21]

Hoover was still frequently called upon for his views on subjects unrelated to the reorganization proposals. Late in April 1949 he responded to a request from Congressman Robert Doughton, chairman of the House Ways and Means Committee, for his comments on pending legislation relating to Social Security. Referring to the enormous expenditures of the federal government, most of which stemmed from the necessities of the cold war, Hoover warned: "Already our economy is up to the limit of endurance under this load. I believe we should go slow and hold further additions to this burden to the absolute minimum. When the cold war is over, we can afford many more domestic improvements." The actuarial basis of the Social Security system was faulty, he charged, and within five to ten years "the general taxpayer will be forced to make up the annual deficit." Hoover recommended that the system be placed on a "pay-as-you-go" basis, with an increase in benefits, but no expansion of the coverage, and that federal grants be given to the states in order "to provide more adequately for the aged and dependents actually in need," because "the real and urgent problem is the need group. It is not solved now, nor can it be solved for many years, by the 'Federal Insurance System' —even if that system can be made to work efficiently." Beyond that, Hoover suggested a study to find a simpler system, because the federal Social Security System and the aid given by the states amounted to expensive dual administration to deal with the same problem. He thought that a "careful inquiry might disclose an entirely different system which would avoid the huge costs of administration and the duplication, which would substitute some other forms of taxation, more simple and more direct for its support, and which would give more positive security to the aged than this complicated system."[22] To Congressman Robert Kean,

Hoover wrote: "I believe some other system must be found if there is to be real protection in old age."[23]

Hoover was also concerned with the deadening effect on individual and local responsibility, which he saw resulting from the excessive involvement of the federal government in nongovernmental activities. One of his concerns was with the expansion of governmental welfare agencies. He agreed that such activities had "a place in American life provided the cloak of welfare is not used as a disguise for Karl Marx," but he found many citizens questioning why they should support voluntary welfare agencies. Why not let the government do it all? Hoover's reply was that the "essence of our self government lies in self government outside of political government," as the "fabric of American life" was "woven around our tens of thousands of voluntary associations." It was from these, not from bureaucracy, that the "inspirations of progress spring," and if these voluntary activities were replaced by the government, "this civilization would be over." They were the "spur to official progress," and without them such governmental activities would deteriorate. "The greatest and in fact the only impulse to social progress," Hoover maintained, "is the spark of altruism in the individual human being."[24]

Queried in June for his views on federal aid to education, Hoover responded by decrying the fact that logrolling had resulted in federal grants-in-aid going not only to states in need of federal assistance, but also to states that did not need help. He was opposed to the expansion of federal bureaucracy that must inevitably result from such a scatter-gun approach to educational assistance, and he was alarmed by the dictation of state and local educational policies by a federal bureaucracy. He regarded the "grants-in-aid system" as "a prime instrument in centralizing the government of the people in Washington." As correctives of the abuses, Hoover insisted that safeguards against federal dictation should be written into the bill more strongly than at present, that aid should be limited to the approximately twelve states that seriously needed it, and that the definition of need should be based on specific educational standards rather than on economic calculations. Such an approach, he argued, would reduce the proposed appropriation in Congress by about half, would limit unnecessary bureaucratic expansion, and would keep the "camel's head" of federal bureaucratic control "out of probably 80% of the nation's educational tents." Furthermore, they would curb the demands from special groups and interests for money, which always accompanied the general grants-in-aid method of governmental assistance. In Hoover's view: "To place a Federal bureaucracy over the whole national system will be, in my mind, a disaster to educational progress—no matter what legal limits are put on it or what advantages are painted."[25]

The opportunity to serve in the United States Senate, which Hoover had sought in 1945, was offered to him in July 1949. The retirement of Senator Robert Wagner of New York created a vacancy, and New York Governor

Thomas Dewey offered to appoint the former president to fill out the remainder of the session. But this time Hoover declined the appointment. He wrote Governor Dewey on July 6:

> I have given the matter prayerful consideration and I feel you must appoint some younger man. I will not be physically able to undertake the necessary strain of the nomination and election campaign four months hence or, if successful, to again repeat such a campaign in 1950. The Republican Party needs young blood on its fighting fronts.

Hoover saw little opportunity for constructive service in the approximately one month remaining in the current session of Congress, and he believed that his best service to the nation was through "occasional special investigation or advice in fields where I have some experience, and with an entire independence of view." He felt that he could not "be so helpful to the country if I surrender such independence to re-enter" the active political field.[26] Governor Dewey appointed John Foster Dulles instead. The fact that the seat had been offered first to Hoover was not made public in order not to detract from Dulles's appointment.[27]

While his efforts in behalf of the Hoover Commission's recommendations occupied most of his time, Hoover spent every available moment on his memoirs. These were now attaining immense proportions, and only a small portion of his drafts would ultimately appear in published form.[28] Late in 1949, however, foreign affairs began once again to capture his attention. The fall of China to the communists in that year led Senator William Knowland to inquire as to Hoover's views concerning the changed situation in east Asia. Hoover recommended that "we should not recognize the communist Government of China; that we must continue to recognize and support the National Government [of Chiang Kai-shek]; that we should, if necessary, give naval protection to the possessions of Formosa, the Pescadores, and possibly Hainan islands." So long as the United States supported the government on Formosa (Taiwan), he asserted, it would exist as a wall against communist expansion and as a "continued hope of some time turning China in the paths of freedom again." It would also prevent the communist regime in China from gaining a voice in the United Nations Security Council, or in peacemaking with Japan, and it would bar the Chinese communists from transforming Chinese embassies and consulates in the United States into "nests of Chinese conspiracies." Continued support of the Chiang Kai-shek regime on Formosa would also, he maintained, contribute to the security of the Philippines and Japan.[29] Knowland released Hoover's letter to the press and wrote him that it had been "given an excellent play in all the newspapers of the Country and I think it has done a great deal to help focus attention on this important part of the world."[30]

Senator Taft agreed with Hoover's position on the need to "prevent the Communists crossing over to Formosa which, after all, is not legally a part of China, until a peace treaty is written with Japan." In the beginning he was more flexible than Hoover, however, on the question of diplomatic recognition of the People's Republic, agreeing with an article by Henry P. Fletcher in *Human Events*, which advocated such recognition. Taft felt that Formosa should probably "be an independent island."[31] Hoover, on the other hand, was willing to abandon the defense of Formosa if U.S. military strategists did not consider the island vital to American security, but he was insistent that the communist regime on the mainland not be recognized by the United States. As he wrote Knowland again, on January 20, 1950:

> We would have the same consequences which have befallen us from every one of our recognitions of eight Communist States—the first in Russia in 1933 and the last in Hungary in 1944–45. . . . Our experience from these Communist States has been consistent—their agents boring within our institutions, revolutionary plots all over the world, maltreatment of our citizens. . . .

Hoover also made a plea for the right of self-determination of the Formosan people, pointing out that the population of the island was only slightly less than that of Greece and that the United States had conducted an election in that country to determine whether the people wanted a communist government. Implicit was the suggestion that the United States ought to consider the defense of the Formosan people against aggression, if they were opposed to communism, even if not a defense of the Chiang Kai-shek regime there.[32] Hoover also suggested to Patrick Hurley, former ambassador to China, that it was time for him to publish the story of his failure to achieve peace between the nationalists and communists in China, since it "might stem the undoubted determination of these left-wingers to recognize and support Mao Tse-tung and the communization of China."[33]

Although both Hoover and Knowland were opposed to the recognition of the People's Republic of China, neither was averse to meeting the famine conditions there with food relief. The two conferred late in March 1950 over the telephone, and the result was a proposal from Knowland to Secretary of State Dean Acheson that surplus American food supplies be directed to the Chinese people, that the people of that country be notified of the American intention to furnish relief via the Voice of America and other channels, and that the food be provided subject to the condition that it go to all those in need and not just to those who supported the communist government. Knowland suggested the creation of a relief commission similar to the Committee for Relief in Belgium (CRB) under Hoover during World War I, with the distribution of food to be handled under the supervision of committees composed of both Chinese and American members. He believed, Knowland told Acheson, "that this should be done as a humanitarian move without in any way necessitating the recognition by this government of the regime in whose area the famine conditions prevail."[34] Acheson, however, believed that for the time being "the disadvantages of attempting to offer governmental relief outweigh the advantages." He did not, however, discourage private relief initiatives.[35]

By late 1949 the recommendations of the Hoover Commission had acquired considerable momentum in Congress, and Hoover was far more hopeful that a significant proportion of the suggested reforms would be adopted. He was pleased with the reception that the work of the Citizens' Committee was receiving and with the growing public interest in the commission's report.[36] Hoover had considered the opposition of Secretary of Defense James Forrestal to be one of the most formidable obstacles to reforms in the military structure, but a more positive attitude was indicated on the part of the Defense Department when Forrestal was replaced by Louis Johnson. Evidence of this new attitude could be seen in Johnson's offer to send a military aide to meet Hoover's train when he arrived from New York to testify before the House Armed Services Committee and in his offer of a military aircraft to fly Hoover back to New York at any time he chose to leave.[37] From the director of the budget came an encouraging message in January 1950: "This Budget reflects something of what you have hoped to attain in the field of Federal budgeting. It is certainly a step, and I hope a fairly extensive step in the right direction."[38] Hoover responded that the "form of the new Budget in the adopting of the performance principle is the greatest step in the advance of this problem since 1920." He was sorry, he wrote, that "few people on this earth will ever fully understand its importance to good government."[39] Little by little Hoover could feel that he was once again contributing to the shape and practices of the federal government as he saw the reforms recommended by the Hoover Commission gradually put into effect.

Having long been critical of the influence of alleged communists and "fellow-travelers" in the federal government, Hoover was cheered by Republican activities in digging out evidence that buttressed his suspicions. In late January 1950, he wrote Congressman Richard Nixon: "The conviction of Alger Hiss was due to your patience and persistence alone. At last the stream of treason that existed in our Government has been exposed in a fashion that all may believe."[40] He was similarly supportive of the investigations led by Senator Joseph McCarthy, and he objected to efforts like those of Senator Millard Tydings, whom he regarded as obstructing McCarthy's probes.[41]

However, Hoover was uncharacteristically silent during the early months of 1949 concerning the gradual evolution of an American commitment to the defense of Europe under the North Atlantic Treaty Organization (NATO). Perhaps his silence was due to the fact that the debate overlapped the final months of the Hoover Commission's work and also because he was intent on the bipartisan effort to get the Hoover Commission's recommendations adopted by Congress. Not even in Edgar Rickard's diary of his conversations with the former president is there any indication that Hoover was monitoring the debate in the Senate over the treaty. But a year later, when the press of lobbying for the commission's recommendations had lessened somewhat, Hoover began to devote attention to the issue. In May of 1950, after meeting with Senator Kenneth Wherry, Hoover sent Wherry a memorandum dealing with Secretary of State Acheson's forthcoming visit to Europe to consult with leaders of NATO. There were, Hoover wrote, "grave questions in this matter as to which the American people need information. In fact, we need a foreign policy." He reiterated his view that the United States was "economically overstrained" and unable to give the American people the "services and relief of taxes that they should enjoy." These enormous expenditures derived from the "Marshall Plan, the subsidizing of European armament and the demands for our own defense."[42]

Hoover insisted that before the United States appropriated more money the people needed to know what the administration's policies were, and what the policies were of the European nations "for whom we are making huge sacrifices and efforts." Pointing to newsmagazine descriptions of Europe's small military strength in comparison with that of the Soviet Union, Hoover asked whether the time had not come "when we should find out beyond any question of a doubt whether the Nations of Western Europe and Southern Asia are willing to do far more themselves for their own defense." He wondered how many of those nations would stand with the United States if the cold war heated up. Hoover suggested that the intentions of the Marshall Plan countries might be tested by insisting upon the use of approximately three billion dollars in counterpart funds, accumulated under the Marshall Plan, for defense purposes, and by asking those nations "to contribute something still more out of taxation." He concluded: "In any event, the American people should know more about this whole business and should know what our policies are."[43]

With the United States already overextended economically and overtaxed, in Hoover's view, a new factor appeared to further test the nation's economy when the communist government of North Korea invaded the Republic of Korea (South Korea) in June 1950. When the United States quickly rushed assistance to the South Koreans, Hoover issued a public statement:

> When the United States draws the sword, there is only one course for our people. Like others, I have opposed many of our foreign policies, but now is not the time to argue origins, mistakes, responsibilities, or consequences. There is only one way out of such situations as this: that is to win. To win we must have unity of purpose and action.[44]

He wrote Truman that he would "be glad to be of any service within my limitations at this time."[45] The president expressed warm appreciation for Hoover's statement and added that, if events required, "you may rest assured that I will want your help and advice."[46]

But beneath his public show of support for the president, Hoover was far from happy with the growing American military commitment in Korea. The limited assistance provided by other United Nations members to that country was proof to him that he had been correct in his doubts concerning the useful-ness of the United Nations and of the will of the west European nations to stand with the United States to repel communist aggression. When Senator Homer Ferguson wrote Hoover in mid-July 1950 to solicit his views concern-ing a United Nations resolution that Ferguson had proposed to "brand any nation assisting the North Koreans directly or indirectly as an aggressor against the United Nations," Hoover responded: "Your and my thinking run exactly on the same line. We must know who are with us and with what?"[47] Hoover concluded that as matters stood, "if we got into war with Russia, we might *perhaps* have the support of *Canada* and *Australia*." After such a resolution as Ferguson had proposed, Hoover suggested that the next step should be a demand for "economic sanctions on [North] Korea. If she was an aggressor that could not be denied under the United Nations Charter." He would then seek a U.N. denunciation of Soviet assistance to North Korea as aggression. After Korean security had been restored, he would "pull back our military actions to the Western Hemisphere. A war with Russia, with the support we now have in sight, could never end until we were economically exhausted—and we will be [economically exhausted] by a condition of huge armament for a few years even if we have no war with Russia."[48]

A few days later, in his annual talk to the summer Bohemian Club encampment, Hoover dropped the usual humor that filled his talks and de-voted himself to a serious review of the problems that faced the United States in the summer of 1950. The United Nations, he argued, was not functioning effectively as an instrument against communist aggression, and it would be even less effective if Communist China were added to the Security Council. The United States should make clear its determination to use the veto, if necessary, to deny membership to the Peoples' Republic of China. The west European nations, with the exception of Britain, lacked the will for a war with the Soviet Union and even the will to adequately prepare for one. Despite the fact that the manpower and industrial capacity of Western Europe were greater in 1950, the nations there had only one-fifth the army divisions that they had put into the field for the two world wars. A successful ground war could not be fought against the Russians with such numbers, and the United States must rely on air and sea power to defend itself. To counter the Soviet Union's obvious aggressive intentions, the free world must be prepared, and a first step should be to call for a U.N. resolution demanding that the members of the United Nations "refrain from economic, military or other aids to any" aggressor nation. If the Soviet Union vetoed it, the next step should be "to put the Communists out of the U.N." Hoover did not, however, expect the United Nations to take such an action at that time. Another possibility, however, was to introduce a resolution "denouncing Russia as an aggressor for having given military aid to [North] Korea," and a still further step might be "economic sanctions against Russia and her satellites for giving aid to an aggressor." If the United States failed in efforts to bring about increased solidarity and commitment among the noncommunist nations in resisting Soviet imperialism, then it should "retreat into the Western Hemisphere to save our own civilization from exhaustion." He did not consider that a desirable course of action, but the United States could be self-sufficient if forced to be. As for "fifth-columnists," Hoover suggested legislating directly against them by amplifying the laws against conspiracy and treason so that the government could "move directly against any publication or any persons attending any meeting of Communists where subversive activities were discussed." He did not object to intellectuals believing in or sympathizing with "abstract Communism," for that was a part of academic freedom, but the moment they attempted to move from theory to discussion of subversive action they ought to be targets of the FBI. Hoover had no patience with those who refused to take a loyalty oath to the government, but he did not favor a federal law to compel it. In conclusion Hoover told his audience:

> Today most of the American people have abandoned that supreme fantasy of all history which has been promoted since the Russian Revolution. That folly was the hallucination that this was one world. There are two worlds. One world is militaristic, imperialistic, aggressive, atheistic, and without compassion. The other world still holds to belief in God, free nations, human dignity and peace.[49]

In mid-August Senator Taft asked Hoover for his views on the need for any economic controls as a result of the Korean War. The former president responded that the United States was involved both in a minor war and in a preparedness program for a major war. The Korean War would cause "scarcely a ripple" in the American economy, but the preparedness effort did require controls. To curb inflation he suggested "indirect controls," including prohibition of hoarding and excessive inventories, limitations on installment credit, an increase in excise taxes on nonessentials in order to discourage unnecessary buying, and cuts in government expenditures. Regarding controls of commodities and processing, he did not believe there was need for them, and there was great danger in all-embracing price, wage, and rationing controls at present. He advocated only some controls over materials and manufacturing that were a military necessity. "Our greatest domestic danger at this time," he wrote Taft, "is shock hysteria in the public which leads the Congress to unnecessary surrenders of freedom."[50]

Early in September the seventy-six-year-old former president contemplated his role in the 1950 mid-term elections. He wrote one correspondent: "I have agreed to do some work in this campaign as I believe it is the last chance for our country as we have known it."[51] Later in the month he responded to a request for speeches in the campaign by writing that he had "been awaiting the outcome of this three ring circus in foreign relations (plus a gall bladder attack) before settling anything in the nature of a public address." For it to be effective, he thought it best that any speech he made not be in a "partisan frame," but rather an analysis of where the Truman policies were leading. He had scheduled a speech over the Columbia Broadcasting System (CBS) for October 19, "by which time we should be able to see more clearly and by which time I shall have recovered some pep."[52]

A few days before Hoover's speech was to be given, Truman would be giving a speech of his own, and Hoover decided that he would have to "take into account what he [Truman] has to say" in preparing his own. Looking ahead to the elections, he concluded that the prospects of the Democrats would be enhanced if the "Truman war" could be ended before the election, but otherwise it would be of less value for them. As for the Republicans: "Our old issues of economy and reduction of government expenditures are practically lost in this mass of military operations." He found the Republicans, however, "fighting well all over the country."[53] The day before delivering his speech, Hoover wrote a letter congratulating Harold Stassen on a speech Stassen had just made; Stassen had, wrote Hoover, done "great service to the country when you propounded certain questions the other night." He wondered, however, if it were not time for Stassen to begin to propose answers, as well.[54]

Hoover's own speech, on October 19, dealt with American foreign policy. He traced the course of American relations with the Soviet Union from the time America "first entered this swamp of lost statesmanship when we recognized the Communist government in 1933." He recalled the communist attempts to subvert the U.S. government, the wartime alliance against Germany, and the broken agreements and the vetoes by the Soviet Union in the United Nations. The Russians had engineered the attack on South Korea, he charged, and "every day they engage in defamation of the American people." The only hope of containing Soviet expansion lay in "an effective organized phalanx of the non-Communist world which will freeze the ambitions of the Kremlin." But Western Europe had shown no disposition to join in such an effort. They could muster only 30 active divisions against the Soviet potential of 175 divisions, and the United States could not supply more than a minor part of the deficiency. Despite all of the loans and gifts from the United States, those nations had created no significant defense capability by 1950. This meager result from American sacrifices was, Hoover said, "deeply disappointing to a growing body of Americans." There were serious questions being asked by Americans as to whether the Europeans, outside of Great Britain, had "the will to fight, or even the will to preparedness." It was time to demand more than words from those nations. The United States should be willing to help the Europeans, but "they must do most of it themselves—and do it fast." Noting that there had been suggestions that ten American combat divisions should be sent to Europe, Hoover argued that such an action could result only in "a slaughter of American boys unless many times that number were standing by their sides. We should say, and at once, that we shall provide no more money until a definitely unified and sufficient European army is in sight. And further that 10 American divisions will not be landed until then." It was time for the other nations of the world to help in shouldering the burden of their own defense, for the United States could not "long endure the present drain on our economy." Said Hoover:

> But if we do not find real military action of powerful strength in Western Europe; if there is no definite and effective mobilization of the other members of the United Nations so as to take up the major burden of their own defenses, then we had better reconsider our whole relation to the problem. In that event, we had better quit talking and paying, and consider holding the Atlantic Ocean with Britain (if they wish) as one frontier, and the Pacific Ocean with an armed Japan and other islands as the other frontier.

He made it clear that he did not want to retreat from the communist front, but if the other nations of the world were unwilling to man that front, then the United States ought to settle for "an uneasy peace within the economic burdens which the United States can bear."[55] Hoover's speech was the opening round of what would come to be referred to as "the Great Debate."

The issue of communist subversion in the federal government had become a major controversy in America by 1950, largely under the influence of the investigations and charges of such public figures as Senator Joseph McCarthy of Wisconsin, and late in that year the controversy brought Hoover another invitation to service from President Truman. The president wrote Hoover that there had "been a great deal of talk about the infiltration of Communists in the government, particularly in the State Department." He had decided to appoint a bipartisan commission from all segments of American life to investigate the extent of communist penetration into the government, and he proposed to appoint Hoover as chairman. Truman told Hoover that if he would consent to serve, it "could not only restore the confidence of the people in the organization of the government, but could help the foreign policy situation very much."[56] Hoover replied that despite his advancing age he did not "wish to ever refuse service to the country." However, he doubted that there were "any consequential card-carrying Communists in the government or, if there are, they should be known to the FBI." The lack of confidence in the government, he suggested, came from "the belief that there are men in government (not Communists) whose attitudes are such that they have disastrously advised on policies in relation to Communist Russia," and that they were still in the government. To examine the past and present behavior of such men would require a widespread and extensive inquiry, including the authority to question under oath and to have access to "all files of all officials and departments over the years." The personnel of such a committee, if Congress and the public were to have any confidence in it, would have to be approved by the leaders of both parties in Congress, and it was likely that Congress would conduct its own investigation anyway. Hoover concluded:

> Therefore, it seems to me that any inquiry as to "Communists in the government" by an informal commission would not be likely to satisfy the public or to restore confidence. I dislike indeed to respond in terms of declination to any request of yours, as I would like greatly to be helpful to you in these troublous [sic] times. In that direction, may I suggest that a statement might be issued by you that you would be glad if the Congress would either create such a commission, or would itself make an inquiry on the broadest basis such as I have outlined, both as to the past and present. That very statement by you would greatly restore confidence in the administration's foreign policy makers.[57]

On September 26, 1950, the North Atlantic Council announced that it had agreed on the establishment of a unified force for the defense of Europe. On December 18, General Dwight D. Eisenhower was designated as supreme commander of the NATO armed forces. On that same date, influential columnist Walter Lippmann attacked American foreign policy. The American people had been "shaken," he wrote, by the "demonstration of misinformation, miscalculation, and misjudgment at the highest levels of decision and command" involved in the decision to allow "virtually all of the American Army and all of its reserves" to be "sucked into a peninsula of Asia in the presence and in defiance of overwhelmingly superior forces." It was time, he wrote, for a new doctrine, the "central principle" of which "would be that North America is an island, a continental island to be sure, but still in relation to the Old World an island. The people of North America can never meet on even terms the armed forces of the Eurasian Continent." Lippmann continued:

> The true American doctrine—both in defense and in offense—is to recognize limitations of and to exploit the advantages of our island character—our inferiority in manpower, our superiority in technol-

ogy and in production, the oceans of sea and air around us which offer us the means of a flexible defense and a highly mobile offense.

The American people, he found, wanted "to increase the military power of the United States and to get out of entanglements like Korea. There is little doubt, I think, that the main tide is running in the direction of an armed isolation." He concluded: "Our allies abroad will be well-advised, therefore, for their own security as well as for our own, to work with and not against an American withdrawal from the overextended commitments of the Truman doctrine."[58] Lippmann followed up by writing the next day, December 19, 1950: "The new doctrine will have to found the defense of the United States and of the Atlantic community upon seapower and airpower—and along with them upon a diplomacy which is conceived and is planned by men who know the limitations and also the advantages of sea and air power."[59]

It was one of the few times that Hoover found himself in agreement with the columnist. On December 20, Hoover reiterated the theme he had begun to enunciate during the summer, in another nationally broadcast speech. He regarded it as one of the most important speeches of his public career. As he wrote to Raymond Moley and others: "In an 'emergency' on June 29, 1941, I made an appraisal of the forces moving in the world. I advised arming to the teeth and a policy of watchful waiting before we committed ourselves. I pointed out the obvious disaster if we jumped in. I was proved right after infinite losses to our country." Hoover predicted that his new speech was "likely to be no more welcome than the one ten years ago."[60] To Taft he wrote: "The task I am setting in my speech on Wednesday night is to align us against commitment of American forces in Europe—or anywhere else until we can see clearly what support we will have this time." Conscious of the attacks that were likely to be launched against him, Hoover added: "I hope I may have some defense if that becomes necessary."[61] He did not, he said, "expect our Eastern seaboard press to be any more enthusiastic about this" speech than they had been about the one in June 1941.[62]

The speech, delivered as American forces reeled back in Korea before the onslaught of Chinese communist "volunteers," began with a survey of the global military situation. By contrast with the 800 million people and over 300 combat divisions of the communist world, only the British Commonwealth and the United States had shown any disposition, he argued, to defend the free world. Between the British Commonwealth and the United States there were some 300 million people, only about 60 combat divisions, but powerful air and naval forces. From this he concluded that there was no possibility of victory against the Soviet Union and its satellites in a land war. Moreover, the United States was "already economically strained by government expenditures." Hoover argued for the defense of the "Western Hemisphere Gibraltar of Western Civilization," and also, through the use of air and sea power, for the defense of the Atlantic and Pacific oceans, with Great Britain as the frontier of American defense in the Atlantic, and Japan, Formosa, and the Philippines the American frontier in the Pacific. This meant that the United States should continue to concentrate on the development of air and sea forces rather than a large army. In this way the United States could, after the initial large expenditures on planes and ships, cut its military expenditures, balance its budget and free itself "from the dangers of inflation and economic degeneration." Economically strong, the United States could continue to feed the hungry of the world and to assist other countries in arming themselves against communism. But before the United States furnished any further military aid to Europe, those nations must demonstrate their own determination to defend themselves, by organizing and equipping combat divisions in sufficient numbers to "erect a sure dam against the red flood." That must also be done before the United States landed "another man or another dollar on their shores." To do otherwise would be to encourage another Korea, which "would be a calamity to Europe as well as to us." The American policy toward Europe should "be confined to a period of watchful waiting." This, Hoover argued, was not isolationism, but just the opposite. And eventually "the millions of non-Communist peoples of the world" would awaken to their dangers, and "the evils of Communism and the disintegration of their racial controls will bring their own disintegration."[63]

Hoover's office reported after the speech a "tremendous, favorable response," with the telephone ringing continually, and a flood of telegrams, which began even before Hoover had returned to his office from delivering the speech. Not one message received had been unfavorable.[64] The gauntlet was down and the "Great Debate" had warmed up, for Hoover's position was in sharp opposition to the Truman administration's commitment to the defense of Western Europe, a commitment symbolized by Eisenhower's imminent departure for Europe to take command of Western defense forces there. A check through the *Congressional Record* for a comparison of comment in Congress concerning the December 20 speech with that for the June 1941 address found that there had been little comment over the earlier speech in contrast "with the amount of comment which the speech of December 20, 1950 is receiving in the Record."[65]

The *New York Herald Tribune*, committed to American intervention anywhere in the world, admitted that the Hoover position was not "isolationist," since it embraced the western hemisphere as well as Britain, Japan, Taiwan, and the Philippines, but it coined a new word to describe Hoover's doctrine—"retreatism." The doctrine had gained "increased stature," the newspaper admitted, because of Hoover's advocacy of it, and it represented "a body of opinion that must be reckoned with in the formation of American policy," because it "appeals to the angry frustration which events in Korea have aroused and because it offers what purports to be a cheaper way to defend

America than by assisting allies."[66] President Truman wasted no time in reiterating the position of his administration that Western Europe's defense was vital to the security of the United States.[67] Hoover would no doubt have agreed, if the Europeans would show a comprehension that their defense was vital to their own security. When Senator H. Alexander Smith defended the Hoover doctrine in the Senate, the former president wrote him: "I know how difficult it is to defend this creature—but you did a great job and I am grateful." He suspected that "Congress is going to get a jolt of public opinion such as it has not seen for a long time!"[68]

Hoover was correct; members of the Congress were inundated with mail and wires in support of the Hoover doctrine. Richard Nixon wrote Hoover on December 22 that he had "already received over 100 wires this morning indicating enthusiastic approval of your speech last night." He told Hoover he was "sure that your comments will have an excellent effect in developing a more realistic approach to the critical problems we face today."[69] Raymond Moley supported the doctrine in his newspaper column and in *Newsweek*; he wrote to Hoover: "I don't think a speech was ever much at so necessary a moment in so clearly reflecting the feeling of the country." He thought it would be "of immense help in creating a real Republican policy in the new Congress."[70] Felix Morley expressed enthusiastic approval and added: "If the Europeans have any real desire to unite for self-preservation your speech will stimulate it. If they have no such desire, you have at least pointed to the course that we shall eventually have to follow." History would justify Hoover's stand, he predicted, "whichever way it goes."[71] Landon thought that it had "been a long time since a talk by anyone has rung the bell as your last one has done." He decried the misinterpretation of the speech by administration spokesmen, but he found general agreement on what "is considered to be the kernel of your talk and that is that we can't save people who are unwilling to save themselves."[72]

In what was widely billed as the administration's "reply" to Hoover, John Foster Dulles, Republican member of Truman's State Department, delivered a speech on December 29. Dulles wrote the former president that he regretted his speech had been billed in the press in this way, since he had planned it, instead, as "a year-end discussion of the critical international situation." He admitted that he planned to express a point of view that was somewhat different from Hoover's, but he added that he agreed with much of what the former president had said and hoped that Hoover would agree with much of what he had to say. "I think it is very healthy to have a great nation debate upon the grave issues of our time," he wrote. Enclosing a copy of the letter to Hoover with one he wrote to Taft, Dulles told the senator: "The State Department publicity people pulled this one on me. Actually, as you will see, my speech tonight pretty much represents the strategic concept which you and I discussed."[73]

Despite the ballyhoo attempted by newspapers like the *New York Times*, Dulles's speech seems scarcely to have caused a ripple among the public. The *Houston Post* found his arguments made with "smoothly flowing rhetoric," but filled with "defects in his reasoning, some contradictions and inconsistencies which leaves one far from convinced or assured."[74] Even the *New York Times* found the response to the speech to be "insignificant" and "disappointing," which it admitted was "in sharp contrast to the heavy public response resulting from the Hoover speech."[75]

In his prespeech letter to Senator Taft, Hoover had expressed the hope that Taft would come to his defense in the event of attacks on his doctrine. Taft did join the fray with a speech in the Senate on January 5, 1951. In that speech Taft took up many of the same points Hoover had posed two weeks earlier and propounded similar policies. He called for reliance on air and sea power for defense not only of the western hemisphere, but of the Atlantic and the Pacific—everywhere that it was possible to exclude communism by other than the use of land armies. He told the Senate:

> Of course, Mr. Hoover's recent speech was completely misrepresented by the Administration press in this regard. He did not advocate retirement to the American continent. He only urged that emphasis be placed on our defense of the Atlantic and Pacific oceans, as it should be particularly if all of our allies should abandon us.

Taft broadened the scope of the American defense perimeter to include Indonesia, Australia, and New Zealand, but, like Hoover, he opposed the commitment of American ground troops for the defense of Europe until those nations showed a greater disposition to defend themselves. Like the former president, Taft was concerned about the implications for the American economy of the massive expenditures on defense under Truman. The United States "must not so extend" itself "as to threaten economic collapse or inflation, for a productive and free America is the last bastion of liberty."[76] Taft regarded his speech, he said, as fundamentally "in accord with Mr. Hoover's theory, although I have tried to make it somewhat less uncompromising."[77]

Hoover's speech had attracted considerable and encouraging support from newspapers and from the public, but it also attracted the predictable distortions and smears.[78] When Senator Knowland queried him concerning the editorial and other response to his speech, Hoover sent him a breakdown from his clipping service that showed that of the newspapers covered by his service, those with 68 percent of the circulation supported his position, those with 8 percent showed partial support, and those with 24 percent were opposed. The survey showed the greatest editorial support in New England, the Midwest, the Middle Atlantic, the Southwest, and the Mountain and Pacific states, with the only areas opposed being the Southern and South Atlantic states.[79] But, as Senator Taft put it: "Unfortunately, the internationalist press in the East and the New Deal columnists are determined to involve us in the project of a large American army in Europe, and they are doing everything possible to smear statements like that of President Hoover or my own."[80]

Typical of the distortions of Hoover's position was the summary of it offered by the moderator of the "American Forum of the Air," on January 14, 1951:

> Former President Hoover has launched the great debate. He has proposed a foreign policy quite different from the Truman doctrine. He wants the United States to pull out of Europe and Asia; to preserve this Western Hemisphere Gibraltar. He would cut off all aid to Western Europe until it showed spirit and strength in defending itself against Red Russia. Administration leaders have called this isolationism, a wave of defeat and frustration, an act of appeasement.

This description, which mirrored the administration's distortions of the Hoover doctrine, omitted his call for defense of the Pacific and Atlantic oceans, with the American frontiers in distant Great Britain, Japan, Formosa, and the Philippines. Fortunately, Senator Everett Dirksen was present in this instance to correct the distortion of Hoover's views.[81] When the *New York Herald Tribune* described a speech by Harold Stassen in mid-January as "aimed at the position of Herbert Hoover," the Minnesotan quickly wrote the newspaper that it was in error:

> I believe that President Hoover's position has been partly misinterpreted by both the administration and by the Republican Senators who claim to adopt it. His basic premise is that if the western European nations are not determined to defend themselves and do not themselves rearm, we cannot attempt to defend them on the ground. This is certainly sound.

Stassen also agreed with Hoover that the first priority should be given to "the building of an extremely powerful American Air Force."[82]

From a number of quarters came appeals that Hoover follow up the December 20 speech with another to keep up the attack.[83] He had already drafted a list of possible elements that might go into a speech of reply to his critics. Among them were an expression of regret "that the debate cannot be carried out with resort to name-calling, such as 'isolationist,' 'retreatist,' 'defeatist' . . . all of which I deny, and all of which serves only to cloud the issues": an expression of hope that his opponents would "substitute for vague promises an analysis based on the cold mathematics of the situation with concrete

documentation"; an expression of the thesis again "that the crux of the difficulties lie in Europe's ability to help themselves *today* . . . not at some indefi-
nite future time"; and the question: "Are we, or are we not definitely
committing ourselves to a land invasion of the European continent."[84] He
wrote to General A. C. Wedemeyer late in December: "There will be more of
this debate—probably more observations from me in the latter part of January."[85] During that month, Hoover began to circulate drafts of a proposed
speech among his advisers.[86]

On January 28, the *New York Herald Tribune* reported that the Democratic National Committee was circulating among Democratic congressmen a
paper written by the committee's publicity division, which accused Hoover
and Taft of being "false prophets of doom." The paper contended that the two
Republicans were advocating the same "wrong" policies which they had supported before World War II. Just as the two "isolationists" had supposedly
misjudged the situation from 1939 to 1941, so they were now deemed to be
misjudging it again. Two men who had been so completely "wrong" a decade
earlier could certainly not be judged competent, the reasoning went, in the
present circumstances.[87] The paper smacked of a resurgence of the Michelson
tactics during and after his presidency, and was a perfect example for Hoover
of the Democrats' tendency to confront opposition with smears rather than to
debate an issue on its merits.

In his speech of February 9, 1951, Hoover addressed himself to this type of
criticism. He pointed to his speech of June 29, 1941, furnishing quotations
from it that had questioned the wisdom of America aligning itself with Russian communism against Germany and added: "Need I remind you that the
grip of Communism in this decade has spread slavery from 200,000,000 to
800,000,000? And we have no peace." There were certain "stark realities"
upon which American foreign policy must be based. The first was the impos-
sibility of defeating the Soviet Union's enormous army in a land war, given the
small number of combat divisions then available in the Atlantic Pact nations.
Another was the desirability and possibility of defending the western hemisphere and making it self-sufficient. "I am not advocating isolationism," he
told his listeners, "but if other nations should fail, we may be isolated by force
of circumstances and against our will." A third reality was the finite American
economic capacity. The burdens proposed by the Truman administration
meant sure economic chaos for the nation, and "the economic destruction of the
United States is one of the means by which Stalin hopes to overcome us."
Another factor was that clearly "the U.N. for the present will not be a substantial protection from Communist aggression." The United States must take into
consideration its commitments in Korea, Japan, and elsewhere before obligat-
ing itself in Europe. The North Atlantic Treaty Organization provided only
that the signatory nations would aid one another in the event of attack. There
had been no attack. Despite earlier assurances from the Truman administra-

tion that American participation in NATO would not mean the stationing of American ground troops in Europe, it was apparent that Truman contemplated exactly that, even though there had been no attack. Did not the disparity between Soviet strength and that of the NATO nations imply that many more American divisions would have to be sent?[88]

Hoover reiterated his own doctrine. The air threat to the Soviet Union, he insisted, was "far more powerful than pouring American divisions into the reach of this Asiatic horde." A ground war, moreover, must necessarily be a defensive war, while in the air the United States could go on the offensive. Moreover, the concentration of American resources on air power would be less of a strain on the economy—for the same amount of money that would be required to maintain even as few as ten U.S. combat divisions in Europe for a year, Hoover calculated, America could "purchase and man 390 B-36 long-range bombers compared to 60 of them at present," and the annual cost of maintaining the bombers would be only one-third of the cost for the ten divisions. But Hoover had altered his doctrine slightly since the December speech, and it was closer now to that of Senator Taft. Where his December speech had emphasized defense, Hoover now contemplated, as had Taft, the use of American air and sea power in an offensive role to aid Western Europe if it were attacked by the Soviet Union. Hoover argued that both Japan and West Germany should be given their independence under representative governments. He said: "During 100 years these nations were the great dams against these Russian-controlled hordes. In the last war we may have been engaged in a great crusade for freedom of mankind, but we certainly destroyed these two dams." In the event that the nations of Western Europe continued to inadequately provide for their own defense, the United States should, as a "prudent nation, have in mind a second line of air and naval defense based upon the foreign shores of the Pacific and Atlantic Oceans both North and South, and I may add the Mediterranean and Indian Ocean." What he proposed, Hoover argued, was neither retreat nor withdrawal. "The essence of this program I have proposed is to effectively restrain our enemies from attack upon our allies or ourselves. It is the best chance of peace—even if it is an uneasy peace."[89]

Air-power advocates were delighted with Hoover's speeches, but the February speech more than the December one. Retired Brigadier General Bonner Fellers, former aid to General MacArthur, wrote in *Human Events* that the logic of Hoover's December speech and Taft's January speech was "compelling." He wrote: "The essence of the Hoover-Taft position is a pragmatic, resourceful attempt to deter war, win it if war comes, and in any event avoid the slaughter of millions of our youth on the Eurasian mainland." A powerful air force was the answer to the dilemma posed by America's inability to numerically "right the world's balance of war." He argued:

To succeed in a program of containment we must be able to strike quickly, not just on the European fronts but *anywhere* about and within Russia's far-flung borders. Only air power has the range, speed and flexibility to perform such a mission. . . . More than anything else, Russia fears air power. It is the one weapon against which Russia's terrific ground forces, enormous distances, and winters are impotent.[90]

Fellers to the contrary, the use of American air power as an offensive weapon against the Soviet Union was not set forth clearly in Hoover's December speech, although it was in his February address. The shift between the two speeches from an emphasis on defense to the offensive use of air power against the Soviet Union itself in the event of war, stemmed in part from the influence of Major Alexander P. de Seversky, noted exponent of air power since before World War II.[91] In a press release of January 16, 1951, de Seversky sharply criticized Hoover's December position for being

a purely defensive strategy based on the Navy and Air Force. But we know that defense has never won a war and never will. It would leave the initiative to the enemy in the wishful hope that the Soviets, if left alone, will disintegrate with time. It would also contemplate abandonment of our Western Allies—an unnecessary step if our strategy is right.[92]

Hoover subsequently wrote to de Seversky concerning his criticism, and the two men began a correspondence in which the aviator explained to the former president the offensive possibilities of air power.

Hoover's new position was made even clearer when he testified before the Senate Foreign Relations Committee on February 27, 1951, in behalf of the Wherry Resolution. That resolution, introduced by Senator Kenneth Wherry of Nebraska, would have expressed it as the "sense of the Senate that no ground forces of the United States should be assigned to duty in Europe for the purposes of the North Atlantic Treaty, pending the adoption of a policy with respect thereto by Congress."[93] In his statement before the committee and in his answers to questions, Hoover rebutted all of the arguments advanced for stationing U.S. ground troops in Europe and raised his familiar arguments against such a policy. He concluded that "there is only one real salvation for Europe at the present moment. That is, to build up the air and naval power of the United States and Britain so as to overwhelm Russia in case of attack."[94] Bonner Fellers thought Hoover's testimony had been "marvelous" and would "do a world of good."[95] Seversky wrote Hoover: "From a professional military point of view, your second speech was much closer to the strategic concept we airmen entertain, and your statement before Congress, from our point of view, was nearly perfect."[96] Hoover was convinced that the Senate hearings had awakened the public mind to the prospect that the United States might be drawn, through the Truman policies, into a Korea-type war in Europe, and that "the American people, outside selected circles, are ninety percent with us."[97] Taft agreed that Hoover's testimony had been helpful in arousing public support for the Wherry resolution. He had heard nothing but the highest praise for Hoover's testimony and he told Hoover: "I believe the smear tactics have failed, and whether we win or lose we will have the majority of the people with us."[98]

While the Senate grappled over the Wherry resolution, Hoover addressed a dinner meeting of House and Senate Republicans in Washington on March 13. The purpose of the meeting, Congressman Clarence Brown of Ohio told Hoover, was to "clarify the [international] problems and help them consolidate their position for the coming battle."[99] The meeting was off the record, but was nevertheless reported in the newspapers. At the meeting, Hoover reiterated his reasons for opposing the stationing of American ground troops in Europe, insisting that it was an "unwarranted gamble." He lashed out at what he described as the "infantry generals" of the Pentagon who could not grasp the strategic potential of air power and argued that the deterrent posed by long-range American air power, more than the stationing of American troops in Europe, would prevent the outbreak of World War III. It was time, he insisted, that civilian control be re-established over the armed forces through the reassertion of congressional responsibilities over foreign and military policy decisions. The West Europeans, he argued, were not worried about the possibility of a Soviet invasion, and some Europeans suspected that the United States was seeking a war with the Russians, Western Europe being the battlefield. Unless the Europeans could get together, he said, "they can offer no substantial resistance to Russia."[100] A month after Hoover's talk, the mystery of the press coverage was solved when the manager of the Willard Hotel, where the dinner meeting had been held, discovered that a zealous reporter had apparently drilled a hole through the partition behind where Hoover had stood and a stenographer had listened and taken notes.[101]

By late March Hoover had concluded of the Great Debate: "We will probably be defeated, but we can at least hope that posterity will realize that we did our best in their protection."[102] Bonner Fellers, who was now an assistant to the chairman of the GOP national committee, acted as a liaison between the former president and members of Congress in furnishing them with information concerning Hoover's position.[103] Early in April the Senate voted by the narrow margin of 49 to 43 to permit four American divisions to be sent to Europe as part of the NATO force, with the condition that Truman seek approval from Congress before increasing these troops. The Wherry

Resolution was then tabled. Robert Taft, who from the beginning had been more compromising than Hoover on the issue, voted for the four divisions and voted to table the Wherry Resolution, as he was satisfied that the point had been made and that Congress had established control over any increase in the American commitment.[104]

Coincidental with Hoover's inauguration of the Great Debate, revisionist historians had launched a timely attack on the policies of the Roosevelt administration of a decade earlier. At the American Historical Association meeting in December 1950, Professor Charles C. Tansill of Georgetown University and Dr. Harry Elmer Barnes, formerly of Smith College, presented a panel in which Roosevelt's foreign policies came under fire for "allowing an unalerted Pearl Harbor to be attacked even though [Roosevelt] knew the attack was coming; of paving the way for Communism's present death grip on China by turning Japan into an enemy of the United States, and then, in World War II, destroying Japan as a bulwark against Russia." Tansill reasoned: "If Japan could be maneuvered into firing the first shot, America could enter a crusade on two fronts. Thanks to the breaking of the Japanese code, Roosevelt and his coterie of advisers had advance knowledge of Japan's intention to strike." Barnes attacked the dominance of the history profession by "court historians" —those who had worked for the federal government during and after the war—who were committed to defending Roosevelt against the truth as raised by revisionist historians. Barnes argued: "The attitude of the public during war time has been maintained by means of propaganda. The United States is likely to undertake the third crusade before it is fully aware of the real causes and disastrous results of the second." He concluded: "A robust revisionism is our only hope of deliverance, if there be one, at this late date."[105] As Joan Hoff Wilson has pointed out, Hoover was actively encouraging the revisionists by seeking financial support for them and by providing them with material from his own extensive files.[106] Such revisionist works not only served to vindicate Hoover's position in 1940–41, but also aided his fight against the new interventionism of the 1950s.

In the spring of 1951 the Great Debate was overshadowed by, and intertwined with, the dramatic dismissal by President Truman of General Douglas MacArthur from his command of U.N. forces in Korea. Convinced from intelligence reports that the Chinese effort in Korea was ebbing for lack of supplies and modern weapons, MacArthur had suggested a battlefield cease-fire to the Chinese commander, thereby undercutting Truman's own diplomatic efforts in behalf of an armistice. Worse, from the administration's standpoint, was the fact that MacArthur coupled his offer of a cease-fire with threats of possible military action against China itself if a cease-fire were not forthcoming. This was in clear opposition to Truman's policies and in defiance of the president's "gag" order to the general. When MacArthur went further, in a reply to a letter from Congressman Joseph Martin, by implicitly criticizing Truman for his failure to make use of Nationalist Chinese troops from Formosa, the president relieved MacArthur of his command.[107]

Hoover's suite in the Waldorf Tower quickly became headquarters for orchestrating MacArthur's return to the United States. Bonner Fellers, who had served as secretary to the general during the war and in the first months of the occupation, now acted as the liaison between Hoover and MacArthur. When MacArthur expressed his intention to return to the United States by ship, Hoover directed the general instead to fly back as soon as he could. Clearly, if he returned by ship the furor over his dismissal would have moderated by the time he reached the United States. According to Fellers, MacArthur told him to inform "the chief" that if Hoover would advise him what he should do he would follow his advice, and when he got back to the United States he would "take his [Hoover's] advice and that of no one else." Fellers later recalled that when he passed the message along to Hoover, Hoover "started giving [advice] right then over the phone—quite a bit—so much that I again called [MacArthur] back that night."[108]

Hoover suggested the content for speeches MacArthur would be called upon to make, recommended that he deny, for the present, the reports that he had accepted a $100,000 a year position with the Remington Rand Corporation since it "is very bad and lowers your stature at this critical moment," and arranged for a great homecoming for him in San Francisco, enlisting the assistance of William Randolph Hearst.[109] He also apparently helped to engineer the invitation to MacArthur to speak before Congress.[110] Fellers told the general that Hoover had also advised him not to "fear their yells of 'creating disunity.' There are things far worse for a nation than disunity over policies. The worst is *wrong* policies that kill the flower of a people."[111] Hoover outlined for MacArthur the cleavage over American foreign policies, as exemplified by the Great Debate. But while others allied with Hoover in the fight against the administration's foreign policies eagerly expected MacArthur's active and effective support of the Hoover position, the former president counseled the general not to align himself with either side, but to "speak above them."[112]

MacArthur later told newsman Richard Berlin that he had expected to slip off unnoticed to a hotel upon his arrival in San Francisco and then to fly east unrecognized. He felt discouraged, even disgraced. But the tumultuous greeting he received in San Francisco buoyed his spirits.[113] MacArthur followed much of Hoover's advice; and Bonner Fellers, reminiscing later, concluded that the general's speech before Congress reflected much of Hoover's influence. He estimated "that possibly half of the points in the speech had been more or less suggested by Mr. Hoover."[114]

Hoover, himself, had been silent on foreign policy, allowing the debate in Congress over the Wherry Resolution and MacArthur's return to the United

States to reveal the opposition to Truman's policies. Late in May he wrote Arch Shaw that he had scaled down his public speaking because he didn't know what further he could add to what had already been said. "You have had about two billion words on the subject during the last month—and an astonishing amount of lies from men in high places," he observed. "I intend to keep still until after this burst of words and lies have gone by."[115] Late in June, however, he was appalled at information he received that alleged Marshall Plan funds were being used in Europe to build three deluxe hotels—one each in Rome, London, and Paris—and a television station in Monaco. This did not strike him as worthy expenditure of money taken from the American taxpayer, and he asked Senator Homer Ferguson to investigate.[116] In early August Ferguson sent Hoover a detailed report prepared by the ECA, dealing with ECA aid to the hotel industry in Europe. Counterpart funds had been used to assist in the construction of 6 principal hotels in Austria alone, along with 43 other newly constructed hotels. In Italy the ECA had been involved, through counterpart funds, in grants and loans to 443 hotel projects. Aid had also been provided to hotel building in other European countries.[117] Hoover was not pleased since he felt "that there are five million American families who need homes more than Europe needs hotels."[118]

In July Hoover returned to the attack with a memorandum to Senators Homer Ferguson and Kenneth Wherry and to journalist George Sokolsky listing the essentials of a bipartisan foreign policy. Bipartisanship, he wrote, could only be obtained through "cooperation of the Administration with the Republicans in the United States Senate and House of Representatives," who were the only "representatives of the Party who can make effective commitments in respect to bi-partisan policies." It no doubt increased the efficiency of the State Department to hire Republicans, he observed, in an obvious reference to John Foster Dulles, but "the American people should not be deceived into thinking it constitutes bi-partisan action," because such Republicans were not "acting under the authority of the Republican members of the Congress." Bipartisanship in foreign policy also meant that the administration should not seek to "avoid the spirit of the Constitution" by making executive agreements and other commitments that did not require the approval of the Senate, nor could there be bipartisanship without consultation with Congressional Republicans in the early stages of any agreements made.[119]

In August Hoover traveled to his native Iowa where he addressed 20,000 people in 96 degree heat at the state fair. He called for a reawakening of interest in the "Old Virtues" —integrity, truth, honor, patriotism, economy in government, self-reliance, thrift, and self-sacrifice, as well as decency in public life. He lashed out at "a cancerous growth of intellectual dishonesty in public life which is mostly beyond the law"; and he said that he saw greater danger in America's "complaisance with evil," "public toleration of scandalous behavior," and "cynical acceptance of dishonor" than he did in foreign threats to the

United States. Referring to the revelations of corruption in the Truman administration, Hoover wondered what the founding fathers of the Republic would have thought "of the 'sacred honor' of the five per centers, mink coats, deep freezers and free hotel bills? Or favoritism in government loans and contracts? Or failure to prosecute evil-doers, cancerous rackets and gambling rings with their train of bribed officials all through the land." The issue in American life today, he insisted, is "decency in public life against indecency." Hoover also attacked secrecy in foreign policy, remarking of the Teheran and Yalta agreements, "which sold the freedom of half a billion people down the river," that if they had been "submitted to the American people for debate and to the Congress for decision" they could not have been approved. "And there is where we lost the peace and wandered into this land of hot and cold wars."[120]

The recommendations of the Hoover Commission had been transmitted to the president and to Congress during the early months of 1949. During 1949 and 1950 a substantial number of the recommendations had been implemented, either by administrative decree, executive order, or congressional legislation. In 1951, however, little was accomplished in putting the remainder of the recommendations into force. The *New York Times* found that during that year "little more than lip service" had been paid to the recommendations, by comparison to 1949–50, and it argued: "This is not good enough when the efficient working of democratic government is at stake, not to mention total savings estimated at $5.4 billions annually." Noting that there would be twenty separate measures for reform before Congress when it convened, the *Times* continued:

> In our view it would be the best kind of politics for the so-called "leadership" in Congress to take an active part in furthering some of these essential reforms in governmental reorganization. We don't think it is true that the people are uninterested. We think that next November they will be very interested in knowing just how much of the Hoover proposals have been adopted, how much rejected—and why.[121]

In December 1951, when Hoover was on the attack once again concerning the scandals in the Truman administration, he argued that the scandals "would not have occurred if the Hoover Commission's recommendations on political appointments had been accepted more than two years ago."[122]

Hoover was unwilling to allow the Great Debate to die. In October 1951, at the age of 77, he planned another major speech on foreign policy, which he hoped would bring into question once again the policies that had been carried into effect by the Truman administration during and after the Senate debate on the stationing of U.S. ground troops in Europe. Felix Morley aided him with the writing of the speech and strongly encouraged that it be given.[123] The speech went through numerous revisions, with the early drafts proposing a mutual withdrawal of U.S. and Soviet troops from a zone in Europe that would begin with Germany and then be broadened. The U.S. troops, having been stationed in Europe by President Truman, should now be used as bargaining chips in bringing about concessions from the Soviet Union. The plan would have included the unification and neutralization of Germany after the joint U.S.–Soviet withdrawal, followed by a general withdrawal by both the Soviet Union and the United States from European countries.[124] By the time the speech was delivered on January 27, 1952, however, these elements were missing, apparently because it was an election year, and Hoover did not wish to propose anything that might embarrass his choice for the Republican presidential nomination, Senator Robert Taft.[125]

The Great Debate, despite the Senate authorization of the stationing of American troops in Europe, was far from over. The issues that had been raised by Hoover and Taft and others were still very much alive, and Taft was a leading contender for the Republican presidential nomination. Less than two weeks before Hoover's speech, General Hoyt R. Vandenberg, U.S. Air Force chief of staff, told the Economic Club in New York City that the United States needed a 143-group air force. The decision on the part of the secretary of defense and the joint chiefs of staff to press for an air force of that size, he told them, had been reached as the result of "a long hard look at the realities of the world struggle against communism." An air force of that size, he maintained, would give the United States "a force so powerful that even a would-be aggressor would shrink from the cost of challenging it; or, if its power to deter should not be enough, a force capable of engaging instantly and effectively in a world of survival." In words that might have been spoken by Herbert Hoover, Vandenberg told his audience: "It seems to me self-evident, on the basis of the Korean experience, that neither this nation nor its allies can afford to adopt a strategy calling for an endless line of garrisons along the entire perimeter of Communist power." The Soviet Union, he argued, was "primarily vulnerable to air power—both land-based and carrier-based."[126]

Hoover's speech of January 27 reviewed the world situation and concluded that the nations of Western Europe had made no progress toward arming themselves in the year since the Great Debate. The only improvement in Europe's defenses stemmed from the presence of the American divisions stationed there, and the European attitude concerning the prospect of a Soviet invasion was still "profoundly different from the attitude of Washington." Only in the United States was there the kind of "war psychosis" that led to air-raid drills. The European nations recognized that if the USSR wanted to overrun Western Europe it could have done so at any time in the previous five years, and that they had not done so was proof to the Europeans that the Soviet Union harbored no desire to do so for a number of reasons. Whether these assumptions by the Europeans were correct or not, they did "contribute to

Western Europe's lack of hysteria and their calculation of low risk and, there-fore, their lack of hurry to arm." This complaisance required that the United States re-evaluate its own policies. In Asia and the Middle East a "prairie fire of revolution" had been ignited against the West, while in Korea Americans continued to die. Americans were groaning under the weight of a war economy and would soon begin to feel the full impact of the gigantic increases in government spending and taxes. The irresistible forces of inflation were being spawned. Again, Hoover advocated his doctrine of reliance upon air and sea power to defend the free world, which "could better halt the spread of Com-munist imperialism." He firmly believed, Hoover told his listeners, "that a third world war is neither necessary nor inevitable."[127]

Hoover received plaudits for his speech from numerous retired military officers, cabinet officers, and diplomats. He gathered them together and issued them to the press the following month.[128] Lieutenant General Leslie Groves, overseer of the work on the atomic bomb during World War II, issued a statement in which he said:

> I hope that Mr. Hoover's words will not be ignored as they were a year ago just because they make unpleasant reading. As he points out, the great danger of our position is overextension in international commitments, both economic and military. It will take courage to revise our present policies, to admit our mistakes, and even to accept minor and, we hope, temporary defeats. As Mr. Hoover suggests, our military policy should be based on air and sea where our great technical capabilities can be put to best advantage, rather than on the ground where the number of bayonets is of prime importance.[129]

Taft wrote Hoover that he had read the speech "with great pleasure and approval." He doubted, however, that "anyone who is actually responsible for foreign policy in early '53 could at that time take as drastic action as you proposed," but if he were nominated and elected he would "move in the same general direction." He believed that the speech would "have a substantial effect on future American policy."[130]

Support for the points made in Hoover's speech also came from an un-likely source. In what Harrison Salisbury, correspondent in Moscow, de-scribed as a "most unusual" action, *Pravda*, the organ of the Central Committee of the Communist Party in the USSR, published the January 27 speech, in full, together with a two-column, front-page editorial, which de-scribed Hoover's critique of American foreign policy as based on realistic facts. And, Salisbury wrote, "when three other important Soviet newspapers—the military organs Red Star and Red Fleet and the Moscow party organ Moscow Pravda—republish Pravda's analysis, as they did today, it constitutes a major event in Soviet discussion." Although *Pravda* referred to Hoover as "one of the most rabid instigators of the aggressive policy of the United States," it published his speech uncut, including the sections that were highly critical of the Soviet Union and of Soviet policy. Salisbury reported that Western diplomats in Moscow were pondering the significance of it all. He speculated that the Soviets had concluded Hoover's views represented such a sizable body of opinion in the United States, that Truman's policies might be changed in a direction that Moscow believed "should reduce the danger of a third World War." The Russians, he suggested, realized that foreign policy was likely to be a key issue in the 1952 campaign and that Taft, sharing many of Hoover's views, would be a strong contender for the GOP nomination. Salisbury wrote: "While a good many conclusions might be drawn from these facts, one that seems to be indisputable to the Russians is that Mr. Hoover's program is less likely to lead to a third world war than that of Mr. Truman."[131]

The reception in the Truman administration, however, was less hospitable, especially in the Pentagon. Bonner Fellers wrote Hoover that the speech had "caused near consternation in the Army Division of the Pentagon. General [J. Lawton] Collins, who was quite upset, cancelled his appointments for the day, called in some dozen top brass to plan how best to meet your views, especially those relating to the Europeans' providing their own ground defense." According to Fellers, Collins had told the other officers: "We can't take this." Fellers reported that the army had "decided to launch a press, radio and magazine educational campaign to discredit your speech" by calling in "key reporters and commentators and then leak such secret briefing information as is necessary to establish a basis to undermine your views."[132]

In that same month, Hoover received a request from the GOP national committee for his views on a statement that had been prepared for use by convention delegates in formulating the Republican platform at the convention. The statement on foreign policy called for repudiation by the United States of the Teheran, Yalta, and Potsdam agreements because they had been "unilaterally violated by the Soviet government and hence are now no longer binding on the United States," because they had not been "submitted to the Senate in treaty form for approval and hence the action of the executive was unconstitutional," and because "they violated the principles of the Atlantic Charter" and had resulted in the "enslavement of Albania, Bulgaria, Czechoslovakia, Hungary, Poland, Rumania, and Yugoslavia." Such repudiation, the statement argued, would serve notice to the Soviet Union that the United States did not recognize their domination of these peoples, would give those nations encouragement in maintaining their "moral resistance" against communism, and would also regenerate American foreign relations. On a more practical level, it was held that such a policy would rally "the foreign language groups in the United States" behind the GOP, since it would be the party standing in favor of the "liberation" of their motherlands.[133] Except for the omission of Latvia, Estonia, and Lithuania from the list of enslaved peoples, this was classic Hoover, and he responded that the proposal "seems good to me."[134]

Hoover was closely monitoring the campaigns for the GOP nomination. On the last day of 1951 he wrote one correspondent that "only the election of a Republican President will save this country. But first we must nominate somebody who has no taint of 'me-too-ism.' "[135] To ensure this, Hoover interested himself again in the nomination of Senator Robert A. Taft. The popularity of General Dwight D. Eisenhower seemed the only possible obstacle to Taft's nomination. In late April 1952 Hoover tried to convince himself that Eisenhower's campaign had peaked and that Taft would now come on.[136] Felix Morley thought Taft's nomination so essential that he suggested Hoover break with his practice since 1933 of not entering into the preconvention fray, and come out openly for Taft's nomination. General Robert Wood even suggested that Hoover might go to the convention as a New York delegate and lead the movement for Taft in the voting. Morley wrote Hoover of Wood's suggestion:

> Of course any such action would bring you down to the arena of politics and would, therefore, temporarily diminish your influence in the vital role of elder statesman. On the other hand, it would also emphasize the vital importance of the coming nomination and would give enormous stimulus to the Republican unity which is shaping up in spite of a relative handful of dissidents.

Morley thought Wood's suggestion worthy of consideration.[137]

While Hoover maintained a public appearance of impartiality through the preconvention months, he was privately active in the Taft campaign to an extent unprecedented for him in any previous preconvention campaign. John D. M. Hamilton, Taft's Eastern manager in 1952, recalled that Hoover had made connections for him in the East, including one with Governor Charles Edison (Democrat) of New Jersey, which were extremely valuable, and when the campaign ran short of money, helped to obtain contributions, including one for $5,000 from Joseph P. Kennedy (Democrat) for the New Hampshire primary campaign.[138]

The nomination would hinge upon the decision reached by the convention over the question of the seating of rival Taft and Eisenhower delegates from several southern states. Great publicity was being given to the charge that the Taft campaigners had "stolen" a number of delegates in those states. Hoover sought to arrange a compromise over the disputed delegates with Senator Henry Cabot Lodge, of the Eisenhower camp, but failed.[139] He was incensed over the tactics of the Eisenhower organization before and during the convention in Chicago, charging that the pressure applied upon the delegates was reminiscent of the 1940 Willkie "blitz" and seemed to have been arranged by the same operators.[140]

For those who favored an American military and foreign policy based on air power rather than a large standing army and commitments in Europe and elsewhere, the contest between Taft and Eisenhower seemed to present a clear issue. Eisenhower, the first commander of NATO troops in Europe, appeared to represent all that the proponents of air power and a "realistic" foreign policy opposed, while Taft's position had consistently been close to Hoover's own in advocating a reliance on air and naval power. This perception of the issues brought such air-power advocates as Bonner Fellers, A. C. Wedemeyer, and de Seversky into the Taft campaign. Early in July the latter sent to Hoover a personal message, which he intended to distribute to the Republican delegates advocating Taft's nomination, and he sought the former president's comments on it.[141] The de Seversky memorandum made the familiar points and drew contrasts between Taft, who had "dealt forthrightly with the urgent need for a correct strategy—one that is within America's means and manpower, resting on America's own potential strength," and Eisenhower, who was described as "a military man raised in the tradition of old-style surface warfare," whose obsolete ideas could lead American youth to be "committed to useless slaughter in Europe and Asia without the slightest chance of preserving our way of life." He called for the election of a civilian as president, and one who recognized that any future war could be won only through "*global command of the air*—a command as clearcut and decisive as was Britain's global command of the seas in an earlier period."[142] Hoover described the appeal as "a clear cut statement and a good one."[143]

On July 8, 1952, Hoover made his second "farewell appearance" before a Republican convention. His speech dealt with familiar refrains—the usurpation of power by the federal government, the loss of freedom in America, the poisoning of the American economy with fascism, socialism, and Keynesianism, the enormous growth of the federal bureaucracy—before turning to foreign policy. Here, too, the refrain was familiar—the betrayal of freedom for hundreds of millions of people by the American surrenders at Teheran, Yalta, and Potsdam. Now the Soviet Union possessed awesome military strength and despite 35 billion dollars of aid that the United States had poured into Western Europe, those nations had shown no serious disposition to defend themselves. Hoover reviewed the economic burden placed upon the American people by the Truman–Acheson foreign commitments and concluded: "If free men are to survive in America we must reduce spending and taxes." The administration was following "the road to militarism in the United States. That is at its base a threat to all freedoms." The only alternative to bankruptcy and militarism was to rely on air and sea power for America's defense. "I do not propose that we retreat in our shell like a turtle," Hoover maintained. "I do propose the deadly reprisal strategy of a rattlesnake." He closed with his farewell, and added that he would continue the fight "for those principles which made the United States the greatest gift of God to free men."[144]

Having failed in another attempt to work out a compromise over the disputed delegates, this time by intercession with GOP national chairman Guy Gabrielson, and upset with the tactics of the Eisenhower campaigners, Hoover finally abandoned all pretense of impartiality in the convention. On July 9, Hoover publicly endorsed a candidate for the GOP nomination for the first time since he had left the presidency. In a press statement he said:

> I have not for many years taken public part in convention choice of candidates, but on this occasion when the issues are so vital to our country, my conscience demands that I speak out. I favor Senator Taft, whom I have known since he was associated with me in World War I. Senator Taft has long proved his forthrightness, integrity and absolute devotion to the public interest, and he has had long experience in government. His leadership in the Senate has provided the Republican Party with a fighting opposition to the currents of collectivism in the country. This convention meets not only to nominate a candidate, but to save America. I have been deeply distressed at the acrimonious discussion in the convention. I can only hope that it shall cease for the sake of the future of our party and the country.[145]

But the endorsement was an act of desperation. By the time it was made it had become all too apparent that the uncommitted delegates in such key states as Michigan, California, Pennsylvania, and Minnesota would not support Taft in the struggle over the contested delegates and probably would support Eisenhower for the nomination.[146] Bowing to the inevitable, Hoover had already begun to cast about for an alternate candidate who might be able to stop the Eisenhower bandwagon. At a meeting in his suite at the Conrad Hilton he suggested that if Taft were unable to gather the votes necessary for the nomination, his supporters should turn to MacArthur if there seemed any chance of his nomination. Wedemeyer was delegated to talk to Taft about releasing his delegates to vote for MacArthur in that event. Taft was certain that no one would win the nomination on the first ballot, but he agreed to throw his support to MacArthur if on later ballots it appeared that he could not be nominated. Queried by telephone, MacArthur agreed to accept the nomination if it were offered to him.[147]

Like most of Hoover's convention strategies, however, this one failed. Eisenhower was nominated on the first ballot. A disappointed Hoover told reporters: "Being a Republican, I shall vote the Republican ticket."[148] The terseness of his statement revealed his disappointment with the result and his disgust with the tactics of the Eisenhower campaigners. To Taft, Hoover wrote: "I am sorry, beyond expression. We did our best."[149] The senator responded that he could not "adequately express my gratitude for the support you gave me throughout the nomination campaign, for your public statement and for your letter of regret." He was "deeply disappointed," he told Hoover, not only because he feared what "we may get in the way of government" if Eisenhower were elected, but also because of the sacrifices that had been made by his supporters in the losing cause. "As far as I am concerned," he concluded, "I am probably better off individually."[150]

Hoover complimented GOP chairman Guy Gabrielson for his skillful handling of a difficult convention, writing that he had conducted it "with great urbanity and fairness in a most difficult situation." He added: "We are now in uncharted waters."[151] Alluding to Dewey's support of Eisenhower, Gabrielson responded that "it looks as though we are going to be called upon to rescue [the GOP] again from the Governor of New York."[152] A bright spot for Hoover was the emergence of Senator Everett Dirksen at the convention. He wrote to the senator: "This is just to say that you are the one who emerged from the convention as the leader of our kind of Republicans. Some day we may be able to stop the left-wing domestic and misdirected foreign policies."[153] Taft agreed that the conservative wing of the party would now have to work to free the GOP of New Deal influences in order that it might win the election and "thereafter conduct a government based on sound Republican principles. We can still carry on that fight both before and after the election."[154]

Like Hoover, Taft showed little warmth for the Republican candidate and no inclination to give him active support. Alarmed at the coolness of the conservative wing of the party toward his campaign, Eisenhower soon sought to build bridges to Hoover and Taft. On July 29, he wired Hoover that he was sorry to have missed him at the convention and hoped that he would "agree to a meeting between us at your personal convenience." He wanted especially, he told Hoover, to talk with him about the Hoover Commission's recommendations, but also hoped to obtain his views "on many other questions facing us today." He reported "gratifying evidence of developing team work and cooperation among major elements of the Republican Party," but added that "to bring this to full success we of course need your help."[155] With little enthusiasm, Hoover responded that he had "a number of long established commitments on the coast," but would be returning to New York "after August when a meeting can be arranged."[156]

Taft had likewise put off any meeting with the nominee until September and had formulated terms that Eisenhower would have to accept in order to win his support in the general election. In late August it appeared that the two rivals might not get together, but Eisenhower was soon feeling the effects in his campaigning of the lack of a unified party behind him, and in mid-September the two met at Eisenhower's headquarters on Morningside Heights in New York City. After the conference the senator felt that he had obtained enough concessions from the nominee in budget, taxation, and labor matters (although Taft did not drive a hard bargain) to permit him to support the general. It was a conference that unified the party, and conservatives like Hoover could now support their nominee.[157]

Hoover waited for a call from Eisenhower. In the meantime, he leaped to the defense of the vice-presidential nominee, fellow Californian Richard Nixon, when he came under attack over the "slush fund" issue. After Nixon made his televised "Checkers" speech, Hoover issued a press release:

> From intimate acquaintance with Senator Nixon since before he entered public life, I can say that if everyone in the city of Washington possessed the high level of courage, probity and patriotism of Senator Nixon this would be a far better nation. There can be but one end of this campaign of smear. The Republican Party will be firmer in the heart and confidence of the American people.[158]

Still the call to assist in the campaign did not come. On October 1, Hoover wrote General Wedemeyer that he had declined many invitations from state and local committees to make speeches in the campaign, but he had "informed friends in touch with the General that I am prepared to make a major speech if he publicly requests." He had received, however, no such invitation and he had heard from friends in touch with the Eisenhower campaign that he was not "wanted in the campaign." That left him free, Hoover concluded, to oppose Eisenhower on important policies if the general was elected.[159]

On the same day that the letter to Wedemeyer was penned, however, Hoover received a wire from the nominee. According to Bonner Fellers, Hoover learned that the farther west Eisenhower went in his campaigning, the more people asked him whether he was supported by Hoover, and when he reached California he was told that he could not carry the state without the former president's endorsement.[160] Whether this was true or not, Eisenhower did wire Hoover on October 7 that he had tried to reach him by telephone before leaving New York for his western swing but the former president had been out of town. He had then hoped to meet Hoover in California, but Hoover was not there. He now hoped to meet with the "elusive" Hoover in New York when he returned there on October 16.[161] Hoover responded quickly that if the candidate wished him to participate in the campaign, October 16 would be too late to make effective arrangements. He told Eisenhower: "If you request it, I will prepare and deliver a major address in your support. . . . However, I want you to feel perfectly free to make such a decision. If you believe it better that I stay out of a public part of the campaign, it will in no way dim my prayers for your success."[162]

Approval was evidently conveyed to Hoover, for he went on the air over CBS radio and television on October 18 with his lone campaign speech. It was the speech that he had often hoped Republican candidates would make, and it was doubtless one of the best of his public career. Hoover told his listeners that he had come out of what he "had hoped was final retirement from political activities" and had done so "at General Eisenhower's request." He had consented "because I believe General Eisenhower and the Republican ticket should be elected." Hoover addressed his speech especially to the 40 percent of the voters—approximately forty million in number—who had "come of age since there was a Republican Administration in Washington," since those forty million knew "little of the Republican Party's background of principles, of its forward-looking constructive accomplishments" because of twenty years of "misrepresentations" about the GOP. He called attention to seven major such misrepresentations. Reviewing the party's record of legislation designed to curb the excesses of big business, beginning with the Sherman Anti-trust Act and the Interstate Commerce Commission, he rebutted the misrepresentation of the party as the instrument of big business and privilege. Tracing the origins of the depression to World War I and voicing his familiar assertion that recovery had begun in 1932 only to be retarded by fear of the New Deal and the consequences of New Deal legislation, Hoover rebutted the view that the GOP had caused the depression and that Roosevelt had rescued the American people.[163]

Hoover then turned to a review of GOP legislation and other actions establishing the Departments of Labor and Commerce, ending the 12-hour workday, establishing the Railway Mediation Board, the Bureau of Housing, Civil Service Commission, and other initiatives, to put to rest the charge that the Republican party was "reactionary" and opposed to change and reform. Pointing out that the GOP had originated "practically the whole idea and all of the agencies of Federal conservation of natural resources," he dismissed the claim that the Republican party was anticonservation. Comparing the record of publicized corruption in twenty years of Democratic rule with that of the GOP before 1933, he ridiculed the claim that the Republican party was corrupt. Describing the GOP's internationalist efforts to preserve peace through the Washington treaties, the Kellogg–Briand pact, the World Economic Conference, and other initiatives, he undermined the assertion that the GOP was incapable of preserving peace and was isolationist. And comparing the 80,000 membership roll of the U.S. Communist party in 1943, with the 13,000 membership roll in 1932, he rebutted the charge that the "Republican depression" had fueled the growth of communism in the United States. Hoover concluded by warning his young listeners that the misrepresentations were not "ancient stuff," for they indicated "the character of the party seeking by such means to retain their hold on Washington."[164]

Judging from the comments in Hoover's correspondence, the speech was well received. One wrote that it had "an almost unbelievable impact, especially on the younger generation."[165] Eisenhower warmly acknowledged the speech, and Hoover told him that it had obviously met with favor for there had been 35,000 requests for copies.[166] By mid-November the number had grown to over 130,000.[167] On October 22, Hoover wrote Clarence Kelland of the irony in the fact that the GOP national committee, "after refusing to pay for the electronics of that speech (for which we had to pass the hat) has now ordered 35,000 copies."[168]

On November 6, 1952, former president Herbert Hoover stationed himself in front of the television set to watch the election returns, confident that after twenty years a Republican would be returned to the White House. Stopping off en route to the Eisenhower suite in the Commodore, Clare Boothe Luce found Hoover "as close to happy" as she had ever seen him. A few hours later, when the results were known, Eisenhower joined his supporters briefly to thank them for their assistance, then returned to his suite where he collapsed on the bed exhausted from the long campaign. Mrs. Luce, who had served as something of a "pipeline" for Hoover's suggestions to the nominee during the campaign, now told the president-elect that before he went to sleep there was one more thing he must do. He must telephone the elderly man in the Waldorf-Astoria Hotel who had been waiting twenty years for this moment. Mrs. Luce dialed the phone and caught Hoover just as he was readying himself for bed. At her suggestion, Eisenhower told Hoover that he would try to bring as much integrity to the presidency as Hoover had, and that he would count heavily on the former president for his advice.[169] Hoover had waited a long time to hear those words from a Republican president.

11

The Last Assault on the New Deal

erbert Hoover regarded the verdict in favor of Dwight Eisenhower as representing "a turning in American life away from bad taste, corruption, Communism, and to some extent, from socialism." Having criticized a succession of Republican presidential candidates for running behind the total GOP vote garnered by candidates for other offices, however, he now faulted Eisenhower for having run ahead of those candidates in 1952, attributing this to the "nature of a campaign centered upon an individual and little interest in the Party as such." Because of this he concluded that it would be necessary to keep up the battle for conservative ideals.[1] Eisenhower's commitment to Republicanism was clearly suspect in the Hoover-Taft wing of the party, but it was no more so than Hoover's own Republicanism had been suspect to party leaders in the 1920s. In fact, the parallels between the former president and the new occupant of the White House were many and striking. Like Eisenhower, Hoover had been considered too "liberal" by the party establishment when he entered the White House. Both men had earned their reputations in time of war—Hoover as administrator of relief and head of the U.S. Food Administration during World War I, Eisenhower as leader of the Allied military forces in Europe in World War II. Both, in fact, had built their reputations largely as administrators, for even Eisenhower's military reputation rested primarily on his ability to deal with complex problems of directing a multinational army and controlling subordinates who frequently disagreed with him on strategy and championed their own national interests. And, like Hoover, Eisenhower would become more committed and orthodox in his Republicanism once he had departed from the White House.

Despite any misgivings he harbored concerning the new president, Hoover was cheered by the numerous letters he received in November hailing the GOP victory as vindication of his labors in behalf of the party for so many years. Congressman Joseph Martin wrote to Hoover: "No one has contributed more to the upbuilding of the Republican Party than you have, and I know the election Tuesday was a great vindication to you. Truth and justice at last prevail."[2] The word vindication was used again and again to describe the former president's relation to the election. Another correspondent wrote that the election represented "the splendid vindication by millions of American voters of those political principles which you consistently espoused and defended against attack, and worse, indifference."[3] And his own contribution to Eisenhower's success was hailed. Congressman Clifford Hope of Kansas was one who wrote Hoover: "The speech which you made near the end of the campaign was a very powerful influence in this part of the country and no doubt elsewhere."[4]

Yet aside from Eisenhower's phone call on election night, the first weeks after the election saw no recognition by the president-elect of Hoover's stature in the party or of any contribution he had made to the general's election. Settled in his offices in the Commodore Hotel, Eisenhower ignored both Hoover and MacArthur in the nearby Waldorf-Astoria, much to their distress. When Albert Wedemeyer was summoned by the president-elect, he went first to Hoover's suite to consult with the former president, who asked him to suggest to Eisenhower the name of Lewis Strauss for a cabinet post as secretary of commerce. Hoover had not been consulted on cabinet appointments.[5] He had come to the conclusion that the Eisenhower cabinet would "be made of pre-Convention Ike men. The solace is that it cannot be as bad as the last."[6] Not until December 23 was Hoover invited to lunch with the president-elect. Present were Eisenhower's choice for secretary of state, John Foster Dulles, and Dr. Arthur S. Flemming, president of Ohio Wesleyan University, who had served on the Hoover Commission and who was part of a three-man committee named by the general to evaluate a study of the organization of the executive branch that was being conducted by Temple University. Many topics were apparently discussed, but judging from the composition of the group, foreign policy and governmental reorganization must have been the principal subjects taken up.[7] Perhaps encouraged by the talk with Eisenhower, Hoover reactivated the Citizens' Committee for the Hoover Report in early January 1953.[8] In that same month he attended the first inauguration of a Republican as President of the United States since he himself had taken the oath in March 1929.

At age 78, the former president remained active. When Stalin died early in March 1953, Hoover thought it best to "go a little slow" with the rearming of the Germans since the new leadership in the Soviet Union, uncertain of its position, might use German rearmament as an excuse to "divert Russia into a foreign adventure." The Soviet armies could, in his view, occupy western Germany in three weeks, thus putting "350,000 American hostages in Soviet hands which could be distributed in Russia," and they could then defy the United States to use its nuclear arsenal against them.[9] Hoover was also being consulted concerning possible reforms in the Defense Department and the Social Security Agency.[10] His suggestions concerning the latter brought an appreciative letter from President Eisenhower, who thanked him for supporting the administration plan.[11] Hoover was also distressed over the organization of the civil service system and sought reform, trying to enlist the support of *Readers' Digest* in the effort. His special concern was "that somewhere between 1500 and 2000 policy-making and policy-advising officials are now frozen into the Civil Service," which meant that Eisenhower could not really get "possession of the Government unless he can appoint or re-appoint these people." An administration whose policies had been mandated by the people and which had been entrusted with the responsibility to implement those policies ought to have "policy-making officials of their choice."[12]

Hoover was also laying the groundwork for a crusade, which he would wage for several years, against public power. In mid-March he wrote Joseph M. Dodge, director of the budget, for figures on federal power enterprises. The Hoover Commission under Truman, he said, had been unable to check the efficiency of public power versus the private utilities because of "the shortcomings of the Federal enterprises' accounting methods," which had not furnished the information required by law of private enterprises, and which had made it impossible for the commission's accountants to draw up comparisons. Hoover wrote the budget director:

> With the background of the Commission's information and my own engineering experience, I have thought I could be of service to further develop this subject and some alternatives. These expenditures now enter in a large way into the budget. I believe it would be of service to your work if the whole investment and operation of these enterprises could be determined.

The information he sought from Dodge would make possible, he hoped, the comparisons that he believed should be made. He told the budget director that he proposed "to open this whole Pandora's Box in an address on April 11th. I start off by absolving the present administration of any part of it."[13] That address would kick off Hoover's final assault on the New Deal.

Although promised, the material did not reach Hoover in time for the speech. He sent a press release of the speech to Dodge, noting that he had received enough information "from other sources to make my initial points." He still needed the requested material, however, as he intended to raise the subject again, and with the additional information he "could more fully indicate possible saving and revenues which might be of use in your many labors."[14] On April 11, Hoover delivered the speech on public power at the Case Institute of Technology. He called for the U.S. government to "get out of the business of generating and distributing power as soon as possible" and gave three "first steps" by which the United States could do so, reducing its annual investment in power enterprises by $600 million a year and also rescuing "free men from this variety of creeping socialism." The three steps included: (1) making no further appropriations for steam generating plants or hydroelectric power generation, since if such projects were economically feasible "private enterprise will build them and pay taxes on them"; (2) ceasing appropriations for multipurpose dam projects unless the power generated was to be leased to private enterprise or states or municipalities or regional authorities for distribution; (3) establishing a temporary commission to reorganize the entire federal venture into the power business.

Hoover cited figures showing that the public sector of power production had grown from less than 1 percent of the national total in 1933, to 20–25 percent by the middle of 1953. He recommended that the temporary commission that he had suggested should: (1) revise accounting methods of public power projects to divide fairly the cost between the various functions of multipurpose dams so that the real burdens to taxpayers caused by the subsidized, cheap power rates could be made apparent; (2) investigate the actual cost and prospective return for each major project contemplated; (3) formulate methods and standard terms for leasing out generating plants, transmission lines, and electric power to provide for interest payments, amortization and arrears on the federal investment; (4) work out procedures for local or state agencies to share in the cost of future capital outlays for generating facilities when they were part of multipurpose dam projects.[15]

A few days later Hoover wrote that he was "having the usual left-wing attack by their battalions, regiments and corps on that power speech."[16] Among those expressing "unqualified disagreement" was Eisenhower's secretary of the interior, Douglas McKay.[17] From the perennial Socialist party candidate Norman Thomas, an ally of Hoover in his attempts before and during World War II to get food relief to Europe, came a challenge to debate the relative merits of public versus private ownership.[18] Hoover responded to the challenge by writing Thomas:

> Over these many years you have held the belief that socialism should be the way of American life. During the same years, I have held the belief that regulated free enterprise should be the way of American

life. I have, during these years, steadfastly opposed your socialism, yet I have respected your high personal integrity. While I do not expect you to agree with my address, it is certain from your letter that you have not read the full text which I am sending you. You suggest a debate, but your mistaken conception of my views, your extension of my speech to include the sale of all public owned electric plants, dams, post offices, forest and public lands to corporations would seem to be setting up wholly false premises for such a debate. In any event, I am associated with no person or organization who holds such views or objectives as you imply. Therefore, I could designate no one to undertake such a debate.[19]

In mid-March, Hoover again considered proposing a mutual U.S.–Soviet withdrawal from European nations. In a draft letter outlining his proposal, the former president wrote that he had presented the idea "to our officials for tentative consideration" a year earlier, and now he wondered if there was "anything practical in the idea."[20] As he outlined the plan:

> The idea I am suggesting for consideration is that we, ourselves, should now propose a unified, disarmed and neutral Germany and Austria, withdrawal of all foreign military forces—Russian and Allies—leaving them with a constabulary for internal defense. It might be proposed that guardianship of any such arrangement be assigned to the United Nations, with the right of constant inspection of activities on the borders as well as control of neutrality within Germany. We might propose that Germany's neutrality be guaranteed by all powers. . . . I do not suggest that in considering this idea that it be complicated by any proposals of world disarmament except Germany and Austria. If other Western Europe States should wish to arm, it will give them time to build up their defenses. I do not suggest that we, or Britain, abandon our great deterrent on Russian military aggression—our air and naval forces. If accepted, it would enable us to reduce our dangers of war on the European flank for some years, strengthen our deterrents, reenforce our own defenses and somewhat reduce our excessive military expenditures by decreasing our ground troops. . . . If the Russians should favor such a proposal it might be followed with a later proposal as to Korea, and to Indo-China, but I would not think that the German-Austrian proposal should be complicated by including them at the start.

Even if the Soviet Union rejected such a proposal, "it might be good propaganda as to our constructive efforts to find peace. Not only would it be useful in that respect in the Middle Eastern, South Asian and Latin American countries, but even among the people of the Soviet Union." His letter was intended, he said, to go to several intimates for their "confidential reactions to it."[21]

However, General Albert Wedemeyer, now vice-president of AVCO Manufacturing Company, responded negatively to Hoover's proposal. He found it based "on two very weak and uncertain premises: (1) That the Soviet Union would abide by an agreement, and (2) That the Germans themselves would accept such a status of impotency when surrounded by bristling guns of distrustful and unfriendly countries." Wedemeyer's solution to the European situation was to allow the West Germans to create an army of 60 divisions and require the other NATO members to mobilize 80 divisions, together with supporting units, with the United States assisting "to a reasonable and proportionate extent after receiving tangible evidence that the NATO countries of Europe were serious about defending themselves and making commensurate sacrifices to do so." He reiterated that any "plan to guarantee the neutrality of the German-Austrian areas would be recognized at once as futile." The Germans were the major military force in Europe. With all of the difficulties that the United States was encountering in persuading the other European nations to create suitable military forces even for their own defense, it would be clear to the Germans that those nations could not be counted upon to defend Germany if the Soviet Union attacked.[22] Somewhat disappointed at the reaction to his plan, Hoover responded that because the lower house of the German parliament had ratified the NATO agreement, he had suspended any further work on his proposal. "However," he wrote, "a new policy is necessary."[23]

On April 19 Arthur Krock wrote in the *New York Times* that the Eisenhower administration was moving "methodically and at a more rapid pace" to carry out its campaign promises, including "taking the Government out of competition with private business to the utmost practical degree." Krock wrote that both the executive branch and Congress had "made long steps toward the goal and have listened with interest to advice from former President Hoover that it make an even longer one."[24] Encouraged, Hoover wrote that he was confident that the administration was "making progress in cleaning up the mess" in Washington. He knew from his years investigating that "mess" through the Hoover Commission, what a task it would be. "It will be a slow job," he wrote one correspondent, "but I am in hopes such progress will have been made by 1954 that we can carry the Congressional elections."[25]

Hoover and other air power advocates were shocked, however, when the first Eisenhower budget envisioned slashing the air force objective of 143 groups down to 110 or 120. As Bonner Fellers wrote Hoover: "The Republican policy to establish American Air Supremacy advocated by you and Senator Taft has been abandoned." Worse still, the Democrats could now be expected to champion the air force issue, especially Senator Stuart Symington of Missouri.[26] But if the administration in Washington had not yet adopted Hoover's policy of dependence on air power, there was some consolation in the fact that, in the former president's words, "the British totally disagree with our European military policies and are advocating my line."[27] On this and other issues, however, Hoover did not feel disposed to openly criticize a Republican administration. As he wrote Ferdinand Eberstadt on another issue late in May 1953: "I am still regarded by many of the public as a Republican leader." If he opposed the administration, Hoover continued, "this will at once be heralded as a split in the Party." The fact was that Eisenhower's was "the only Republican Administration we can have or hope to reelect in our time." He did not rule out the possibility, however, that some issue might eventually compel his "conscience to speak up."[28]

Meanwhile, Senator Homer Ferguson and Congressman Clarence Brown had introduced in their respective houses of Congress a bill to establish a new Commission on Organization of the Executive Branch of the Government. The legislation differed from that establishing the first Hoover Commission in several important respects. For one, the Ferguson-Brown bill called for "eliminating non-essential services, functions, and activities which are competitive with private enterprise." For another, it did not require that the commission should consist of an equal number of Republicans and Democrats. And finally, it provided the new commission with the power to subpoena witnesses and to recommend legislation or constitutional amendments.[29] When queried by Congressman Brown on possible appointees for the new committee, Hoover wrote: "The House Committees have declared themselves for private enterprise. Unless that Commission is set up under men who believe in it, certainly I want no part of it." After suggesting several possible members, including Lewis Strauss, Hoover added that it "would be a good thing if the President appointed Dr. Arthur Flemming from his official staff. As you know, he was a member of our Commission." He promised to send more names.[30]

Hoover continued to press his crusade against federal power projects. On June 8, 1953, he dined at the White House and on the following day he prepared a memorandum on "Projects for Navigation, Flood Control, Irrigation and Electric Power," which he noted had been prepared at Eisenhower's request and was to be transmitted to him by Lewis Strauss. In the memorandum, Hoover pointed out that the completion of all projects authorized by Congress or proposed by government agencies or local communities would cost approximately $50 billion. Given the state of the economy, many projects would have to be delayed or postponed. To determine which these should be, Hoover suggested again the establishment of a "Commission for Review," which could examine all such projects and decide which should be continued or begun. By "a nation-wide review of our Federal electric power now in operation or under construction," it could also be determined "which could be more profitably administered by private enterprise or by the municipalities or the States or by a combination of States covering river basins." Private enterprise and state participation should also be brought into the financing of such projects. "Our purpose," Hoover insisted, "must be to restore the vitality and responsibility of local government in the administration of these projects. By doing so we can give release of the States from Federal dictation and remove taints of Socialism." In his covering letter to Strauss, Hoover pointed out that "by the character of his appointees on the new Commission for Reorganization of the Government now passed by Congress," the president could accomplish the creation of the "Commission for Review" that he had recommended in the memorandum.[31] A few days later Hoover sent Senator Herman Welker of Idaho a copy of his April speech and added that he had sent it because "it would appear that the President has now adopted this policy."[32]

On July 10, 1953, President Eisenhower signed into law the Ferguson-Brown bill creating a new Commission on Organization of the Executive Branch of the Government, and three days later he wrote Hoover to ask if he would consent to serve on it.[33] With Hoover's consent, the president named him as one of four presidential appointees to the commission, along with Attorney General Herbert Brownell, Jr., Dr. Arthur S. Flemming, the director of defense mobilization and a member of the first Hoover Commission, and Democrat James A. Farley, postmaster general under Roosevelt. Vice-President Richard Nixon, acting for the Senate, appointed two Republicans and two Democrats, as did Speaker of the House Joseph Martin. Both Senator Ferguson and Congressman Brown, sponsors of the legislation, were selected for the commission. In appointing three Republicans and only one Democrat, President Eisenhower created a majority of 7 to 5 on the commission in favor of the Republicans. This was entirely permissible under the law, but it did diminish the aura of nonpartisanship that had surrounded the first commission and it laid the basis for later criticism of the commission's recommendations.[34]

Meanwhile, early in 1953, Hoover's longtime and close friend, Ohio senator Robert A. Taft, was afflicted with cancer. The Ohioan, now majority floor leader of the GOP-controlled Senate, fought a courageous battle against the disease. Despite his own advanced age, the former president managed frequent visits to Taft's bedside. In July, Hoover flew to California for the annual Bohemian Club encampment. By this time Taft's malignancy was well advanced, and on the last day of July he died. In a statement to the press, Hoover recalled that Taft had been his "devoted friend for over thirty-five years since he joined in public service during the first World War." He described the Ohio senator as "more nearly an irreplaceable man in American life than we have seen in three generations."[35]

The next day, August 1, Hoover delivered his annual off-the-record speech at the Bohemian Club camp. Beginning with an appraisal of the international situation, he now concluded that Stalin's death would lead to a period of tranquility in the Soviet Union's relations with the rest of the world until a new leader was able to consolidate his hold on the government. He still considered that any Soviet expansionist aims were in Asia, not in Western

Europe, but he still found the Western Europeans no better prepared to defend themselves than they had been at the beginning of the Great Debate nearly three years earlier. Again he called for a reappraisal of American policies toward Europe. Of the new Hoover Commission, he noted that, unlike the first commission, this one had "far wider powers," including the authority to "make recommendations for surgery on everything except the Congress and the Judiciary." The issues before the commission he saw as dear to his own philosophy. That he viewed the commission as an opportunity to wage renewed warfare on the remnants of the New Deal and Fair Deal is clear. As he told the Bohemian group:

> The Commission can at least serve to expose certain overall growths in the Federal Government during the past 20 years which cry for remedies. The first is to lessen this invasion of State and local governments by a Federal bureaucracy from Washington. The survival of free men rests on local government.
>
> The second is to make a contribution toward lessening Federal expenditures, toward balancing the budget and toward reducing taxes. This continued inflation, unless quickly stopped, will undermine all freedom in the United States.
>
> The third is creeping Socialism. The Federal Government has today more than 500 activities in economic competition with the private citizens. The new authority specifically requires us to propose surgical operations on these spots. Among them is the so-called public power. My objections are not directed against building dams for water conservation or for generation of electric power. I do object to the use of power distribution to socialize the electric industry.

The commission, Hoover told his audience, "could do a better job if we had dictatorial powers, and the right to have about one man hung every month without trial." Its main purpose was "to help clean up the mess which General Eisenhower inherited. But it will take time." He closed his talk with a eulogy of Senator Taft.[36]

Back in the business of reorganizing the federal government, Hoover considered it best "to keep still on any partisan matter for the present," since he was trying to put the new Hoover Commission "on a non-partisan basis— at least bipartisan."[37] He wrote to Leonard Hall, chairman of the GOP national committee: "You will have to count me out on all speeches for some months to come. I have to be careful if I am going to do the job now in front of me." He was sorry, Hoover said, that he could not be of more service to the party.[38] No doubt the former president was aware of concern already being expressed that the commission intended an all-out assault on the New Deal. As one Brooklyn College professor put it in a letter to the *New York Times*, the second Hoover Commission, "if permitted, will serve as the front for the

Republican party to turn the clock back to the Nineteen-twenties and the political philosophy of Herbert Hoover."[39] Certainly the potentials for such an assault by a committee dominated by Republicans and headed by Hoover, working together with a Republican administration and a GOP-controlled Congress, seemed enormous. According to such a view, it was only the reelection of Truman in 1948 that had blunted a similar design in the case of the first commission. But clearly the new "grand design" would require either that the new commission complete its work before the 1954 Congressional elections, or that Republicans remain in control of Congress in 1955–56.

The new commission held its first meeting late in September 1953, and Hoover was quickly elected chairman. In a press release, he reviewed the task before the new Hoover Commission. The first commission had made a total of 273 recommendations for reforms in the government, he pointed out, of which about 122 items remained as "unfinished business." The earlier commission had been primarily concerned with the reform of the executive agencies of the government. One result of its work had been that the heads of agencies were granted authority to effect their own reorganization "toward greater efficiency and the elimination of waste." But many of the problems of inefficiency and waste could not be solved through the action of individual agencies as they involved more than one. Hoover had suggested that the new commission should "specialize in such fields," including such multi-agency problems as "the methods and problems in accounting, budgeting, and procurement of supplies and personnel." The president was overburdened by "an appalling number of agencies" that reported only to him and that lacked adequate supervision or overlapped the responsibilities of other agencies. Some activities were participated in by a number of different agencies—housing, medical services, lending, and others. The commission was also, Hoover noted, specifically charged with inquiring into areas where the government was in competition with private enterprise. It would proceed as the first one had, "by setting up task forces composed of men and women who have had experience in these fields and who are independent of any special interest."[40]

Hoover had already drawn up lists of prospective task force members and had won at least grudging approval for them from the commission, as well as authority to name other members to the task forces without consultation with the commission. A study of the second Hoover Commission notes: "As a result the membership of all the task forces eventually was named by the former President even though the 1947 Commission had voted as a body on such appointments."[41] In selecting the areas of inquiry for the task forces and naming their members, the chairman had clearly put his own stamp on the commission's inquiry and recommendations to a far greater degree than with the first commission. Even at the first meeting there was uneasiness on the part of some of the commissioners, especially with the scope of the inquiry by the task force on water and power resources which, some commissioners felt, seemed to echo Hoover's April speech in which he had expressed his antipathy to federal involvement in the generation and distribution of electric power. As the *New York Times* reported: "While commission members declined to be quoted, some privately expressed the fear that the issue could be prejudged."[42] Another issue that would later draw some fire was Hoover's refusal to provide for the selection of a vice-chairman, even though the legislation establishing the commission clearly mandated that one should be chosen. It has been suggested that Hoover's failure to put the question to the commission stemmed from "his desire to retain unrestricted control over the Commission since he may have found the presence of Vice-chairman Dean Acheson a personal hindrance in 1949."[43] While this may well have been one reason, another was doubtless the fact that both Senator Ferguson and Congressman Brown, the cosponsors of the legislation establishing the commission, desired the post.[44] Thus, Hoover may have left the vice-chairmanship vacant to avoid alienating either of these friends.

The commission's inquiry into public power continued to be the lightning rod drawing most adverse comment concerning the commission's work. Only weeks after the commission held its first meeting, the *New York Times* observed that the water and power resources task force, headed by retired admiral Ben Moreel, now chairman of Jones and Laughlin Steel, would, if it followed Hoover's personal inclination, probably follow the advice of the former president's April speech. The newspaper argued that the issue of public power was not, however, as simple as that. There were areas in which private enterprise was efficient, but others in which public ownership seemed essential. The *Times* hoped that the task force would approach the issue of electric power with an open mind and that it would "contribute new ideas in this field."[45] Only a few days later, two groups—the American Public Power Association and the Cooperative League—charged that the Moreel task force was weighted in its membership against public power. The American Public Power Association charged that none of the 25 members of the task force was a public power advocate, and it feared that the task force would recommend specific methods for implementing the position that Hoover had taken in the April speech.[46]

In mid-December 1953 Hoover wrote Hugh Gibson that he had been "working at my job in Washington 3 to 4 days a week since mid-September." Of his relations with the Eisenhower administration, he wrote that at first "there was coldness—and even some hostility. Gradually that has evaporated, but I am not in any inner circle of influence." With the exception of a few people in the administration, he found that he still belonged "in outer darkness." Hoover found hopeful signs, however, that his "three year campaign on obsolete methods of war" had "now had a mite of acceptance as witness the budget which will be presented next month."[47] He reiterated this latter view to another friend and added that there was also a growing feeling in Washington that "Europe does not intend to help itself so long as we keep up the money stream. If these tendencies continue, we may see daylight." Referring to his work on the reorganization commission, Hoover added that he had "taken on a most trying job merely in the hope that I can contribute something to keep the ADA [the liberal Americans for Democratic Action] from running the United States."[48]

The next month Hoover wrote Hugh Gibson that he was "having no joy in trying to reorganize this situation, but the State Department has decided to go back to my recommendations of four years ago and begin there, which is something." He was leaving for a fishing trip in Florida to "recuperate from some rough sessions with the politicians in my new commission. My relations with the New Dealers four years ago were more pleasant." He found pleasure, however, in the fact that "the administration, without admitting it, has adopted my proposals in the Great Debate—of course without any acknowledgments as to where they got it. Anyway it is all to the good. And somehow the republic lives."[49] Indeed, by the time of the Hoover letter to Gibson in mid-January 1954, the "New Look" defense policy of the Eisenhower administration was clear and it was compatible with the former president's views in its emphasis on air power, nuclear weapons, and flexible response.

Hoover had continued to express his opposition to the recognition of the People's Republic of China. When the issue heated up in May of 1950, Senator William Knowland sent the former president a copy of the letter written to President Truman and signed by 35 U.S. senators, which urged the government to make clear its opposition to recognition of "the communist regime in China" and to any efforts by the Soviet Union "to unseat the representatives of the Republic of China and to extend membership to the representatives of the communist regime of that Country in the United Nations." The 35 Senators declared their firm conviction "that a prompt clarification of our position in this matter is in the national interest." The signers of the letter, one of whom was Senator Robert Taft, represented both political parties.[50] Hoover approved, writing Knowland that "the recognition of the Moscow satellite government in China would be a further surrender in the cold war" and "further acceptance of the sweep of the Kremlin's aggressive militarism, agnosticism and Red Imperialism." The United Nations, he insisted, if it were "ever to be useful to the human race. . . . must free itself of Communist domination—not add to it."[51] Hoover's letter was released to the news services, and Knowland felt certain that it would "be of great help in this matter."[52]

Late in 1953, a small group of opponents of the admission of the People's Republic of China into the United Nations launched a drive to secure several hundred prominent signatures on a petition opposing such a move. Hoover agreed to sign the petition in September.[53] Word of the petition leaked out, however, and the organizers were so deluged with requests to sign that they decided to change it into a Committee for One Million to obtain that many signatures on petitions. Charles Edison, Congressman Walter Judd, and former diplomat Joseph C. Grew sought to enlist Hoover as a sponsor in order to attract financial support and further signatures.[54] The former president did support the effort, issuing a statement in January at the request of the committee, which said:

> One of the greatest dangers the cause of freedom faces today is uncertainty in the minds of both governments and peoples abroad as to the position of the United States in relation to Communist China. The nations in the Far East are in constant danger of their aggression. In the meantime, they work and conspire to break down the morals of these free peoples of Asia; endeavor to create disunity and spread lies about the stand of the United States.

The position of the United States must be clarified, Hoover stated, and to this end the Committee for One Million was endeavoring to gather signatures.[55] An old foreign policy ally in Kansas, however, was disturbed by the circulation of the petition by what he termed "Hoover's committee." Alf Landon did not favor the admission of mainland China into the United Nations, but he did wish, he said, to permit flexibility in American foreign policy in the event it might someday be possible "to woo this government away from the Kremlin," and he feared that the committee's work was making such flexibility impossible.[56] Thus, the two septuagenarian GOP statesmen were at odds over the issue, and Landon spoke out in Kansas against the petition campaign.[57]

While avoiding partisan speeches, Hoover continued to preach on those issues that were dear to him. In January he told the International Ben Franklin Society that the federal government had shown "some lack of adherence" to Franklin's notions of thrift. He noted that, for Franklin, government borrowing and debts "were the road of sorrow and in general the destroyers of liberty."[58] Two months later he predicted that if the recommendations of the new Hoover Commission were followed, $5 billion to $7 billion might be saved per year. In a speech to the National Press Club he expressed pessimism, however, that all of the commission's recommendations would be adopted because about two hundred pressure groups "occupy themselves pressuring the Government for more spending or in opposing any reductions."[59]

In April 1954, Hoover responded to a request from Senator Alexander Wiley for his views on possible revisions in the United Nations Charter by sending him a memorandum. The Senate Foreign Relations Committee was considering possible revisions since the charter provided that revisions might be proposed at the 1955 meeting of the United Nations. Hoover argued that the United Nations should be retained, even though it had not "fulfilled expectations." He pointed out similarities in structure, purpose, and authority, and difficulties between the United Nations and the defunct League of Nations. Both the league and the United Nations, he noted, had suffered from a dissolution of the spirit of wartime unity, neither was prepared for "the destructive effect upon peace or upon the organizations by totalitarian governments," which were "by nature militaristic and aggressive and, therefore," were "poor material upon which to build international laws and morals." The dominance and disparate views of the major powers had rendered both the league and the United Nations "impotent to prevent aggression by a major power." Neither organization was able to make progress toward disarmament, which meant that on this and other questions the nations of the world had been forced to seek solutions outside the league, and the "same thing is taking place outside of the United Nations today." The failures of the league had led to a resurgence of balance of power concepts, the formation of alliances, and the division of the world into armed camps. This, too, had been the case since World War II, despite the presence of the United Nations. He also found the United Nations' failure to adequately apply unified action in Korea comparable to the league's failure to adequately apply sanctions against Italy for its aggression in Ethiopia.[60]

Hoover conceded: "In view of the attitude and the purpose of the Communist nations and the difference of interests between non-Communist nations, it does not, at the present time, seem possible to make such changes in the Charter as would remedy" the difficulties he had enumerated. Such changes would have to "await a great change in the whole Communist attitude." In the meantime, the United Nations could continue to "build toward more unity in the field of pacific action to settle disputes especially among secondary nations; in the promotion of scientific research; exchange of knowledge; public health; philanthropy; and such contributions to general prosperity as are possible." Hoover then reviewed the suggestions he had made at the time the charter was being written, while acknowledging that "in view of the Communist attitudes and division of interest among other nations there would seem little likelihood of adoption of many or any of them at this time." He noted suggestions that Secretary of State Dulles had made for revisions, implying approval of them, and added one new suggestion: "That all treaties suggested by [the United Nations] subsidiary economic, social or other organizations for submission to nations should be subject to revision and approval by the Security Council before their submission to individual nations."[61]

During May and June of 1954, as the French reeled before Viet Minh attacks in Indochina and British Prime Minister Winston Churchill visited the United States, foreign affairs loomed important in Hoover's thoughts. A visitor late in June drew him out at length on the subject in an eight-hour conversation. The former president was convinced that the United States would not send ground forces to aid the French in Indochina, and that such an intervention "would be much worse than Korea" and would mean "the end of the Republican Party" if Eisenhower embarked upon it. Such an intervention in Southeast Asia would be "just what Russia would like to have us do." Hoover was opposed to a Southeast Asian military alliance, but he was also concerned over the necessity for Japan to trade with her Asian neighbors in order to reduce her negative balance of trade, so he favored, instead, an "Asiatic economic alliance including Burma and India." He dismissed the idea "that hunger causes communism," arguing instead that "it is the intellectuals who fall for communism." He shared the view of Secretary of Defense Wilson that the false ideas of communism could not be destroyed by bullets, but must be countered and destroyed "with the truth, with superior ideas and sound philosophy." Hoover recognized the tenseness of the current world situation, but did not "share the view that if we start drawing in our horns and minding our own business that Russia will advance every foot we retreat until we will eventually find North America standing alone in a communist world." This "unreasoning fear" Hoover called "silly." It ignored, he said, the forces of nationalism, "the fact that no people anywhere like to live under the Russian yoke," and "the fact that the farther Russia spreads out the weaker the control."[62]

Late in the same month, Hoover spoke at a Hall of Fame Dinner in Chicago and discussed the methods by which the United States could get along with other free nations. First, Americans must recognize "that there are wide differences in social inheritances, economic and political objectives in each of the free nations," and that "military alliance or peacetime collective action can endure only as long as there are common objectives and purposes among the participants." Those "interests, objectives, and policies of nations constantly shift with this rapidly changing scene," as could be seen in the shift of American policies and attitudes toward the Soviet Union, Germany, and Japan. Americans must also recognize "that the atomic bomb and the steady growth of Communist military strength have contributed to shift the policies of some of the free nations." The United Nations was paralyzed by the communist members and by the lack of unity among the free nations, with the result that many free nations had been "forced into a multitude of military alliances." Others had sought refuge in neutrality, and "some of our military allies are faltering in the march." The American people must realize that collective security through the United Nations was nonexistent and that the world was back to the ancient concepts of balances of power "and ancient forms of diplomacy." The American people must recognize that "in dealing with these gigantic problems of today we must have patience, tolerance, and understanding of these differences of interests and objectives of the free nations," and must not expect miracles of those who "must pilot our foreign policies." But Americans should not abandon hope in the United Nations, nor should they give up "the ideal that someday, somehow, unity for peace can be built in the world." Americans should recognize the importance of nationalism in the world and should not denigrate it at home, for love of country was a source of strength that could keep the country free. Finally, Hoover concluded that "our people must realize that our own right arm plus some deterrents unhealthy to the aggressor are our major reliance for our defense."[63]

In August, the former president returned to his birthplace in West Branch, Iowa. In a speech there he decried the fact that the division of powers between the federal and state governments, and between the three branches of government, had "become seriously confused, corroded and weakened during the twenty years before this Administration," as the federal government had fastened its grasp upon "many of the vital functions of state and local government." The result had been an incredible growth in the federal bureaucracy. Innate in bureaucracy, he asserted, were "three implacable spirits," which he identified as "self-perpetuation, expansion of their empires, and demand for more power. Bureaucracy rushes headlong into the visions of the millennium and sends the bills to the Treasury." In foreign relations there had been "a special encroachment of the Executive upon the legislative branch. This has been through a new type of commitment of the United States to other nations"—joint statements with foreign officials that committed America "without the specific consent of the elected representatives of the people." Hoover reviewed such commitments, which had "resulted in a shrinking of human freedom over the whole world" and had led to the "jeopardies of the 'Cold War.' " A by-product had been the shrinking of American freedoms "by crushing taxes, huge defense costs, inflation and compulsory military service." Such misuse of power must be forever made impossible. As for the present foreign situation, the history of the world since World War I had, in Hoover's view, only confirmed his predictions as an opponent of intervention in World War II. After reviewing the threats posed by communism, socialism, and the welfare state, and championing the uncommon man, he concluded:

> There are voices in our country who daily sound alarms that our civilization is on the way out. Concentrated on the difficulties of our times, they see an early and dour end for us. But civilization does not decline and fall while the people still possess dynamic creative faculties, devotion to religious faith and to liberty. The American people still possess those qualities. We are not at the bedside of a nation in death agony.[64]

Where foreign affairs were concerned, however, Hoover had pulled his punches due to the presence of a Republican in the White House. His real feelings about the international situation are better revealed by a memorandum that he wrote on September 4, 1954, "simply to file away for the record" the points he had omitted from the Chicago and West Branch speeches. In the memorandum he began by noting: "The state of mind of all thinking Americans is one of complete frustration over our foreign policies." Despite the clear intention of "the Kremlin to spread Communism over the earth by infiltration, conspiracy or military conquest," the United States had, from 1933 to 1946, undertaken "military alliance and political collaboration and appeasement with the Kremlin," and then "from 1942 to 1950 we undertook at the same time to support the Chinese Nationalists and collaboration and appeasement with the Chinese Communists." He added:

> The result has been a long line of tombstones over 21 free peoples and 900,000,000 human beings engraved with the words, "Recognition of Communist Russia, 1933," "The Atlantic Charter, 1940," "The Tacit Alliance with Russia, 1941," "The Moscow Conference, 1942," "Casablanca, 1943," "Tehran, 1943," "Yalta, 1945," "Potsdam, 1945," "Hiroshima and Nagasaki, 1945," "United Nations, 1945," "The Marshall Mission to China, 1946," "Defeat of China, 1950," "The Aggression Against Korea, 1952," "Indo-China, 1954," "The Defeat of the European Defense Community, 1954."

Recognition of the Soviet Union had brought communist conspirators into the United States who, along with fellow travelers, attained important positions in the federal government where: "(a) they influenced American national policies to further Communist calamities upon civilization; and (b) they stole our national secrets of policy and of military invention, including both the A- and H-Bombs."[65]

By the alliance with Stalin and Churchill during the war, not only was communism spread over the world, but the unconditional surrender policy "destroyed the German 1000-year dam against the swarming of Asiatic hordes over Western Europe and the Japanese 75-year dam against the spread of Russian conquest of Asia." The major successes of the United Nations organization had been "the spread of further Communist infiltration; the frustration of every effort to secure peace, and a world forum for the defamation of the United States." The policy of containment, launched in 1946, had led to the stationing of 300,000 American servicemen in Europe, air bases on the periphery of the Soviet Union, "gigantic giveaway programs of money, commodities, and arms under the Marshall Plan and other agencies, to a total expenditure of $70 billions, or enough to have rebuilt every subnormal home, school and church in the United States." When in 1950 the communists "began a policy of military aggression by their satellite countries," the United Nations had responded in South Korea. But, Hoover noted: "The nations who voted for this action in the United Nations, have about 1,500,000,000 inhabitants and armed forces of about 2,000,000 men. Yet those who voted contributed only 5% of the United Nations Armies. We, with 10% of the number of inhabitants, furnished 95% of the military forces and lost 150,000 casualties." The Allies, principally Great Britain, had intervened to prevent victory in Korea and MacArthur had been removed. Allied compromise in Korea was regarded in Asia as a defeat for the United States and the United Nations, and that defeat had been followed by another in Indochina for the West. By its support of Britain and France in the maintenance of their overseas empires, the United States had been given "the stigma of colonial exploitation which we little deserve in view of our long history of sympathy with peoples trying to be free. . . ."[66]

From all of this Hoover came to some conclusions: "We must at last recognize one positive fundamental in international life. The economic and expansion aims, ideals, objectives, traditions, fears, hates and national interests in all nations are different." The United States must also recognize the power of the spirit of nationalism in other nations. Military alliances endured only so long as "the aims, ideals and interests and safety of nations run parallel." The policies of Italy, France, and the nations of South Asia were also profoundly influenced by the presence of powerful communist parties in those countries. NATO was still utterly incapable of putting up any significant defense against a communist attack. More and more nations were embracing a new international phenomenon—neutralism, together with an emphasis on "peaceful coexistence." These forces meant that "the whole North Atlantic Treaty Organization has gone with the wind," and not even Britain or Japan could any longer be counted upon as an ally in the event of a war with the Soviet Union. Hoover wrote:

> That there is failure and disaster which besets our present foreign policies should be now evident. We have tried cooperation with the Kremlin. We have tried since the war to find peace by (a) diplomatic organization; (b) military alliances for "containment"; (c) resistance of Communist satellite aggression; (d) economic support to nations. All of these policies have gone by the board. There is no wonder that thinking Americans are in a state of total frustration over our national policies.[67]

Hoover then addressed himself to the policies that the United States should pursue in the face of the new situation in the world. First of all, he concluded, the government should be frank with the people about "where we find ourselves," and that "a new line of foreign policies must be worked out." The United States should not oppose movements toward neutralism, and opposition would be futile in any case. Nor should the United States oppose "any agreements between nations and Russia looking to 'peaceful coexistence.' If they think they can get protection from aggression by those means we ought [not] to object to their trying it." The United States might keep "a feeble flame of resistance alive by arms and subsidies to such governments as pledge themselves that there will be no 'neutralization' agreements to 'peaceful coexistence.' " That might include such nations as Germany, Belgium, Holland, Greece, Spain, and Turkey, but "we should furnish nothing more even to these nations except upon request. Then we could make our demands as to what they intend to do, and how?" Economic aid should be ruled out as "an antidote to Communist penetration," because "no amount of American activities could so rebuild European lower classes' standard of living as would counteract Communist infiltration and much of our aid is blatantly being diverted to the rich, not the poor." West Germany should be given complete independence and be allowed to rearm, so that they could "rebuild the only safety of Western Europe—the German dam. Whether Russia would sit by and see Germany re-arm is itself problematical but is worth trying." Japan could "only survive by raw materials from China and that market for manufactured goods," so the United States "should encourage her to set up all such trade relations" with China in order that American subsidies to offset her deficit in trade could be eliminated.[68]

Hoover concluded that most of America's rehabilitation measures should be concentrated on Latin America—"and there only upon their request and upon our stipulation that their government set up their own organization for this purpose to which we could contribute on a 50–50 basis. These steps are essential to maintain wise use and to maintain their own national pride." Meanwhile, the United States should "build our air, atomic and missile weapons intensively and at once to such dimensions as will deter any Communist attack upon us. We should build our radar and other electronic defenses to the utmost degree." Ground armies, "except for internal defense," he now considered obsolete, as well as battleships. Foreign military and economic aid should be diverted to America's own economic rehabilitation. The United States "should cease to support colonial exploitation even by our friends" and "reaffirm the American doctrine of freedom of peoples." And finally, Hoover concluded, "above all, we should realize that only in our own strong arm and the Western Hemisphere is our safety and sanctuary. We should not destroy them by chasing mirages."[69]

Although Hoover felt constrained not to voice his views in public lest they embarrass the Republican in the White House, he accepted Eisenhower's invitation to go fishing with him in Colorado in late August, shortly before the memorandum was dictated. No doubt Hoover acquainted the president with his views on the international situation while they fished for trout in the mountain streams near Denver.[70]

In October, two months after his eightieth birthday, Hoover hosted an "after-glow" party at the Waldorf-Astoria Hotel for his guests at various Bohemian Club encampments over the years. In a speech before the group, he touched on many topics including the work of his reorganization commission. As an example of the "nightmare" they were confronting, he pointed out:

> The Federal Government is engaged in 1500 socialistic business enterprises in competition with the citizens; it has $25 billions invested in them; 12 agencies give contrary advice on the weather; and 41 agencies give assorted medical service. That does not include the Federal Hospitals of which there are 38 in the New York area alone—each with empty beds. The Government possesses obsolete commodities costing $30 billions and that does not include 22 years' supply of toilet paper. After listening to lists of some of these commodities, I suggested to the Pentagon that I had no doubt the General who fought the first battle with gun powder kept his crossbows in storage for 40 years.

Of the controversy that had been generated by the charges of communists in the government by Senator Joseph McCarthy of Wisconsin, Hoover told his guests:

> I may mention that Moscow has not stopped recruiting agents among our fuzzy-minded intellectuals just because Senator McCarthy is to be stopped by Senator [Ralph] Flanders. McCarthy is the seventh King-pin to be bowled over by the left-wingers in ten years. But we still have two King-pins standing up. They head other Congressional Committees at work on this job.

The former president argued that such committee investigations of communists were vital.[71]

As for foreign relations, Hoover told his guests that he detected a rise in the spirit of nationalism everywhere but in the United States. The atomic and hydrogen bombs, he suggested, had "transformed all our alliances, all allegiances and all international relations," for no matter how much other nations might wish to support the United States, they would no longer dare to go to war with the Soviet Union on this nation's side lest they be obliterated by Soviet nuclear weapons. The funneling of American money into the pockets of other nations had won no dependable friends for the United States, he concluded, but "they still want our money." Of the United Nations he remarked that: "No one can believe that this organization could or would protect us from a major military aggression," but it ought to be retained, nevertheless, if only because "they have electronic devices by which we can give and receive the best oratory of denunciation in five languages all at once." There was always the possibility that the United Nations might some day become "a rallying ground for unity in the free nations," and if it did nothing else it made contributions in public health. Of the fate of the American people, Hoover concluded that there were "less war tensions in the world than a year or two years ago." Recent years had seen advances in science and technology of revolutionary import, and there was no sign that the pace was slackening. And the resultant productivity, he noted, had "produced a higher standard of living than we had before the second World War."[72]

In mid-October of 1954, Hoover accepted an invitation from Chancellor Konrad Adenauer to visit West Germany, and later in the month Adenauer called on him in New York to finalize the details of the trip, which would take place late the following month.[73] Before he left for Germany, the off-year elections of early November 1954 swept the Republicans out of control in Congress, which did not augur well for the adoption of the Hoover Commission's recommendations. A few days before leaving, Hoover wrote Clarence Kelland that he was hopeful conservative Democrats would join with conservative Republicans in the Congress "in opposition to further socialism," but he did not expect much help from "middle-of-the-road Republicans." He expected that the Hoover Commission report would "throw many jolts against all this, but beyond registering, it will not likely be decisive." He had confidence, however, that the Republican party would eventually awake to the fact that the United States was not a socialist country. Hoover expressed support for Dulles, Secretary of Defense Charles Wilson, Secretary of the Treasury George Humphrey, Secretary of Agriculture Ezra Taft Benson, and Sherman Adams. "The trouble," he wrote, "comes from other quarters from outside the White House and the Cabinet." He was, he told Kelland, "leaving for Germany on Sunday to help Adenauer, for he is the only bulwark against the sweep of Socialism over Europe."[74]

In Germany, Hoover was greeted at the airport by Adenauer and hailed by the German leader as "one of the great men of the world who has placed himself in the service of humanity."[75] At a dinner hosted by the German chancellor, he was described as a great American who had helped pave the way for West Germany's recovery from the ravages of war.[76] On November 24 Hoover delivered a speech in Bonn, in which he expressed faith in a healthy German nationalism. He reiterated his belief that "the German people have before now been the bastion of Western civilization which deterred its destruction by Asiatic hordes. My prayer is that Germany may be given the unity and full freedom which will restore her to that mission in the world." He told his German audience that the fundamental reason for the presence of U.S. armed forces in Europe was not the defense of the United States—that, he said, could be done much more cheaply—but to preserve Western civilization in Europe and the freedom of the nations there. He expressed the hope that Europeans would take up more of the burden of defense, noting that the patience of the American people was not inexhaustible. He expressed hope that tensions with the Soviet Union were abating, but warned that "from our many years experi-

ence with the Communists we should learn more about what peaceful coexistence means. What we must await are works rather than words."[77] Upon
leaving Germany a few days later, Hoover recalled that when he had last
visited that country eight years earlier he had concluded that it would be
"many, many years" before Germany would be on its feet again, and he
described the accomplishments of the past eight years as "brilliant." "Today,"
he told Adenauer, "under your wise statesmanship, West Germany is about to
attain her independence and to become a partner in the defense of freedom
from the common danger."[78]

Upon his return to the United States, Hoover reported to President
Eisenhower on the trip. Eisenhower responded by writing that he had noted
"with great satisfaction" that the trip

> had been as successful as I knew it would be and a real tribute to the
> humanitarian spirit of America which you personify. Let me thank
> you for your readiness to undertake this mission. At this decisive
> moment in the history of American-German relations, it would be
> hard for me to think of any man more eminently qualified to convey
> to the German people the feelings of friendship with which the
> American people welcome the return of Germany to the family of
> Western nations.[79]

It would not be the last overseas mission that President Eisenhower would ask
the former president, who was in his eighties, to undertake.

Back in the United States, Hoover was once again absorbed in the work of
the second Hoover Commission. In mid-February 1955, the commission's first
report was filed with Congress. It recommended a government employment
program to attract and hold more top talent, including the creation of a "senior
civil service group" of nonpartisan, well-paid professional administrators possessing special skills and experience, and higher pay for top administrators, as
well as better training programs and greater use of merit pay increases. The
report also called for revisions in the conflict-of-interest rules, revisions in
reduction-in-force procedures, the extension of civil service to more government jobs including U.S. marshals and customs officials, and the payment of
"prevailing wages," especially to employees in lower wage brackets. The
report estimated that if the high rate of turnover in government jobs could be
reduced by such reforms, it could save nearly $50 million a year. The report,
however, had not been adopted unanimously. Two Democrats, Congressman
Chet Holifield of California and James A. Farley were in opposition, as well
as Republican Congressman Clarence Brown.[80]

A week later the second report of the commission was released dealing
with paperwork and estimating that $255 million could be saved if the recom-
mendations for cutting red tape were put into effect. The report urged a

presidential executive order creating a paper management program, with the General Services Administration (GSA) supervising paperwork management in the executive branch, and with an official in each agency assigned the task of eliminating nonessential reports and copies of letters and simplifying forms.[81] The commission's third report, issued a week later, dealt with federal health services. It recommended the closing of uneconomical hospitals and an end to excessive building of federal hospitals. It sought an end to free medical care for merchant seamen and restrictions on care for veterans with non-service-connected disabilities, as well as contributory medical and hospital insurance for civilian employees of the government and dependents of servicemen stationed in the United States. It urged the creation of an advisory council to help coordinate federal medical services. It recommended that most of the hospitals and clinics of the Public Health Service be closed, and that armed forces hospital services be regionalized. It also called for the creation of a national library of medicine, the creation of a central authority for medical care in the event of a nuclear attack, and reorganization of the Food and Drug Administration.[82]

As the reports of the task forces flowed into the commission, were debated, and modified, and the resultant recommendations passed on to the Congress, Hoover wrote Clarence Kelland that he had "never worked harder nor longer hours than on the present job." He had, he wrote, "little hope that our views will be adopted, but at least the American people will know what their government is doing." He was not "as frightened over wars and rumors of wars as much as Washington and the Press" were. He wrote:

> To keep up such tensions is good setting for military legislation and spending. With 8,000,000 persons, directly or indirectly being employed in the Military field and the present inflation of every business activity, we would have a bigger bump than that of 1931 if peace came all of a sudden. And with an unbalanced budget inflation is still working.[83]

The fourth report of the commission was the most controversial to date, and it passed the commission by a narrow 7–5 vote, with three Democrats (Holifield, Farley, and Joseph P. Kennedy) as well as Brownell and Flemming in dissent. It called for drastic changes in the federal role in lending activities, including major cuts in favor of private enterprise, and cited potential savings of $200 million per year. Included in the recommendation were proposals that the Production Credit Corporations, Agricultural Marketing Act Revolving Fund, Federal Farm Mortgage Corporation, and loans for college housing construction all be liquidated, that crop loans to farmers under price supports be substituted for purchase agreements, that the Rural Electrification Administration (REA) be put on a self-supporting basis and merged into private enterprise, that Federal Housing Administration (FHA) programs be re-organized to obtain financing from private sources subject to federal regulation, that the president be allowed to raise down-payment requirements for FHA-insured loans, and that the Export-Import Bank end short-term commercial loans and become the only federal source of long-term exports and loans to foreign governments. It also recommended that the Small Business Administration and other agencies raise their interest charges to cover their operating costs and pay interest to the Treasury equal to the cost of money to the government, and that the Federal National Mortgage Association, Federal Intermediate Credit Banks, and Banks for Cooperatives be merged with private enterprise through "mutualization." The commission also asked Congress to review the International Monetary Fund to determine whether it was still needed by the United States.[84]

The fifth report, issued in early April, was less controversial. It dealt with transportation functions of the federal government, particularly in the Defense Department. The report recommended the creation of a transportation director in the Defense Department to strengthen central direction of transportation functions. It urged pay raises for government traffic management personnel, ending the shipping of private automobiles abroad by servicemen on government vessels, the transfer of mail from military to civilian aircraft, greater use by the military of commercial cargo and passenger ships and tankers, and more group movements of military personnel instead of individual movements; it scored the unnecessary and uneconomical use of government ships in competition with commercial ships and found such usage at odds with the aim of Congress to build a strong, privately operated merchant marine.[85]

In the report on federal legal services and procedures, even Hoover joined with five other members of the commission in abstaining from voting on some of the proposals, but approved their submission to Congress for consideration. The report urged the establishment of a U.S. administrative court for tax, labor, and trade regulations, as well as the creation of a legal career service. The aim was to separate the administrative and judicial functions, which were centered in some federal agencies, thus to give greater protection against abuses of power and arbitrary bureaucratic action.[86] The report on federal surplus property followed a few days later and urged the compilation of a catalog of all federal property. It criticized the federal government for poor inventory keeping and lack of coordination of government agencies, which had led to the huge accumulation of government supplies, especially by the armed forces.[87]

In the midst of his work on the commission and the controversy being generated by the reports of the commission, Hoover finally agreed to testify in person on possible changes that might be made in the United Nations Charter. In his testimony before the Senate committee, the former president made it clear that he had "no notion that we can abandon any organization of nations that makes for peace." The United Nations had not fulfilled the hopes of those who looked to it, but it had "served to secure settlement of some disputes among small nations," and it had "performed many good economic and philanthropic services." He did not believe "that under present circumstances the Charter can be very effectively amended because of the Communist veto in the Security Council," but that did not mean "amendments should not be prepared and ventilated to the world at large." He then reviewed the suggestions he had made in his memorandum a year earlier, which were, in turn, the suggestions he had made in 1945. Hoover was asked by Senator H. Alexander Smith if he thought the United Nations should expel the Soviet Union from membership. He responded that he had at one time suggested that either the Soviets should be expelled "in order to give entry to 14 nations" who were being excluded by the Soviet veto, or that "we might consider a new organism to include only the free nations." He now felt that neither course was viable. "My own conclusion," Hoover told the committee, "is that we have to go on and worry with the Russians and with the hope that things may be better sometimes."[88] The *New York Times* reported that anti–United Nations forces in Congress had hoped for Hoover's support for their efforts to reduce the power of the United Nations or to take the United States out of it, but that his testimony had given them no "comfort."[89]

A few days later the next Hoover Commmission report went to Congress, dealing with federal buying of food and clothing. The report claimed that better management could save $340 million each year and recommended new central agencies in the Defense Department to buy and distribute and control supplies of the armed forces. It urged the abolition of competitive bidding and expected savings if the GSA handled all government purchases except those under farm price-support programs. It urged "cross-servicing" arrangements between the GSA and the armed forces.[90] In mid-May the commission urged the federal government to end over 1,000 enterprises that were competing with private business and advocated a gradual end to the Postal Savings system, an increase in parcel post rates, an end to chemical research by the Tennessee Valley Authority (TVA), and an increase in the price of TVA-produced fertilizer to cover all costs, including the loss of taxes that could otherwise have been paid by private producers.[91] Predictably, these recommendations by the commission aroused considerable controversy.

Meanwhile, Hoover had already taken to the stump in support of the commission's recommendations. Early in May he told the U.S. Chamber of Commerce that the federal budget could be balanced "overnight" if the recommendations of the Hoover Commission were implemented. Some of the problems that the commission had found in government, he said, arose from the "fabulous growth of the Federal Executive branches by about fourteen times the size of twenty-five years ago." Others were "due to obsolete legislation which obstruct progress," and some arose from "the tenacity of Government agencies to the idea that their empires are sacrosanct." Yet others were "due to the pressure groups that profit from the present set up of these agencies and resent all change." And finally, he said: "Some of these systems are due to the primary emotion of all bureaucracies that their sleep be not disturbed."[92] Later in the month he told the National Industrial Conference Board that all of the commission's recommendations, if adopted, could save taxpayers $6 billion per year, and produce a return of $7 billion to the Treasury through liquidation of government agencies and functions that competed with private business.[93]

Late in May, the commission reported its recommendations on federal storage. It urged modern operation and wider use of private warehouses, envisioning savings of $235 million per year. It found much duplication of storage space by the armed forces and proposed that Congress authorize the GSA to force coordination in the storage of civilian records.[94] The commission next recommended expansion of civilian and military research and development, especially in weapons development. It asked for more federal assistance to medical research and cited inadequate public and state support for medical schools. It proposed a standing committee of scientists in the Department of Defense to spur weapons development.[95]

The commission's report a few days later on foreign aid found little agreement among the members of the commission. Hoover was the only member who supported the entire report. A majority of the commission argued that the recommendations should have included one for reduction in foreign aid. The report did say that certain nations no longer needed extensive aid, that technical aid to the original NATO countries should end, and that aid for large manufacturing or industrial projects in Asia should not be undertaken except perhaps in Japan, that the United States should not duplicate the programs of the United Nations, and that all overseas nonmilitary personnel of U.S. agencies should be put under the chief of the U.S. diplomatic mission in whatever country they were stationed.[96]

The next report recommended that rates charged for power by federal power projects be raised to cover the costs that private utilities must pay, including taxes; it urged that the Federal Power Commission should set rates, and it suggested that charges be levied against users of inland waterways aided by federal funds, that a water resources board be established to advise on all water and hydroelectric power projects, and that the federal government should not undertake development projects when state and local governments or private interests could do the job. It also recommended that as far as possible new federal power facilities should be self-financing.[97] The commission next attacked the waste in federal real estate management, pointing out that some agencies bought property while others had idle land and buildings. It urged that the Bureau of the Budget and the GSA be given greater control over real estate management.[98]

The reports were being issued at a more rapid pace now, as the Hoover Commission was due to expire on June 30, 1955. One of the most important of the reports was that recommending changes in preparing the federal budget and the form of congressional appropriations, which would save $4 billion a year, the commission claimed, if private business methods were adopted. The commission recommended new powers and staff for the Bureau of the Budget to control spending and perform management duties; it proposed an accounting office under an assistant budget director to plan for accounting and budgeting in executive agencies; and also proposed that the bureau place its own experts in major agencies, with each agency to have a controller chosen with the help of the assistant budget director. The commission urged that Congress limit its practice of obligating funds years ahead of payment and suggested that the budget and appropriations be shifted from an "obligational" basis to "accrued expenditures," which would end large balances of unspent appropriations. Brown, Farley, and Holifield dissented from the recommendations.[99]

On June 24, the second Hoover Commission held its final meeting and paid tribute to Hoover, while the former president hailed the contribution made by the commission members.[100] On June 26, the *New York Times* wrote: "For former President Herbert Hoover that last public service is done." With the expiration of the Hoover Commission on June 30, it reported, "Mr. Hoover, its chairman for eight years, at 81 and with forty-one years of almost constant and almost wholly unpaid public service behind him, will retire to private life." There was some irony in the fact that the *New York Times* had also retired the former president after the first Hoover Commission had expired. The *Times* reporter who interviewed Hoover found "traits the public rarely sees. He was warm and friendly, a hint of humor lurking in his speech. With a well-caked black briar pipe clutched in his left hand, he rose to shake hands. The high starched collar had been replaced by a shirt with almost no starch at all." Hoover told the press that of all the commission recommendations the one on the civil service was "nearest my heart's desire." When asked of the philosophy that had guided the commission's work, he responded: "The purpose was to save the taxpayers money. But more important than savings was the realization that the whole social and economic foundation is based on private enterprise."[101]

Two more reports appeared after the final meeting of the commission. The first recommended the creation of a fourth branch of the Defense Department which would be a civilian-run Defense Supply and Service Administration. The commission estimated that it could save $2 billion per year. The commission also proposed modifying the conflict-of-interest laws so that appointees to government positions would not have to liquidate "lifetime business" interests, suggesting that instead such employees take an oath that they would not participate in decisions affecting their financial interests.[102] The last and one of the most controversial reports was the one on water resources and power. The recommendations of the commission were, however, less sweeping than those of the task force. The report of the commission urged higher rates for electricity produced by federal agencies like the TVA; a ban on new generating projects by the federal government where state, municipal, or private funds were available; permission for private companies to buy a "fair share" of federal power for resale; requirements that agencies like TVA finance themselves by issuing public securities; that government cease its preferential treatment in power sales to nonprofit agencies like cities and cooperatives; that government no longer build transmission lines where non-federal agencies could provide the service; and that Congress adopt a clear statement on national water supply. It also advocated a "user charge" on inland waterways; that a water resources commission be created to advise the president; and that the rates for federal electricity be made high enough to provide payments in lieu of taxes to state and local governments, such as private utilities would pay. The commission report, however, did not follow the task force recommendation that called for the sale of federal facilities to private enterprise.[103]

At a news conference on the final day of the Hoover Commission's existence, Hoover brushed aside criticism of the water resources and power report and made public the recommendations of the task force, which were much more drastic. He noted that the commission estimated that a total of $8.5 billion per year might be saved if all of the recommendations were adopted, and that $15 billion could be salvaged for the Treasury through the recovery of investments, liquidation of liabilities, and property sales. Asked if he thought there was a need for yet a third commission, Hoover replied "somebody else" would have to organize it.[104] A press release from the commission recommended that 33 independent agencies then reporting to the president be placed under the supervision of "some official within the President's office." It noted that the commission had made 145 "administrative" recommendations that could be carried out by the various departments and agencies and 167 that required legislation. The commission identified 50 administrative actions that had already been taken and 40 bills that had been drafted covering many of the legislative recommendations. But the *New York Times* editorialized that "the Administration and Congress have been so slow to act upon this year's Hoover reports that one can fairly wonder how many of them will be put into effect at all." It found this in marked contrast with the enthusiasm shown for the report of the first Hoover Commission.[105]

Hoover was prepared for criticism. He wrote Congressman Clarence Brown of the commission: "I expect a lot of venom from the left."[106] Brown, who was encountering criticism of the commission's recommendations in the

House, wrote the former president: "I am sure you appreciate it is not easy for me to, almost singlehanded, combat those, both in and out of Government, who for their own selfish reasons would like to belittle and besmirch the efforts of the Hoover Commission."[107] Hoover was not very sanguine that the recommendations requiring legislation would be adopted, but he felt that those that could be put through by administrative action were "being rapidly adopted by the Republican administration." He feared that "we may have to await a Republican Congress to have rapid motion in the legislative matters." But, no matter what the record of adoption, he thought the reports would "have educative value to the less instructed."[108] When the press reported that Hoover would now probably retire from public service, the former president thought their speculation a bit premature, writing Joseph Dodge: "If the history of the first Commission on Organization is any guide, I will, in the next few years, be before 20 Congressional Committees explaining what we meant and 20 audiences trying to convince pressure groups the error of their ways." He was, Hoover said, "neither going to get 'retirement,' nor do I want it."[109]

In an interview published in the August 5, 1955, issue of *U.S. News and World Report*, Hoover admitted:

> In the Commission's work, the large majority favored the philosophic foundation under which we would operate. It's very simple— that the whole social-economic system of this country is based on private enterprise, properly regulated to prevent unfair competition and to prevent monopolies; that the Government should provide those services which people cannot do for themselves.

It was to this test that the commission had submitted all of the agencies it had examined. "That part of our work," he confessed, "was not so much a matter of savings as strengthening our vital structure of individual, State and local government rights." In addition to "trying to strengthen the philosophical foundations of our country," the commission had sought to reduce expenses without injuring the security of the nation or disturbing "the justifiable social services of the country." When asked if there had been enthusiasm demonstrated in Congress for the recommendations of the commission, Hoover responded that he "couldn't say one way or the other." He added: "With the philosophical foundation I told you about a minute ago, I imagine that all the 'left-wingers' in the Congress are opposed to everything we suggested." He considered the federal government "immensely too big," because it had "undertaken functions which ought to be left to the States and the people." He observed that approximately 70 percent of the recommendations of the first Hoover Commission had been adopted, "but it took six years." Asked how much money the first commission had saved the taxpayers, Hoover pointed to the GSA, created as a result of the recommendations of the first commission, which already showed specific savings of $150 million per year. The enormous budget increases that had resulted from the Korean War, however, had obscured other possible savings. Asked how much success he expected from Congress with the second report, Hoover responded: "I expect more, because we have a more emphatic public opinion behind us now." He admitted, however, that "there is a very considerable element who are on the 'left wing' side who do not believe in these recommendations."[110]

The September issue of the *Democratic Digest* carried a partisan attack on the second Hoover Commission in the name of the Democratic national committee. The article implied that the commission had been politically partisan, that Hoover had stacked the task forces, particularly the one on public power, with adherents to his own philosophy, and that President Eisenhower did not approve of the commission's recommendations. The former president responded with a statement on August 16 denouncing the "infamous smear" in the *Digest*. Hoover maintained that the commission had "never divided upon political grounds. Every recommendation was by a majority and was voted for by some if not all of the five Democratic members." That the work had been done "fairly and patiently" was attested to, he said, by a statement signed at the final session by all members of the commission, including all the Democrats. There had been no representatives of the public utilities on the water resources and power task force, Hoover insisted, because the commission was "conducting an objective inquiry and not a Donnybrook Fair." As to the president's attitude, Hoover pointed out that Eisenhower had already "directed the Departments to set up machinery for the implementing of the Commission's administrative recommendations."[111]

Already past his eightieth birthday during the heaviest work of the commission, Hoover had worked hard. Participants in the commission's activities marveled at the effort he put in at the sessions. Herbert Brownell later recalled that he and Joseph P. Kennedy had admired the former president's ability to work "like a Trojan." According to Brownell:

> That's my recollection of him during that time—how hard continuously he worked. He just begrudged every minute we took out for a sandwich and coffee in the middle of our all day meetings, you know, because he wasn't getting something done. We used to joke with him a little about it and he would laugh about it, but he'd go right on with business during lunch.

Brownell also attested to the influence Hoover exerted over the final recommendations of the commission.[112]

Throughout 1955 and 1956 Hoover delivered a number of speeches on the work of the second Hoover Commission. He even consented, after declining for years, to appear on "Meet the Press" in order to publicize the work of the commission to the public.[113] After that broadcast, Lawrence Spivak, the moderator, wrote Hoover that when he decided to retire "there is a place for you in television." He thought that Hoover had done "a wonderful job" on the broadcast and concluded by writing: "The only criticism I have to make—and that really isn't a criticism—is that you did not smile more frequently, because when you did your face lighted up in an extraordinary way and brought out qualities of humor and kindliness which are not often enough associated with your greatness."[114] A letter to the editor of the *St. Louis Post Dispatch* referred to Spivak's "kidgloves" treatment of Hoover on the television broadcast:

> Like an art lover looking at the Mona Lisa in the Louvre
> Was Lawrence Spivak of Meet the Press questioning Herbert
>   Hoover.[115]

Through such appearances and the work of the Citizens' Committee for the Hoover Report, Hoover endeavored to build public support for the committee's recommendations to ensure that they would be carried out.[116] Rolling back the New Deal was not an easy task.

Hoover also continued to speak out on political and international issues. He told the press that he foresaw the possibility of "an endurable peace for years to come" as a result of the forthcoming Geneva summit conference in July, but he cautioned that this was the best to be expected, and by no means a "lasting peace."[117] When President Eisenhower challenged the Soviet Union to exchange full military information with the United States, Hoover called it a "master stroke" by which to force the Soviets to demonstrate the sincerity of their professed desire for world peace. Eisenhower's proposal, he told the press, had "really put the Russians in a spot this time."[118]

On his eighty-first birthday, August 10, 1955, he spoke in Newberg, Oregon, where he had spent much of his childhood, on the theme of the "American Way of Life." He recalled his boyhood in the Oregon forests and fishing in the lakes of the region. Such reminiscences, he mused, would probably be regarded as "an expression of longing to go backward in American life." While he denied this, he did lament that "during the last score of years our American way of life has been deluged with criticism." He had, himself, joined in some of the criticism, "because of my anxieties over mistaken policies and especially the influence of Karl Marx on our way of life." But in the midst of the criticism, it was also important, he insisted, to "lift our eyes unto the hills from whence cometh our help. We should occasionally mention something good about ourselves." He pointed to the unequalled level of American productivity and standard of living, the constantly improving health and life expectancy of the American people. He recounted other positive features of America and concluded that "freedom of mind, of spirit and of initiative still lives in America. . . . Here alone, even with all its defects, is human dignity not a dream but an accomplishment."[119] Despite the optimism of his speech, however, Hoover confided a few months later: "I don't like for the American people, each with their own problems, to be as discouraged over the future as I am."[120]

Hoover's relations with the Democratic former president were also becoming more cordial. Early in 1954 he had declined an invitation to attend a dinner celebrating Truman's seventieth birthday, writing James A. Farley:

> My presence there would cause a mass of gossip and ventilation of old issues, more especially in this case, in view of Mr. Truman's many personal attacks upon me. I have never made a personal attack upon him, and I gave much of my energies for nearly four years to aiding his Administration. We have differed on public policies, but that is the legitimate and necessary process of American life. I have had a higher opinion both of Mr. Truman personally and of many of his policies than many of my political colleagues. I have no desire to avoid meeting him. Indeed, I am confident the time will yet come when he and I can join to forward matters of public interest.[121]

In mid-October 1955, the Democrat paid a courtesy call on the Republican in New York City, and later in the month, Hoover joined the sponsors of the Harry S. Truman Library, Committee of the Southwest, in seeking to raise $200,000 in that part of the country as part of the $2 million needed to build the library in Independence, Missouri.[122] The next month, Hoover was pressed into service by the Republican in the White House to represent the president at the Armistice Day ceremony at Arlington National Cemetery where he laid a wreath on the Tomb of the Unknown Soldier. It was a day, Hoover remarked, for consecrating the nation once again to peace. "And we dedicate ourselves," he added, "to maintain respect of nations for our preparedness and our might to defend ourselves against aggression."[123]

It had been a busy year for Herbert Hoover. In December he wrote a friend:

> As I have launched about 300 reforms needed in Washington, I shall have to spend my next months with Congressional committees and government agencies bent on devices to avoid them. However, it is a blessing to keep busy. To be sure of that, I am at odd times writing some more volumes to be published after I have passed on. That delay is in order that I won't need meditate on the reviews which this great center of intelligence [New York] will produce.

He had decided to spend the holidays fishing in Florida, he said, "because out in a skiff on the blue water and with no radio, television, telephone or tabloids with their scoops of murders, and with only a bonefish for an objective, one can recover some stability from the jars and shocks of the time."[124]

12

The Active Octogenarian

lthough Hoover had passed age 81, his pace seemed hardly to have slackened. His routine remained the same: part of the summer he spent in the West, with fishing in Oregon, visits to San Francisco and Stanford University, and the Bohemian Club encampment among the redwoods; part of the winter he pursued bonefish and other varieties of gamefish off the Florida coast; and the rest of his time he divided between the New York apartment and activities in Washington, adding an occasional trip for speech making. He continued his work on behalf of the Hoover Commission's recommendations, and he remained abreast of world and domestic affairs.

In December of 1955, Hoover made a return appearance on "Meet the Press," thereby setting in motion what he would later refer to as the "Double Cross." During the broadcast he referred to the burdens of the presidency and proposed "an Administrative Vice President" to relieve some of those burdens. It was an unfortunate choice of terminology for what he clearly intended to be a sort of chief-of-staff to whom the president could delegate some of the responsibilities of his office, since the use of "vice president" suggested a change of constitutional importance. Called to testify on his proposal for the Senate Subcommittee on Government Organization, Hoover gathered material for his testimony, only to find his position undercut by the Eisenhower administration, which feared that the public would interpret such a proposal as evidence that Eisenhower did not feel capable of handling all the duties of the office due to his heart attack of September 1955.[1] Eisenhower did not endear himself to the elder statesman of the party by his position, but former president Truman also opposed the proposal.[2]

After weeks of bonefishing, Hoover went on the attack against Marxism in April. In a speech before the Inter-American Bar Association in Dallas, he concentrated on the threat that Marxism was posing to the western hemisphere. Centered in Moscow, it was "carrying on aggression against the Western Hemisphere by conspiracies among our fuzzy-minded to overthrow our governments." The socialists who sought to gain their ends through the legal use of free institutions no longer used the word socialist, he said, but rather tried to conceal their objectives by adopting words like "liberals" and "progressives," and by advocating what they called real "democracy" and "public welfare." Hoover reiterated his thesis that economic freedom was indivisible from all other freedoms. The experience of Britain and France with socialism, and the record of the Soviet Union's eight satellites, did not bear out the high claims for socialism made by its advocates. "Certainly the exhibits of Karl Marx elsewhere," Hoover concluded, "would not indicate that his philosophy has anywhere produced a Utopia."[3]

But Hoover found few signs that his own philosophy had made much headway in Washington, despite the presence of a Republican in the White House. When one correspondent wrote him of the Eisenhower administration that "one would almost think the New Deal was still doing business," Hoover replied that it was "the Neo-New Deal."[4] Despite his campaign against public power the Senate had approved a bill for Niagara power, which meant, for him, only more "creeping socialism."[5] Meanwhile, Hoover was devoting more and more of his time to writing. One secretary wrote that he had been as "busy as ten bird dogs" with the work on his books, while another wrote: "At the moment the chief is busy on four different books! We can't write another two—yes I know that HH can!"[6]

In 1956, for the first time since he had left the White House, Hoover showed no enthusiasm for attending the Republican national convention. Instead, he had made plans for a fishing trip over the week of the convention. He wrote to GOP national chairman Leonard Hall: "I had made other plans than attending this year's convention. I said last time that was my last appearance. If the President wishes me to do it, I will see what I can do to rearrange matters."[7] From Eisenhower came the request that he do so. The president wrote: "You exemplify in more ways than I am sure you realize the dignity and spirit of the Republican Party, and I know that every delegate to the Convention would be keenly disappointed, as would I, if you were not there to lend your counsel and advice."[8] Hoover had, he wrote a friend,

> planned and engaged all of the paraphernalia by which I would
> leave here on August 8th for the woods of Wyoming until both my

birthday and the convention were over. However, I have a pressing letter from the President that I speak again. . . . The world is somewhat better of these last three years, and on this basis I will try to be as cheerful as possible.[9]

To Eisenhower, he wrote: "I am also much more than even grateful for a President who has, amid stupendous difficulties, kept the world at peace and lifted American public life again to the levels of integrity. As you wished I will make a short speech at the Convention. It will not be an earthquake."[10]

Before the convention, Hoover relaxed in the Bohemian Club woods and delivered his yearly off-the-record speech. He criticized the high taxes and pointed out that the Hoover Commission had produced recommendations that would save $7 billion annually if adopted. Many of those recommendations had been adopted, but Congress, he noted, "does not always act with the speed of light." It had taken five years for 70 percent of the recommendations of the first Hoover Commission to be adopted. Turning to academic freedom, he observed:

> If freedom is to survive, it is the particular responsibility of men of learning. And any intellectual man who has to defend his doings by yelling "Academic Freedom" has something the matter with him. The two things that bite at the vitals of this small minority group are not the lack of Academic Freedom. They are either the lack of intellectual integrity or are fuzzy-mindedness.

He closed his talk by touching upon fishing. Hoover confided to his audience the reason why all presidents took up fishing:

> The simple reason is that the American people concede privacy on only two occasions. Fishing and prayer—and presidents cannot pray all the time, even if the activities of the public need it. Moreover, if the President wants to leave the White House, no citizen questions the purity of his motives if he is just going fishing. Any other destination requires a press conference and news releases.[11]

A few days later, on the eve of his eighty-second birthday, Hoover told the press that he detected a lessening of world tensions, but he refused to estimate the prospects for peace. He credited President Eisenhower and Secretary of State Dulles with having contributed an "enormous amount" toward reduction in world tensions. Hoover was described by reporters as "ruddy and in good health," and somewhat apologetic for having slowed down to only a twelve- to fourteen-hour workday. He expressed his opposition to retirement, which meant centering one's life on ills and pills and associating only with others of the same preoccupation. He told the press: "Any oldster who keeps at even part-time work has something worth talking about. He has a zest for the morning paper and his three meals a day. The point of all this is not to retire from work or you will shrivel up into a nuisance to all mankind." The *New York Times* added:

> On his annual summer visit to the West Coast, Mr. Hoover has fished four or five days in the Mackenzie River of Oregon, his favorite trout stream. He has attended the annual encampment of the Bohemian Club. . . . He has sat in at board meetings of many organizations of which he is chairman or a member. He has helped launch a financial drive for a Stanford medical center as honorary chairman of the campaign. He keeps a staff of eight secretaries and research assistants on the move here and in New York. Although Mr. Hoover's speechmaking now is limited, he receives fifty or sixty letters a day asking him to give talks. Once in a while, one invitation draws an affirmative answer. After that address, his secretaries are swamped with mail.[12]

The 1956 Republican national convention marked the centennial of the GOP, and Hoover thought it an appropriate occasion for dispensing with the usual political platform to issue, instead, a declaration of Republican principles. He had prepared such a document and submitted it for consideration. His draft affirmed a commitment to peace as "the first obligation of statesmen and governments," and to the maintenance of such defenses as "will deter the menace in the Kremlin from attack upon us and the free world." He held that "the road from the era of international chaos is the right of peoples to their own independence and that cooperation between nations for their economic welfare and their common defense is indispensable for peace in the world." Hoover's statement affirmed a commitment to limited government, fiscal responsibility, and a regulated free enterprise system. The role of the federal government was to "aid in the conservation of our forests, our soil, our water resources, and in construction for navigation, flood control, and airways," as well as in "education, medical and scientific research; protection from unemployment and in old age," as well as the care of "dependents of veterans whose lives were lost in war, care of the war-disabled, and medical attention for veterans who are destitute."[13]

In his speech before the Republican convention on August 21, Hoover noted that in each of his past six convention appearances he had stressed "our responsibility to maintain the safeguards of free men," and he opined that this was still "America's most vital issue." Freedom, he found, "threatened and even overwhelmed by the revival of old ideas and the spread of a host of new ideas dangerous to free men." The Eisenhower administration had reduced international tensions and had "stemmed the malign forces which have beset us from within and without," while increasing prosperity and maintaining "two vital forces in the minds of free men" —integrity and religious faith. It was the responsibility of the centennial convention of the Republican party to "generate a spirit which will rekindle in every American a love not only for his country but a devotion to its true ideals." He had only faith in the future of the country because of "the genius of our people, their devotion to personal liberty and their sustaining religious beliefs."[14]

In the Democratic convention that year, the son of Hoover's old friend Joseph P. Kennedy was nearly nominated for the vice-presidential spot on the ticket. John F. Kennedy had served in the House of Representatives before moving to the Senate in 1952. As chairman of the Senate subcommittee responsible for reviewing the legislative recommendations of the Hoover Commission, he had been in close touch with Hoover. Another Kennedy son, Robert, had worked with the second Hoover Commission until he resigned in February 1954.[15] Hoover's own son, Herbert, Jr., was an under secretary of state in the Eisenhower administration. In September, Hoover wrote Joseph Kennedy: "You and I need another joint session. I don't know that we can do anything about things. At least we can take satisfaction in two sons in public life who are carrying on the battle."[16] Kennedy replied that they both could "take immense satisfaction in the jobs being done by Herbert, Jr. and Jack, but I was thrilled to read while abroad of the way you 'stole the show' while on stage at the Republican convention."[17]

The Republican elder statesman had one other consolation in 1956. While there was much that Hoover found objectionable in Eisenhower's policies, the president did not regard him as a pariah to be shunned. In 1956 the Eisenhower campaign sought his assistance once again through a speech on nationwide television. As the director of public relations for the GOP national committee wrote to him gushingly in mid-October:

> We are delighted at your consent to make this important telecast, and I am sure it will be one of the most important in the entire campaign. I know how well your speech at the convention was received throughout the country, and I am sure your talk will be instrumental in swinging many millions of votes for President Eisenhower.[18]

The chairman of Citizens for Eisenhower in Philadelphia sought Hoover's help in that city. Pennsylvania was likely to be crucial for Ike's reelection, he wrote Hoover, and Philadelphia would affect the state's vote. The city had gone for Stevenson in 1952, and Eisenhower's campaigners sought "an informal press, radio, or television interview with you when you arrive in Philadelphia on Tuesday, October 23, to receive the Systems and Procedures

Association award."[19] Hoover's new popularity with the party must have amazed him. However, he had to decline the Philadelphia invitation as he did not plan to accept the award in person.[20]

On October 29, 1956, Hoover aired his brief speech in behalf of the Eisenhower–Nixon ticket. Of only five minutes duration, it was delivered in a New York studio of CBS. The objectives of the American people, he said, were "advancement of peace in the world, and preparedness for defense in the meantime," as well as a rising standard of living and maximum employment, economy in government, reduced taxes, a balanced budget and a stable dollar, care of those unable to care for themselves, and "public improvements which the people or the States cannot accomplish for themselves," governmental integrity, and the preservation of freedom against encroachment by government. "In all these vital segments of American life," Hoover asserted, "the Eisenhower Administration has already succeeded or is driving toward these objectives." The candidate of the other party, he suggested, would "have an uphill battle against these accomplishments." He concluded that the voters of America would "be happier if you vote for President Eisenhower, Vice President Nixon and a Congress friendly to them. Anyway, may God bless you all."[21]

Hoover had meanwhile become involved in what was to be his last international relief activity. The refugee problems resulting from the Hungarian uprising in 1956 were made to order for Hoover's talents and energies, and for the pool of aging, but experienced, relief workers who still remained active from the day when he had directed them in other such efforts. In late October 1956, a meeting of prominent Hungarian–Americans was held at the instance of Dr. Tibor Eckardt, and the group decided to form an organization known as First Aid for Hungary. The group, working through a field office in Vienna, began its activities early in November with a shipment of medicine. It was incorporated on November 5, 1956, with Hoover as honorary chairman. By early the following month, First Aid for Hungary was shipping medical supplies to five hospitals inside Hungary and had established seventeen first-aid stations on the Austro-Hungarian border, four field kitchens in Austria, and three mobile field pharmacies in the border area. They also supplied materials to Hungarian refugees immigrating to the United States.[22] Hoover also advised President Eisenhower on how the governmental aspect of the refugee problem might be handled. First Aid for Hungary was, in the words of one Hoover associate, "intended to mean just that" —a first-aid, temporary type of program. The main task was left to the larger organizations and to governments.[23] By February of 1957, Hoover concluded that the organization had fulfilled its "first-aid" function and that future and larger relief efforts would have to be the province of governmental agencies. First Aid for Hungary ended its operations in that month.[24]

Early in January of 1957, Hoover was asked to testify before the House

Foreign Affairs Committee on President Eisenhower's request for standby authority to use American armed forces in the Middle East and for $400 million to be used for economic assistance in the region.[25] Hoover responded that he was in Florida recovering from colds and bronchitis and that a visit to Washington would be against the advice of his doctor. Instead, he sent a telegram that gave his views on Eisenhower's proposals.[26] Hoover had been concerned about the situation in the Middle East for some time, particularly the evidence that the Soviet Union was gaining influence in that vital part of the world through "international conspiracies." As early as November 1955, he had written that "unless the west is prepared to hold the Persian Gulf, the Arab States, and North Africa away from the Communists—by force, if necessary—we had better get into our own shell and establish the outposts to warn us of attack."[27] He now wired Congressman Gordon, chairman of the House committee, that he could condense his opinion of the president's proposals into one sentence: "On the understanding that these proposals extend only to Russian Communist military aggression and to economic aid I am in full agreement with the President."[28] Later in the month he responded to a similar request for his views from Senator Alexander Wiley by writing that he certainly supported the president's proposal "that the United States should use its military forces to aid Middle East states to repel any military aggression," and also his proposal for "continued economic aid to the region." He considered it "essential to the peace of the world that the Soviet government should be under no misapprehension as to our position with respect to any military aggression which they might contemplate in the Middle East."[29] At first glance it might appear that Hoover had moved a long way from the position he had maintained during the Great Debate six years earlier, but the American national interest was clearly involved in the oil of the Middle East and the protection of the Suez Canal, and the issue here was not, as in Europe, an unwillingness on the part of the countries involved to prepare adequately for their own defense.

During 1957 Hoover continued to monitor the progress of legislation to implement important reforms suggested by the Hoover Commission in budgeting and reorganization of the Defense Department, working closely with Senator John Kennedy and Congressman Clarence Brown.[30] In July he traveled to Independence, Missouri, to join Chief Justice Earl Warren, Eleanor Roosevelt, Senator William Knowland, House Speaker Sam Rayburn, Congressman Charles Halleck and others for the dedication of the Truman Presidential Library. In a short speech, Hoover asserted that it was "of extreme importance that we do not concentrate the history of the United States in Washington, D.C. I am happy to witness an event wherein the history of the American people is being brought closer and closer to them."[31]

Hoover's speeches had grown less frequent, his travel to all but his accustomed haunts more circumscribed. He continued with his busy writing schedule and issued occasional "blasts" from his apartment in the Waldorf Tower. As he wrote to an old friend late in 1957:

> I have gone into this comfortable monastery not to illuminate the margins of old manuscripts like the monks of old, but to write manuscripts myself and occasionally peep out and say something to the American people. I get hundreds of supporting editorials on these occasional peeps, but of course nothing happens. They, however, comfort me that I am still sane. The first book will be out in April or May on *The Ordeal of Woodrow Wilson*. It will illustrate some lessons on the old world and prove that Woodrow Wilson would be a "reactionary" in present estimation. It is friendly to Wilson and I hope you will like it.[32]

Even during his fishing trips to Florida in pursuit of bonefish, Hoover put in many hours at his writing.[33]

The Ordeal of Woodrow Wilson, published in 1958, is a unique historical document—a study of one president of the United States written by another president of the opposing political party. While much of the work actually deals with Hoover's own activities during the armistice period, the portrait of Wilson is a sensitive and sympathetic one. Hoover first established that Wilson's "liberalism," was at variance with the current definition of the term. He wrote: "As a Jeffersonian Democrat, he was a 'liberal' of the nineteenth century cast. His training in history and economics rejected every scintilla of socialism, which today connotes a liberal." Wilson's philosophy had been based upon a regulated free enterprise system, with federal intervention "justified only when the task was greater than the states or individuals could perform for themselves." He then described the story of "the President's plans, his obstacles, his methods, his successes and the causes of the tragedy which came to him in his efforts to bring lasting peace to the world."[34] As one reviewer wrote:

> Hoover's book is essentially a documentation, a blueprint of the Wilsonian ordeal. He shows in detail how Wilson captured the imagination of a warshocked world with the promise of a just peace and a League of Nations to tidy up the international madhouse. He then shows how Old World hatreds and greeds, together with homegrown suspicions, turned Wilson's dream into a patchwork of drab compromises.[35]

For the most part, Wilson scholars reacted positively to Hoover's book.[36]

In January of 1958, Hoover was queried by Senator Estes Kefauver of Tennessee concerning his views on the question of possible inability of a president to perform the duties of his office. The question seemed particularly relevant and timely because of President Eisenhower's two serious illnesses during his first term of office. Kefauver sought Hoover's testimony before his standing subcommittee on constitutional amendments, particularly his views of where he would "place the responsibility for determining the President's inability to perform the powers and duties of his office."[37] Hoover responded with a letter from the Key Largo Anglers' Club in Florida. In the interests of the separation of powers, and of the mandate given to the president's political party by his election, Hoover argued that "a President's inability to serve or his possible restoration to office should be determined by the leading officials in the Executive Branch, as they are of the party having the responsibilities determined by the election." He believed "that a simple amendment to the Constitution (or possibly statutory law) could provide for such a commission made up from the Executive Branch to make the determination required."[38]

The following month Hoover left his "monastery" to deliver two "peeps" to the American people. On February 22 he spoke at Washington's Birthday ceremonies at Valley Forge, Pennsylvania, delivering virtually the same address that he made there in 1931. Again he asserted that the independence of the individual must be preserved "from the deadening restraints of Government," yet government must also "equally assure his fair chance, his equality of opportunity from the encroachment of special privileges and greed or domination by any group or class."[39] A few days later he spoke on the economic recession in America to the New York Chamber of Commerce. He called the recession a "minor slump in business and employment" and recalled that "once upon a time my political opponents honored me as possessing the fabulous intellectual and economic power by which I created a worldwide depression all by myself. At least I might claim from these tributes that I must know something about depressions." To aid with recovery, Hoover called for a freeze on wage and price increases, the elimination of waste and the reduction of nonessential government spending until the budget was balanced. He found hopeful signs that the president was pursuing at least the latter policy. But Hoover advocated pushing beyond a balanced budget "to the point where we can have a tax reduction. This would be the greatest possible stimulant to recovery." But taxes could only be reduced if there were corresponding cuts in government expenditures or a balanced budget. If people doubted that such cuts could be made, Hoover said, they had only to consult the recommendations of the Hoover Commission.[40]

The implementation of those recommendations was proceeding. Senator Hubert Humphrey, chairman of the Senate reorganization committee, reported early in February 1958 that 270 recommendations of the second commission had been put into effect either wholly or in part. This represented about 53 percent of the total, he said, but he noted that many of the commission's proposals for "revolutionary change" were still under study.[41] Hoover was exerting influence to assist the passage through Congress of a bill that would implement some of the commission's recommendations in the Defense Department. On June 11, President Eisenhower wrote Hoover that he appreciated Hoover's "telegram in respect to defense reorganization." Eisenhower noted that he had harbored some reservations concerning provisions of the House bill, but that Hoover's telegram had powerfully supported "the basic approach which I have been striving to advance, and I am most grateful to you for it."[42]

As Hoover approached his eighty-fourth birthday, President Eisenhower asked him to travel to Europe again, this time to represent the United States during its "official days" at the Brussels World Fair, June 2–3, 1958.[43] Hoover was just recovering from the removal of his gall bladder, but he consented to make the trip.[44] Another leading American, Vice-President Richard M. Nixon, went abroad during May and learned at firsthand the discontent in Latin America with the United States. After his return he called upon Hoover in New York City for an hour, emerging to report that the former president had given him "some constructive suggestions with regard to United States policy toward Latin America."[45]

Hoover's trip to Europe was less eventful. He flew to Brussels in the presidential airplane, "Columbine," and was met at the airport by Prince Albert and Belgian and American officials. In Brussels he stayed in the simple quarters of the Foundation Universitaire, an institution for exchange students, which he had helped to found. He met with old Belgian and American comrades from his relief days, was received in audience by King Baudouin, and visited the Dowager Queen Elizabeth at her palace. On July 4 he gave a speech at the fair. In his address, Hoover noted that "in this climate of friendly competition, criticism of other nations would be entirely out of place," but it was in order, he declared, "that the representatives of a particular nation should interpret here the ideals, the aspirations, and the way of life of his own people." He reminded his European audience that Americans were descended from every nation in Europe and that therefore they had "some responsibility for these invisible forces radiating from my country." He called attention to the two "major methods of government among free peoples" —the American form, "where the executive is separated from the legislative powers, and the election of the individual executive and legislative officials is for fixed terms," and the parliamentary form, "which combined the legislative and administrative powers, and their officials are periodically subject to election—all at the same time." Since World War I there had been a proliferation of "fractional political parties" in Europe, which had hampered the ability of governments to govern effectively. "The American method is not perfect," Hoover admitted, "but for 182 years it has sustained stability in our country through every crisis and in the main, brought an orderly progress in the midst of new inventions and ideas." That system might, he concluded, have "uses for other free men."

Hoover touched on the economic progress of America and the "spiritual and moral impulses and ideals which motivate the lives of peoples." After dealing with technological advances, he turned to "the false legends, misrepresentations, and vicious propaganda" that were being disseminated concerning the United States and that often depicted this country "as living under the control of wicked men who exploit our economic life through gigantic trusts and huge corporations." Hoover picked such misrepresentations apart. Far from being imperialistic, as some charged, the American people had "willingly borne back-breaking taxes" without any hope of returns in order "to aid in protecting the freedom of mankind and to relieve people from poverty." They had also fought and died in three great wars "that more freedom would come to mankind and that the world might have a lasting peace," while after none of these victories had the United States asked "for an acre of territory, except a few military bases to protect the free nations." Nor had the United States "ever asked for reparations or economic privileges," but on the contrary had "made gigantic gifts and loans to aid nations in defense and reconstruction, including Communist Russia." He told the Europeans: "I would not have believed in the face of this worldwide record that peoples with a free press could be imposed upon by such propaganda." But such "misrepresentations and propaganda are inciting physical attacks upon American citizens, upon our officials, and abuse of our country." If they continued, Hoover warned, they could lead to a resurgence of isolationist feeling in the United States.[46]

The following day was decreed "Hoover Day" in Belgium by Premier Gaston Eyskens. Hoover spoke on the Belgian relief work and on the Belgian American Educational Foundation, which had resulted from it. That foundation had granted nearly 2,000 fellowships to Americans and Belgians. Premier Eyskens was one of four Belgian premiers who had benefited from such a fellowship, and he paid tribute to Hoover's career of public service and spoke of the esteem and love all Belgians harbored for him. That day Hoover left for his return to the United States.[47] On July 7 he reported to Eisenhower that he had "completed your mission to Belgium." He told the president: "Judging by both the Belgian, the continent and the American press, your idea proved of value. Certainly the Belgian people are grateful to you for this and many other reasons. I am indebted to you for the honor of representing you and for your making the path smooth with the Columbine."[48]

The *New York Times* editorialized that the dispatch of Hoover to Brussels had been "an unusually felicitous idea." It described his Brussels speech as "a very good one, indeed." Hoover, it noted, had spoken "with a vigorous forthrightness" on "the elements of strength in our form of government and political society," and his "reply to the constant criticism of the United States was thoughtful and well taken." The newspaper concluded: "Once more Mr. Hoover has been an honor to his country."[49]

The next month, on his eighty-fourth birthday, the *New York Times* wrote: "Herbert Hoover, who marks his eighty-fourth birthday today, engaged in good-natured polemic against the Russians, offered cautious advice on foreign affairs, extolled the virtues of fishing, and gave an account of an ex-President's private life in an interview last week." Hoover had invited the press and television newsmen into his "comfortable monastery" in the Waldorf Tower and given them "an hour's display of the Hoover wit." If the Soviet Union wanted peace, he told them, it must "stop conspiring to upset free governments and stop the hate talk about the United States and other free countries." He had no expectations, however, that the Russians would do so. "We are all hopeful there is going to be a change of mind and heart and if they make an attempt at it we will grasp it with both hands," he said. In discussing Hoover's private life, the newspaper reported that he had kept himself busy at writing during the past year with the help of four secretaries and a research assistant. He had received 1,620 invitations to speak and had accepted 30. "I'm my own 'ghost,' " he told the press, "and I revise and revise to make my speeches short. I revised those thirty speeches 154 times." He had also written 55,952 letters, "not counting acknowledgments," had taken "part in the dedication of the Truman Library, a school and nine of the forty-one new Boys Clubs of America clubhouses, was active in fund-raising for twelve causes, received ten honors, and published another book." He had also found time for trout fishing on the Mackenzie River and had pursued bonefish in two trips to the Florida Keys. His birthday, the *Times* reported, would be spent in Greenwich, Connecticut, with his son, Allan Hoover, and his family, where "he throws dignity and Quaker sobriety to the wind and has a romping good time."[50]

Perhaps Hoover's most memorable birthday present was the passage of the bill providing for reorganization of the Department of Defense along the lines recommended by the second Hoover Commission.[51] With the passage of this act by Congress, the Citizens' Committee for the Hoover Commission Report disbanded. Hoover claimed that the adoption of the commission's recommendations had reached the point where taxpayers would be saved "upwards of $3,000,000,000 a year." The Citizens' Committee estimated that 64 percent of the commission's recommendations had been adopted, with both the reorganization of the Defense Department and the modernization of the federal budget system having passed in 1958. These Charles Francis, chairman of the Citizens' Committee, called "two of the most significant and far-reaching recommendations ever made in the name of the bipartisan Hoover Commission."[52]

Reviewing the work of the second Hoover Commission and the results, *Newsweek* wrote in October 1958 that the Citizens' Committee had "struggled against great odds." It pointed out that the public had been more apathetic where the second commission's recommendations had been concerned, government bureaucrats had not been sympathetic, nor had the White House always been cooperative. The magazine added:

> Even so, the Citizens Committee, by mobilizing public opinion and bombarding Washington with thousands of letters, was extraordinarily successful. In all, some 60 per cent of the Hoover commission's 314 recommendations were adopted by Congress or implemented by the President, at an estimated savings to the taxpayers of between $3 billion and $4 billion. One of the committee's most notable successes was the new law putting budget expenditures on an annual basis, thus saving many millions in holdover appropriations.

The magazine then listed the major proposals that had been implemented, including the inauguration of a government-wide program to reduce paperwork and cut storage costs, liquidation of the assets of the Reconstruction Finance Corporation, streamlining of the Pentagon's research and development programs, higher salaries for career technicians and other government employees with professional and scientific skills, establishment of a Federal Career Executive Board to offer greater career incentives for management personnel, elimination of duplicate hospital services in the same area of the country by more than one military service, greater utilization of private business for the government's "housekeeping" chores, the curtailment of about six hundred federal activities that were in competition with private business, greater use of commercial vessels and airlines for routine shipments and travel by the Department of Defense, as well as others. But *Newsweek* found many other proposals still pending, including some that were dearest to Hoover's philosophy.[53]

A *New York Times* editorial on November 2 likewise lauded the work of the Hoover commissions, noting that the reports of the two commissions "represent a milestone in the history of American Government, for they included far-reaching proposals that took form in the Reorganization Act of 1949, the Military Unification Act of the same year, creation of the General Services Agency and the Department of Health, Education and Welfare, improvements within the State, Labor and Post Office Departments and the Bureau of Internal Revenue, and the passage of the Defense Reorganization and modern budgeting acts this year." But it added:

> No discussion of the work of the Hoover Commission can be complete, however, without pointing to the fundamental reforms that have been proposed and not yet acted upon because they are politically unpalatable, or because there are powerful special-interest

lobbies working against them or for other equally bad reasons. Out-
standing is the need for reorganization of the Veterans' Administration and veterans' services, and also the unification of the vast array
of Federal medical services. Of equally great importance is the necessity for a reorganization of our natural resource agencies, with
special attention to elimination of competition among them and to
coordination of river development policies. Even without the help of
the Citizens Committee, strong leadership at the top of the government could do much to clear up the major unfinished business in the
field of organization reforms.[54]

But Hoover had never entertained much hope that his "conservative"
philosophy would get strong support from the Republican in the White
House. He had only modest expectations when Eisenhower first became president in 1953.[55] Six years of the Eisenhower presidency did not lessen his
concern for the future of the Republican party. He remained distressed by the
apparent assumption on the part of Eisenhower and other Republican candidates that they must court "liberal" voters, and that "conservative" voters,
having no other place to go, would support the GOP candidate in any case.
Hoover regarded that assumption as a "fallacy."[56] He viewed the Republican
defeats in the 1958 mid-term elections as proof that "Republican radicalism
can get nowhere."[57] Late in the year he wrote that the Republican party still
did not "seem to comprehend that the only way they can live as a vital party is
on the conservative side." The ideals of the self-styled "liberal" or "modern"
wing of the party had already been "fully preempted by the opposition."
Republicans, he insisted, did not seem to comprehend the four major issues
that the party "must embrace." These were, in his view: the problem of
communism; the necessity for "preservation of the American way of life and
freedom, itself, from socialism"; the necessity to reduce expenditures and
balance the budget to head off inflation; and the need to free the people from
the domination of "wicked" labor unions. The GOP, Hoover maintained,
could "save the foundation of American life by these corrections."[58]

It was with Eisenhower's domestic policies that Hoover found the most
fault, for he had mellowed toward the president's foreign policies. He supported American military intervention in Lebanon, telling the press that
Eisenhower had "taken the only course possible if the freedom of nations is to
be protected from militarist conspiracies."[59] In an appearance on the conservative Manion Forum, Hoover observed that the greatest problem before the
United States was "to find some road to lessen the repeated tensions created by
the Communists over the world," such as their provocations over Berlin.
Behind the tensions between the two great superpowers lurked "the dangers of
a war more dreadful than mankind has ever known." The free world had for

40 years sought a "workable relationship or some basis of peace with the Communists" and had learned from bitter experience that the Reds harbored an entirely different concept of international relations than did the rest of the world—one based, he concluded, on no "code of morals such as that to which we must adhere." The USSR had violated a long list of treaties, and before the United States could consider any future agreements with them, such as reduction or limitation of military capabilities, there must be set up "independent machinery to enforce such agreements on both sides." He noted with approval that "President Eisenhower has stood firm on this principle."[60]

Hoover had lost none of his disillusionment with America's European allies. In September of 1958 he wrote Richard Berlin of the Hearst newspapers: "Between you and me it amounts to the fact that no nation in Europe neither can nor intends to join with the United States in a nuclear war with Russia—and the American people have never been plainly told this bare fact. However, these European alliances improve the propaganda front."[61] The European nations were simply too close to the Russian borders to put up any defense, and their only hope was "a victory by the United States." Hoover's familiar conclusion was: "Therefore, the only real balance of power available to us is the Western Hemisphere if we keep Communist governments out."[62]

On the day before his eighty-fifth birthday, Hoover appeared on the nationally televised "Meet the Press." The communist leader of the Soviet Union was soon to visit the United States, and there were high hopes that better relations would result between the two superpowers. Hoover, however, warned that such a result was unlikely. "The tactics of the communists may change," he told the reporters, "but their determination to dominate the world continues." He did believe, however, that tensions might be temporarily lessened and that the world could then be tided over to "a period in which there may be hopes for greater steps to peace." He was confident that President Eisenhower would not "compromise with or appease the evil forces in this world." Asked by newsman Chet Huntley which of his services to the nation had made him the proudest, Hoover pointed to his relief activities. He described his work on government reorganization as "a very happy job, but it had some good consequences, and some were indifferent." He noted that about 70 percent of the recommendations of the first commission had been adopted, but only claimed 30–40 percent for the second commission, which was far less than the estimate of the Citizens' Committee. He continued to warn that the United States had involved itself in too many foreign crises and that the nation badly needed to "clean up our own household" because of dangers from inflation, unbalanced budgets, and the "huge growth of crime." Asked if there was any hope that the GOP would ever again become the majority party in the United States, Hoover responded: "Being a longtime Republican, I'm always in hope." The broadcast ended on a health note:

Mr. [Bob] Considine: "I've got a good question, Mr. President: On the eve of your 85th birthday, how do you feel?
Mr. Hoover: I feel physically perfect.
Mr. Considine: Good.
Mr. Hoover: About 68 I should think.
Mr. Considine: Good.[63]

The following day, Hoover issued a statement to the press on his eighty-fifth birthday. He had, he told them, "six jobs as yet uncompleted." He was keeping an eye on the dangers to the country, hoping to be of service if needed; he was writing three volumes on the history of his relief activities under the title *An American Epic*; he was working with the Boys Clubs of America; there were his continuing efforts to build up the Hoover Institution on War, Revolution and Peace; he was responsible as a trustee or chairman of a dozen institutions; and he attended baseball games. Hoover had not, he told the press, retired.[64] Two days before his eighty-fifth birthday he had thrown out the first ball at the "Old Timers" game at Yankee Stadium with millions of baseball fans watching on television. The *New York Times* found Hoover's "eye is still good and his arm strong. Few would have suggested that he would be celebrating his eighty-fifth birthday today. But it is typical of the man that he seems to get stronger as he gets older."[65]

The "peeps" from his comfortable "monastery" continued. As indicated by the "Meet the Press" interview, Hoover had become increasingly concerned with the growth of crime in the United States. In June, his short article, "We Must Know More About Crime," appeared in *This Week* magazine. Hoover argued that the information on crime was deficient, particularly data on the efficiency of procedures and methods of justice in stemming crime. He suggested that the Census Bureau conduct a special census that would include the names of all criminals arrested during the previous two years, together with details of the crime and the disposition of the case. This would provide information on the ratio of arrests to crimes, the length of time before arrest, and the length of time spent in prison for each category of crime. From such data it might be possible to learn where the judicial system had been "lax or effective." "The story from this Census," Hoover thought, "might bring realization to the American people that freedom in the United States is in more jeopardy from crime than from all the Communist conspiracies within our borders."[66]

At this point in life, Hoover clearly believed that he could make a greater contribution in the years remaining to him through the completion of the books he was writing than by public activities, particularly since the latter now exerted a greater strain upon him. On a normal day he put in ten to eleven hours at his work, but he frequently awakened in the middle of the night to write further. He rose at 7 A.M., and after breakfast at 9:00 he began work on his writing, assisted by his secretaries and research assistants. After lunch at 1 P.M., he napped at 2 P.M. By 3:00 he was back at his desk writing until 5:30, after which he read the afternoon newspapers and listened to the 6 P.M. newscast. At 7:15 guests arrived for dinner, at which Hoover consumed the one dry martini he permitted himself daily. Evenings were filled with conversation or canasta. By 10:00 he was preparing for bed. Author Jim Bishop, profiling Hoover for *American Weekly* magazine, wrote:

> He is alone, yet not lonesome. He is accustomed to doing his own thinking and his own work. At the age of 85, no one helps this man—this rock—with his shoes or his tie. He believes in God and he subscribes to the credo that God will help those who help themselves. Don't forget, he plans to complete four more books.[67]

But Hoover remained somewhat active publicly. In December of 1959, he consented to become a member of the board of trustees of the conservative Americans for Constitutional Action, but only on condition that it did not require any work of him. This group, which included on its board former New Jersey governor Charles Edison, Robert E. Wood, Edgar M. Eisenhower, and Felix Morley, was dedicated to the election of candidates for public office who subscribed to conservative, constitutional principles.[68] And he could not resist an occasional opportunity to give his views on the state of the world. In mid-February 1960, he told the annual meeting of the Eastern Area of United Presbyterian Men that the United States was "plagued with the infection of Karl Marx in both the thinking of our people and the affairs of our government." It had been "frozen in" by the time Eisenhower took office. It had been spread through the nation "by deluded and misled men and by disguised organizations, fronts and cults," who, like "hermit crabs" had crawled "into such terms as 'liberal,' 'progressive,' 'public electric power,' 'managed economy,' 'welfare state,' and a half-dozen others." But experience had demonstrated clearly that government-managed commerce and industry led to dictatorship. Another crisis was the moral slump in America and the failure of the judicial system to imprison lawbreakers. "I know of nothing in the Scriptures," Hoover pointed out, "which advocates the release of mad dogs on to the streets. In fact, I interpret Christ's words on 'casting into outer darkness' to include an effective sentence in prison."[69]

When Republicans sought yet another "farewell" from Hoover at their 1960 national convention, he tried to avoid it. When the subject was first raised early in March, he wrote to Congressman Clarence Brown:

> I will be on the edge of my eighty-sixth year with many commitments that I have to complete. I have already said four farewells to these bodies, which would seem to be enough. Also my advice on

these occasions has had but little effect. Therefore, with your great art in political sciences, can you not bury this request?[70]

Hoover told another correspondent that he had "concluded some time ago not to enter upon this campaign. That is the job of the vigorous younger generation."[71] In April Hoover also declined the president's request that he represent him at the dedication of two memorials of the American Battle Monuments Commission in Belgium, writing Eisenhower: "In order to conserve my strength for already existing obligations and administrative burdens, I am not able to take on additional commitments."[72]

Republicans were not willing, however, to pass up the opportunity of yet another "farewell" appearance from their only ex-president. If Hoover would not make a personal apperance at the convention, it was proposed to present him with a gold convention badge on national television that could be watched on a wide screen by the delegates.[73] This and other such proposals prompted a letter from Hoover telling GOP national chairman Thruston Morton:

> It seems certain that you and many of our leaders are going all around Robin Hood's barn to get me into the Chicago convention! All together these ideas include such things as taped television recordings to be put on screens in the convention hall, live TV with statements from distant cities, and a message to be read at the convention. I, of course, will do anything that I can physically manage to help the party. From all this discussion, I have decided that if you think it important for me to take part in the convention, the direct thing for me to do is to go to Chicago and make a short address. I can do this if it is staged in the earlier part of some evening session and on live nationwide TV. This plan would enable me to fly from San Francisco (where I will be) to Chicago during the day, retire at some hour like 10:00, and return to San Francisco the next morning. This plan would avoid all the above complex arrangements.[74]

The convention scheduled him for 8 P.M. on Monday, July 25, and Hoover set to work drafting a speech. It was destined to be his last personal "farewell" appearance before a Republican convention.[75] But he had also scheduled two speeches in California and a television appearance for September. As he wrote Patrick Hurley, there would be "no summer vacation for me," for between speeches he was "chained to my desk."[76]

On June 8, six weeks before the convention appearance, John D. M. Hamilton called on him and found "his mind was as bright and clear as ever," though there was evidence of some physical deterioration since he had seen him last. In a two-hour talk, they ranged over a variety of topics. Hoover was convinced that there would not be a war soon as the United States was superior, in his view, to the Soviet Union in every category of warmaking potential except ground troops. He was still uncomfortable, however, with the presence of American ground troops in Europe. He felt complimented by the fact that all of the potential Democratic candidates for that party's nomination had been to see him except Adlai Stevenson and Hubert Humphrey, and he attributed this courtesy to his friendship with Truman. As for the Republicans, the assumption was that Vice-President Richard Nixon would win the nomination, and the discussion centered on possible running mates. Hoover expressed a preference for Senator Barry Goldwater of Arizona, but recognized that he had no chance of nomination since it would leave the GOP with both candidates from Western states. Of the Eastern possibilities he preferred Henry Cabot Lodge over Nelson Rockefeller because of Lodge's qualifications and his experience in the United Nations, and because of his concern that Rockefeller was dangerous to a conservative form of government.[77]

Meanwhile, Hoover had appeared on "Person to Person" in May and expressed his lack of interest in a seat for former presidents in the Senate. He told the reporters: "Twenty years ago I would have been enthusiastic about that, but at my time of life, I don't look on the prospect of sitting on a hard cushion for several hours a day and listening to speeches as being attractive."[78] In mid-June, he spoke at the laying of the cornerstone of the $12 million United Engineering Center in New York City. He told the audience that the "unextinguishable spark in the minds of men to be free" might yet save progress and civilization despite the inroads of communism. Communism controlled 600 million people, he estimated, but progress in the past century had flowed from "free and productive minds in the civilized parts of the world—that is, the nations possessed of independence and personal freedom."[79]

On July 25, Hoover interrupted his vacation in California to fly to the Republican convention in Chicago. He opened his speech that evening by saying:

> I had not expected to speak at this Convention. In each of your last three Conventions I bade you an affectionate good-bye. Apparently, my good-byes did not take. And I have been bombarded with requests to do it again for the fourth time. Unless some miracle comes to me from the Good Lord this is finally it.

Hoover briefly alluded to the foreign dangers and to domestic political, economic, and social issues, but he concentrated primarily on what he described as "a frightening moral slump" in the United States. Part of the difficulty lay, he asserted, in the Marxist infection, which was a destroyer of all morals. Religious institutions and other agencies for character building in youth needed help. The nation needed "a rebirth of that great spiritual force which has been impaired by cynicism and weakened by foreign infections." He called that force nationalism—a belief in America. "The re-echo of the word *America*," he maintained, "might resurrect conscience away from crime and back to manhood." It might also restrain the demands of special interest groups and stimulate "anew the initiative and enterprise of tens of thousands of our youth who from fear of the future seek refuge in the bureaucracies of industry and government," and it might bring about insistence "upon a revision of our weakened courts." He called upon Republicans to "stop this moral retreat; to lead the attack and recapture the meaning of the word—America."[80] A few days later Hoover confided: "I am just too old to be traveling about. The trek to the Convention proved it."[81]

Hoover was no doubt cheered by the choice of Henry Cabot Lodge as Nixon's running mate. He had expressed a preference for Lodge in his talk with Hamilton, and it was well known that Lodge was his choice. The *New York Times* had reported that fact before the choice was made, and after the nomination the newspaper reported: "Mr. Nixon's decision was bolstered, . . . sources said, by the fact that President Eisenhower and former President Hoover also wanted Lodge."[82]

Freed from his convention duty, Hoover flew back to San Francisco where, a week later, he spoke to the press and the Union League Club, addressing himself to questions that they had submitted. After discussing his own activities, Hoover turned to the question of federal enforcement of civil rights. His own view was "that the states and local governments must and in the end will, obey the law of the land as declared by the Supreme Court," but he did "not believe the Federal Government should ever use force against the states, except in rebellion." He criticized the federal government for failing to adopt the remainder of the Hoover Commission recommendations, but saw "some hope from the likelihood that both parties in this campaign will attack the other for this failure." He called for "an entire reorganization of our tax laws," because they were "destroying initiative." The problem of food sur-pluses, he suggested, could be solved by the federal government leasing "for 20 years all the marginal land for an annual rental and leave the farmer to live on his farm, but to use it for food supply to his family and to release it to pastorage and reforestation." As for the surpluses that had already piled up, he would "say to every nation of low standard of food supply—send your ships here and you can get it for nothing." He continued to oppose federal aid to education and was against disarmament without adequate controls. He favored con-tinued nuclear testing, both above and under the ground. He still opposed the admission of the People's Republic of China into the United Nations and felt that if "the Communists and African groups become a majority, its usefulness to the United States is likely to be less than nothing." He opposed summit conferences, holding that the president's voice was more powerful from the White House. Hoover was obviously not against U.S. military action being taken in Cuba. "Too many people," he said, "rise in horror that any action on our part would be an act of aggression," but "when a man comes at you with a dagger pointed at your heart, it is not aggression to kick his pins out from under him."[83]

A week later Hoover was back in his "monastery" in the Waldorf, where he submitted to yet another birthday interview. Asked about the possibility that voters might reject the Democratic nominee, Senator John F. Kennedy, because of his Catholicism, Hoover responded: "I think it's a dreadful idea. I abhor bigotry in every form." He noted that he had denounced such bigotry in his own 1928 campaign against Alfred E. Smith. He refused to answer other political questions since he had received "many touching tributes" on his birthday from both Democrats and Republicans and did not wish to be "offensive to my many friends on the other side." He would, however, vote for the Republican nominee. He thought that the thousands of letters of praise for his "moral slump" speech at the GOP convention showed "surely that some force is stirring our people beyond the satisfactions of increasing standards of living." He did not believe that the United States was "in its decline and fall," but on the contrary believed "that with growing strength and determination we can influence the expansion of freedom in the world." As for Soviet Premier Khrushchev's prediction that this generation's grandchildren would live under communism, Hoover answered: "Well, that ain't so." He supported the Twenty-second Amendment to the Constitution, which limited the presidency to two terms for one person, because "eight years in the White House is enough exhaustion for any mortal." As for his own work, he reported that he continued to put in ten hours a day, sometimes seven days a week, on his books. The second volume of *An American Epic* was to be published the following month, the third was in page proof, and the fourth was "in the oven" —in the process of being written.[84]

Both of the presidential candidates in 1960 were well known to Hoover. Hoover, along with his son, Herbert, Jr., had been instrumental in encouraging Richard Nixon to enter politics in California in 1946, and the two had maintained close contact ever since. On the Democratic side, John F. Kennedy was the son of Hoover's long time friend, Joseph P. Kennedy, and the former president had worked closely with the nominee when Senator Kennedy was chairman of the subcommittee reviewing the legislative recommendations of the second Hoover Commission. It seems clear that Hoover grew somewhat disenchanted with the Republican candidate during the campaign. For Hoover, who liked the feeling of being involved and useful, the failure of Nixon to call upon him when he was in New York City campaigning was inexcusable.[85] Hoover did not take an active part in the campaign, but he did offer Nixon advice. After the first televised Nixon-Kennedy debate, Hoover suggested to him that reporters be eliminated from any further debates as in their questions they were "prejudiced and laying deliberate traps for Nixon." He also suggested that the vice-president stop agreeing with Kennedy's "goals" during the debate, since "Kennedy's goals are not those of the people from whom Nixon must get his votes," and the goals were "evil—they are stupendous spending (with inflation); they are socialism disguised as a 'welfare state.' " Kennedy was clearly determined, in Hoover's eyes, to set up "a new and greater New Deal." Hoover also suggested that Nixon do a better job of making-up for his subsequent television appearances, since, in the words of one broadcaster whom he quoted, "Nixon looked like a made-over stiff."[86]

After the four scheduled debates between the two candidates, Kennedy challenged Nixon to yet a fifth confrontation. On October 20, the Republican nominee met with a number of friends and advisers at the Waldorf to discuss the challenge. Among those present were Hoover and Thomas E. Dewey. Hoover's advice was to decline the challenge by claiming that Nixon's time was all "booked up."[87] This was Nixon's position the following day, but he modified it slightly a day later, consenting to debate Kennedy if he could find room for such a debate in his schedule.[88] The time, of course, could not be found, and a fifth debate was not held. Hoover also suggested to GOP national committee chairman Thruston Morton that Nixon attack the spending proposals of the Democrats and point to the inflation and higher taxes that must result; that Nixon announce "a program of *reduced* expenses of government," which would include demands that Europe take over 80 percent of the foreign aid program, the liquidation of "government activities in competition with private enterprise," and the implementation of "Hoover Commission recommendations as to the 'common use services' in the Department of Defense," which he claimed would save $3 billion per year.[89] Hoover found the campaign confusing and was disappointed that "the great big vital issues to our future" were not being mentioned.[90]

After Nixon went down to his narrow defeat, Hoover departed New York for the pursuit of bonefish off the Florida keys. In January both of the 1960 candidates were also relaxing in Florida—president-elect Kennedy in Palm Beach, and Vice-President Nixon in Key Biscayne. On January 11 Hoover traveled to Palm Beach for a reception in his honor on the eve of the dedication of Hoover Dike, an 85-mile-long structure that contained the waters of Lake Okeechobee. The dike had been started during Hoover's administration and was being renamed for him the following day. At the reception, both Joseph Kennedy and the president-elect called on Hoover. It is possible that at this point the elder Kennedy suggested the desirability of a meeting between his son and Nixon to demonstrate postelection unity in America, although Hoover later told Nixon that Joseph Kennedy had phoned him with the suggestion.[91] As Hoover recounted the episode to journalist Neil McNeil, the president-elect's father had noted that both Nixon and Kennedy were vacationing in Florida and suggested that it might be useful to bring the two men together to show that the bitterness of the campaign was over. He told Hoover that if he would arrange for Nixon to receive his son, he would make sure that the president-elect called on the vice-president. According to Hoover's account, contained in McNeil's oral memoir, Nixon was at first reluctant, but finally consented to meet with Kennedy.[92]

Shortly after the election, Hoover wrote to the former head of one of the task forces of the second Hoover Commission that he had "a curious feeling that you and I may be surprised by favorable consequences of the election in important directions."[93] He was obviously referring to the possibility of further action on the remaining Hoover Commission recommendations. The following month he wrote that he was especially hopeful that 1961 would see "further implementation of the Commission recommendations." Hoover found bases for hope. During 1960, more had been accomplished in getting recommendations adopted than in any year since the commission had made its reports to Congress, and the results were especially gratifying in the defense area. And the president-elect, while a senator, had been involved in reviewing the commission's recommendations and was, therefore, "fully familiar with the recommendations and during the past campaign cited their further implementation as a means he would use to increase efficiency and reduce governmental expenditures."[94] Hoover was now serving as honorary chairman of the Committee of Hoover Commission Task Force Members, which had replaced the Citizens' Committee as the group lobbying for the adoption of the commission's recommendations.

Despite the apparently wide ideological gap between them, Hoover felt close to the new president. In spite of his eighty-six years, he attempted to fly from his fishing club in Florida to Washington for Kennedy's inauguration, only to find the Washington airports closed by the weather.[95] The young president obviously felt close, too, to Hoover. At the reception in Palm Beach he asked Hoover if he had any advice for him. The former president responded that he had none, but not to worry since "everybody has advice for a new President."[96] In March 1961 Kennedy invited Hoover to become honorary chairman of the national advisory committee for the Peace Corps, but Hoover declined, citing the fact that he was too busy to be of much value.[97] The following month, George McGovern invited him to become honorary chairman of the advisory committee for Food-for-Peace in the Kennedy administration.[98] Again Hoover declined to serve because of his many responsibilities, but he did offer to give advice if it were needed, and he took the opportunity to suggest that the Food-for-Peace organization undertake a survey to locate the truly hungry peoples of the world. He also suggested that those nations that possessed the resources to buy food should be eliminated from consideration by the agency, but that "antagonism of some nations to the United States" ought not necessarily to disqualify them from receiving relief. Hoover would "not eliminate even Red China if they would accept control of distribution by

American staff." Assurances were needed in any case, he said, to insure that food reached the intended recipients, and this could best be done by the creation of "joint commissions comprising their own nationals and Americans."[99]

Meanwhile, on April 17, 1961, a U.S.-planned invasion by anti-Castro Cuban exiles took place at the Bay of Pigs on Cuba's southern coast. Denied U.S. air support by the Kennedy administration, the invaders were crushed in less than 72 hours by Castro's armies. Embarrassed by the fiasco, Kennedy, in the words of the *New York Times*, "sought the counsel of two elders of the Republican party . . . in his quest for national solidarity in what he has called a period of peril." On April 28 the president called on both Hoover and Douglas MacArthur in their respective apartments in the Waldorf Tower, spending twenty minutes with Hoover and over an hour with the general.[100] According to Hoover's memorandum of his discussion with Kennedy, he had "assured the President of his support in any action he must take to defend the United States." This country had the right to defend itself against such menaces as Cuba under the Monroe Doctrine, he asserted, and that doctrine had never been repealed. A communist regime in Cuba, 90 miles from the United States, Hoover regarded as "an intolerable menace to the safety of our country" and "a center of conspiracy to overthrow all free governments in this hemisphere by violence." It was "daily perpetrating every form of brutality and violation of primary human rights." He suggested to Kennedy two methods of dealing with the situation: (1) an air strike to destroy Castro's military equipment, followed by an invasion by Latin American troops "to restore order and a free election," or (2) "leave him alone in his accumulating miseries." Hoover preferred the second method for the time being, but he promised to support the president in whichever course he chose.[101]

A week later former vice-president Richard Nixon also called on Hoover and MacArthur while on his way to the Midwest for a series of speeches in "loyal opposition" to the Kennedy administration. After 45 minutes with the former president, during which time they discussed foreign policy and the subject matter of his forthcoming speeches, Nixon emerged from his suite to say that he was "always amazed" at the way Hoover stayed "on top of world affairs."[102]

At this point in his life his doctors had told him, Hoover wrote a friend, that if he wanted to complete all of his projects, he must "not go out nights," "must not eat anything except this list (which excludes all good food except cranshaw melons)," "must not climb steps or hills," "must not take automobile rides of more than two or three miles," and "must not ride in vibrating planes—i.e., go only where the jets go."[103] He had cut his baseball viewing down to the annual old-timers game and the World Series, since he didn't want to catch a cold "for anything less than a major game."[104] From a 90-year-old friend came the warning to the nearly 87-year-old Hoover that "one loses a lot of strength between 87 and 90."[105] Hoover responded: "It is good to hear from you despite your gloom over what is coming to me these next three years. However, I can finish my job in three years more so that fact is cheerful."[106] As it turned out, the former president had only slightly more than three years to live.

Late in June 1961, Hoover traveled to Philadelphia for a speech in Independence Square. In an address carried over a nationwide radio network, he told American young men and women that the "validity of our beliefs in freedom is at stake on a global battleground." He warned them:

> You will inherit the costly burden of our defense against the implacable foe who lurks in the Kremlin. While we hope for the cooperation of other nations in the defense of mankind, in the end the safety of America must rest upon our own well-armed right arm, whatever sacrifice this entails. I am confident of your courage. What I am saying to you is not a recital of trite banalities, for these rights and responsibilities are the base of our American way of life, and, in fact, of our civilization.

Hoover recalled that he had "lived and worked in countries of free men, of tyrannies, of Socialists, and of Communists," and had "seen liberty die and tyranny rise." He had "seen slavery again on the march." Whenever he returned from overseas, each homecoming "was for me a reaffirmation of the glory of America."[107] The following month he spoke in San Francisco on his way to the Bohemian Club encampment and appealed for support for privately financed higher educational institutions as part of a $100 million fund drive for Stanford University, his alma mater.[108]

Hoover also continued to monitor the progress of the recommendations of the second Hoover Commission. In June 1961, he wrote to President Kennedy to call his attention to the fact that a Senate bill embodying recommendations for further reforms of budgeting and accounting, which Kennedy had sponsored while in the Senate, had passed the Senate and gone to the House where it was in the Rules Committee. Hoover wondered if any of Kennedy's assistants "could help get the bill before the House."[109] The president responded that "separation of powers" made any such intervention by the White House "a sensitive issue," but he would "endeavor to do everything possible to insure House consideration of the measure." Meanwhile, he informed Hoover:

> Within the Executive branch we are continuing to make budget improvements along the lines recommended by your Commission, including particularly the extension of cost-based budget practices. We expect to achieve most of the benefits which we had in mind a few years ago under the legislation which was then enacted.[110]

Kennedy also extended the former president the courtesy of a "year-end brief-ing" in January 1962 and solicited Hoover's opinion concerning the proposals he had made in his January 24 message to Congress.[111]

On August 8, 1961, Hoover submitted to another interview by the press two days before his eighty-seventh birthday. The *New York Times* writer found: "The once brown hair is thin and gray. The step is slow and deliberate. The voice is thin and lacks some of its old decisiveness. But the spirit still is vibrant." Again Hoover scored the increase in crime, blaming it on "the restrictions upon our courts and the practices which have developed within them." He suggested that American bar associations should "look into the methods of the British courts where there is no such appalling record as that in the United States." He denigrated charges that Americans were "soft." "Too much attention is paid to what goes on in the cities," he told reporters. "Out in the countryside, in the small towns, on the farms, Americans are just as patriotic as they ever were, ready to meet any emergency, any challenge."[112]

Hoover's opposition to the admission of the People's Republic of China into the United Nations remained inflexible for the balance of his life. In response to an appeal from the Committee for One Million to furnish a message for a rally to be held in New York City in September 1961, Hoover wrote: "Over the years I have opposed the admission of Red China to the United Nations and my views are the same today."[113] Some of those involved in the fight against the admission of mainland China to the United Nations, also opposed the use of force by that organization against the attempt of Katanga to split away from the Congo and establish an independent African state. Hoover refused to join in a general protest against the U.N. action, but he did issue a press statement on December 21, 1961, in which he deplored the grant of American assistance to the United Nations in the suppression of the Katangan movement, saying: "It is a sad day for the American people when American resources are applied to the killing of people who are seeking for independence and self-government free from Communist domination."[114]

In the early months of 1962, Hoover enjoyed what would be his last visit to Key Largo in pursuit of bonefish. He had been told by his doctor, Hoover wrote a friend, "to remain in this land of escape until New York reforms its weather habits" and would not return until some time in April.[115] As Hoover's secretary described the life there: "We live aboard the boat, we fish—after bonefish and big ones—we go sightseeing for we have a car with us, we cruise about—and life is not strenuous or dressy."[116] In mid-February, Hoover's secretary reported: "At the moment the Chief is bonefish champ of the K[ey] L[argo] A[nglers'] C[lub] and is on the board with a 9¾-pound bonefish and also on the board for a tarpon!"[117]

Early in 1962, Hoover agreed to serve with former presidents Truman and Eisenhower as an honorary chairman of the Atlantic Council of the United States, a group formed by former secretary of state Christian Herter to promote unity in the Atlantic community.[118] He also sent a message of support to a rally of the Young Americans for Freedom, a conservative young people's group inspired by conservative intellectual William F. Buckley, Jr.[119] Afterward he wrote Senator Barry Goldwater that he had heard the rally was a "great triumph for you and the Young Americans for Freedom," but more than that it had "established a great movement of conservative thought in our country. And we have needed that leadership for a long time."[120]

In March, together with former president Truman, Hoover expressed support for President Kennedy's resumption of nuclear testing, since, he told reporters: "We can do no other if we are to survive."[121] When astronaut Scott Carpenter was welcomed to New York City after his voyage into space, Hoover insisted, against the advice of his doctor, on appearing with Truman at a luncheon in Carpenter's honor. He said of Carpenter: "He has given us a lift and he has given us prestige all over the world."[122] A month later Hoover made what would be his final visit to California, where he told reporters that he sympathized with President Kennedy in the current economic downturn. "He came in just before a big bust in the stock market and with a Congress opposed to him," Hoover observed. "He's going down the same weary path, and my sympathies are with him," he said, with obvious reference to his own experiences with the stock market and an unfriendly Congress. Hoover also expressed his bewilderment with the pace of change in the 1960s when he said of the Telstar satellite broadcasts: "The electronics men have just gone beyond my comprehension. I belong to a generation that just doesn't grasp all that."[123]

On his eighty-eighth birthday, Hoover returned to his birthplace of West Branch, Iowa, for the dedication of the new Herbert Hoover Presidential Library located but a stone's throw from the two-room cottage in which he had been born. As Hoover had participated in the dedication of the Truman library in Independence, Missouri, the Democratic former president was on hand for the ceremonies in West Branch. At the dedication, Hoover and the others addressed a crowd estimated at 45,000 who had come to pay tribute to Iowa's most distinguished son. Reporters found the GOP elder statesman speaking with a firm voice, though "thin of hair and slightly stooped." In his speech, Hoover called on Americans to realize that the United Nations had "failed to give us even a remote hope of lasting peace," and had, instead, "added to the dangers of wars which now surround us." The problem was the communist nations, who "for forty years, have repeatedly asserted that no peace can come to the world until they have overcome the free nations." As a result, they had "destroyed the usefulness of the United Nations to preserve peace." Hoover suggested:

> The time is here. If the free nations are to survive, they must have a new and stronger world-wide organization to meet this menace. For purposes of this discussion I may call it the Council of Free Nations.

It should include only those nations who are willing to stand up and fight for their freedom and their independence.

The foundations for this organization have already been laid by the forty nations who have taken pledges in the five regional pacts and they have obligated themselves to assist each other with military forces against aggression. And there are other free nations who should join.

He did not suggest that his proposed council should replace the United Nations, but "when the United Nations is prevented from taking action, or if it fails to act to preserve peace, then the Council I have suggested of free nations should step in." He suggested an analogy with the Concert of Europe, which had maintained peace in Europe after the Napoleonic wars.[124]

A few days after his speech, Senator J. William Fulbright, Arkansas Democrat, endorsed Hoover's proposed Council of Free Nations on the "Issues and Answers" radio and television program.[125] President Kennedy agreed that the Hoover proposal deserved study, but told a press conference that the real challenge was to breathe new life into existing institutions, like NATO, rather than create new ones.[126]

Despite his advancing age, Herbert Hoover had scarcely curtailed his travel in 1962. The winter fishing trip, extending into the early months of 1962, the annual trek to California, and the birthday visit to West Branch, constituted a good deal of travel for one of his age. It would, however, be the last year of his travels. On August 20, 1962, Hoover entered the hospital in New York City for what was described as an annual checkup. Predictions that he would be released within a few days were revised when tests disclosed a growth on the interior of his large intestine. Surgery was performed and doctors reported: "The pathological study revealed an ulcerated polyp of the transverse colon. A portion of the polyp had undergone malignant change. There was no evidence of any spread beyond the polyp. A segment of the colon which included the polyp was removed and no recurrence is anticipated."[127] The prognosis was too optimistic, but the former president would live for two more years.

13

Epilogue: The Last Two Years

n mid-September of 1962, Herbert Hoover was released from the hospital and returned to his "comfortable monastery" high in the Waldorf Tower. Early the next month he wrote that he was recovering, but in the beginning had been allowed no phone calls, no visitors, and no work. He told a friend. "I expect that next week I will be able to put on pants."[1] That month he watched developments in the Cuban missile crisis and was consulted, along with Truman and Eisenhower, by President Kennedy before the U.S. government replied to Premier Khrushchev's proposal for settling the crisis.[2]

In December, Hoover addressed a poignant letter to another aging former president, Harry Truman, and told him:

> Yours has been a friendship which has reached deeper into my life than you know. I gave up a successful profession in 1914 to enter public service. I served through the first World War and after, for a total of about 18 years. When the attack on Pearl Harbor came, I at once supported the President and offered to serve in any useful capacity. Because of my varied experiences during the first World War, I thought my services might again be useful, however there was no response. My activities in the second World War were limited to frequent requests from Congressional committees. When you

came to the White House, within a month you opened the door to me to the only profession I knew, public service, and you undid some disgraceful action that had been taken in the prior years. For all of this and your friendship I am deeply grateful.[3]

It was apparently soon after the attack on Pearl Harbor that the former president began to research and write fragments of an exposure of the fallacies of the foreign policies of the Roosevelt administration. As time went on, the work, which came to be referred to as the "magnum opus" by those around him, broadened to include the record of appeasement of the Soviet Union under FDR and his successors. By the 1960s, the one consuming ambition of the aging statesman was to complete the work before he died. His health, however, was interfering with his plans. As he wrote an old friend late in January 1963:

> I have taken a bad licking with a setback thrown in. However, I am doing better now. But I am not allowed any more journeys away from New York. I do see people, play a limited amount of canasta, and above all am trying to finish five more books before my time runs out. The book on fishing will be out in May. The fourth and final volume of An American Epic is in the last stages of completion. But the big job of three volumes on "Who, When & How we got into the Cold War" has already had 20 years of work and requires two more. I hope to leave them as a sort of "will and testament" before I finally vanish.

Intimates, including radio commentator Hans V. Kaltenborn, had read them, he reported, and they were "enthusiastic that they are great and needed books." Hoover obviously chafed at his continued confinement in the apartment, but the doctors had admonished him, he said, that: "You can provide any climate in your present abode, so why go out into the cold and meet a dozen kind of bugs which wish to kill you!"[4] While there would obviously be no fishing trip to Key Largo, Hoover still hoped, wistfully, that he might be able to take part in the annual Bohemian Club encampment in California in the summer.[5]

In March, Senator Claiborne Pell wrote Hoover concerning a resolution he had introduced that would give former presidents a seat in the U.S. Senate as senators-at-large, with the right to speak on the floor and to participate in the activities of any committee, but without the authority to introduce bills or resolutions, make motions, or vote.[6] Hoover responded that he had long supported the idea: "At my time of life, however, I no longer desire to sit for days on a hard-bottomed chair and listen to speakers. I prefer to read their speeches from the Record."[7] In May, President Kennedy, in New York City for a birthday party, called upon the Republican elder statesman.[8]

In June 1963, Hoover was stricken again with gastrointestinal bleeding and received transfusions. His sons Allan and Herbert, Jr., were in constant attendance in his apartment.[9] The *New York Times* wrote: "Once a remarkably robust man, Mr. Hoover has appeared thin and drawn, almost frail, the last nine months."[10] Yet a few days later the doctors termed the former president's recovery from the latest bout "almost miraculous."[11] On his eighty-ninth birthday, August 10, 1963, Hoover for the first time was unable to meet the press for his annual session. He was in poor health and unable to walk. The *New York Times* reported: "His condition, however, is improving steadily and he is impatient to complete another book, one he considers his magnum opus, a history of the last 30 years." His books, the newspaper noted, were "an important source of revenue for the Boys' Clubs of America, to which he gives the royalties." Although he could not meet with the press, Hoover issued a brief statement in which he said: "I may be permitted to remark that I have lived a long time and have seen great changes in this world of ours, and that the longer I live and the more I see, the more confidence I have in the American system of constant goodwill and service to other nations, and of free enterprise and personal liberty. We have a great way of life—let's keep it that way."[12]

The following month Hoover wrote restaurateur George Mardikian that he was "making slow progress, but my major job, the case history of the Second World War and its betrayal of freedom is now completed except my staff overhaul to check every sentence for its accuracy. The staff can now complete it in about another year."[13] He was, he wrote Mrs. Joseph Kennedy, confined to a wheel chair like her husband, but "I am in a better way than he for I have begun to walk with the help of two good nurses."[14] When he asked one visitor what she wanted out of life, and was told that she was happy with the status quo, Hoover's expression, she recalled, "was one of total horror, and he said, 'How can you say a thing like that, because *I want more*. I want to write a *better* book. I want to have *more* friends—*I just want more*—and I think you should never sit back and say, 'I want the status quo.' "[15] According to Felix Morley, the former president felt that he had outlived his time, but since he had been given the additional years through no virtue on his part, he felt compelled to make good use of them.[16]

By early November 1963, he could write that he had experienced "a little luck." He told Clarence Kelland:

> Blood transfusions seem to have restored my red blood cell percentage. Hence, I am doing everything except walk and function as an intellectual. The Reader's Digest have accepted the Magnum Opus and it will probably start in about six months. They seem much

excited about it, and I am full of forebodings as to mud volcanoes which will arise from the left who are still adept in that field.[17]

A few weeks later, the aged former president, who felt he had outlived his time, grieved for a young president struck down by an assassin's bullet before his time. In a statement for the press on the assassination of President Kennedy, Hoover said: "I am shocked and grieved to learn of President Kennedy's assassination. He loved America and has given his life for his country. I join our bereaved nation in heartfelt sympathy for Mrs. Kennedy and their two children."[18]

When President Lyndon B. Johnson visited Hoover early the following month, while in New York City for the funeral of Herbert Lehman, he recalled for the press that Hoover had, through his son, conveyed by telephone his willingness to help the new president in any way that he could, though acknowledging, sadly, that there was little he could do at his age. Hoover had also expressed his appreciation for Johnson's support of the Hoover Commission recommendations during his years in the Senate. Accompanying the president on his visit to Hoover's apartment were Chief Justice Earl Warren and New York mayor Robert Wagner.[19]

At about the same time, Hoover wrote his sister:

> I have had some bad luck this year: too much time in bed, six good nurses, five good doctors, 12 pills daily! We have been making some good progress against them, and I am promised I will defeat them before I pass the 100 mark, so that is my health report. And I am doing everything to help.[20]

On Christmas Day, President Johnson phoned the former president and in a press conference a few days later reported that Hoover had "given me some very constructive suggestions on the operations of the Federal Government that grew out of his retirement. We are studying those suggestions. We are applying them where they are appropriate. The Hoover Commission reports have been very carefully evaluated since I became President."[21]

Early in February 1964, Albert Wedemeyer visited the former president and wrote of the visit:

> He was sitting up in a chair in his bedroom. He has a tiny Siamese kitten which crawls all over him, and when I entered took a dim view of my intrusion, so much so that the little rascal jumped from the Chief's lap and then up into mine and when I tried to fondle it the little devil bit me. This amused the Chief a great deal. Actually, he was glad to have it jump out of his lap into mine because he was

adjusting his earphones and the little rascal kept pulling it out of his
ear and biting the cable to the battery.

Wedemeyer found that Hoover had "lost considerable ground," but had "a
wonderful sense of humor as always." They visited for about an hour and
discussed the 1964 presidential election, with the former president expressing
doubts that Barry Goldwater could defeat Johnson, if the Arizonan were the
GOP nominee, unless the Bobby Baker scandal cost the president votes in the
North and his civil rights stand took votes away in the South.[22] Former vice-
president Richard Nixon also called on Hoover, according to a memorandum
in the Hoover papers, and asked for the former president's support in gaining
the 1964 nomination. But, according to the memorandum, Hoover replied
"that at 90 years—with six nurses and five doctors, I was under instructions
not to get into any more controversies." He had, according to the memorandum, given "the same reply to his principal opponents."[23]

Later in February, Hoover was again stricken with internal bleeding,
combined with a respiratory ailment. In a few days the crisis passed, however,
and on February 28, the *New York Times* reported that the former president
was able to sit up in bed to eat his breakfast. According to the *Times*: "As a
nurse approached with his scrambled eggs he said to her, jokingly: 'Faster,
faster.' "[24] The following month, Congressman Charles S. Gubser, who represented Hoover's old district of Palo Alto, California, paid tribute to the
former president in the House of Representatives and was joined by many
other Congressmen who added their remarks.[25] Hoover wrote Gubser:
"Never have I received a greater get-well incentive than yours and your
comrades' in the Congress. I do not feel I deserve such a tribute, but if anything
will get me feeling completely well again, you and your colleagues have made a
major push in that direction."[26] Incredibly, Hoover had begun to contemplate
the writing of yet another book. In mid-April 1964, he wrote Bonner Fellers:

> I am doing another book. It covers recent history I didn't touch on
> [in] my previous volumes. You and I played a role in the arrange-
> ments for General MacArthur when he returned from Tokyo. Do
> you have a diary or other notes you made at that time which I could
> have copied to amplify my own material? I will return them to you
> promptly.[27]

Some of Hoover's intimates hoped that he would support Senator Goldwater for the Republican nomination. At some point in the California primary
campaign, the former president dictated a letter to Senator William Knowland
in which he told the California senator that if it were considered useful he
could issue a statement from Hoover recommending that his friends in Cal-

ifornia support the Arizonan because: "A great need of the Republican Party and indeed a need of the two-party system is for a fighting campaign. Senator Goldwater can make such a campaign." He added in the letter to Knowland: "At 90 years I prefer not to get into the controversy, but I trust your judgment as to its usefulness."[28] The letter, with the statement, was never mailed to Knowland, however, on the advice of one of Hoover's intimates, journalist Neil McNeil.[29] Goldwater did, however, visit with Hoover in May and, according to Jeremiah Milbank, Jr., who accompanied the Senator, the candidate and the former president had a high regard for one another.[30]

In July 1964, Hoover was not able to make yet another "farewell" appearance before the Republican convention. Instead, he prepared a message to be delivered before the convention by Senator Everett Dirksen of Illinois. Hoover wrote the senator: "Since I am unable to attend the convention, I deeply appreciate your willingness to read my statement. I have long been grateful for your devotion and dedication to our country and our party. I shall be there in spirit!"[31]

Hoover's message was a declaration of those principles that he believed Republicans should adhere to. It made the familiar points that the evangelist of the party had been making since he first broke his public silence early in 1935. Hoover called for the maintenance of American defenses and argued that "the rights guaranteed by the Constitution are the foundation of individual liberty." He called for the "strict division of powers and the primary responsibilities of state and local governments" and for the balancing of budgets and the reduction of taxes. The "social and economic system must be based upon private enterprise, regulated to prevent monopoly and unfair competition," and the federal government "should divest itself of thousands of . . . enterprises it now operates when the emergencies for which they were created are ended." Businessmen and farmers were "entitled to a fair profit and labor to a fair wage." Marxism must be rejected as "leading to slavery." The United States, he concluded, could only "survive by binding together the forces of free men— men of religious faith, of loyalty to our American traditions, of integrity in public office, who deeply love our country." And he told his audience, "we hold the long record of the Republican Party gives the best assurance that these principles will prevail in the United States, and with the help of God they will."[32] According to the *New York Times*, Dirksen "stirred the convention to a long outburst when he said 'the grand old man of the Grand Old Party is listening to this program. What better way to exhilarate his spirit than to give him an ovation to lengthen his span of years. Let him hear you,' he said. The delegates cheered and waved their banners."[33]

In the midst of the convention, Goldwater phoned Hoover to advise him that he had tapped Congressman William Miller of New York to be his vice-presidential nominee. He asked Hoover for any comments or objections he might have and added: "We miss you."[34] Goldwater had also sought to visit Hoover a few days earlier, but found him resting. Hoover wired the Arizonan that he regretted not having been able to meet with him on that occasion, and also his disappointment that he could not "take part actively" in the campaign, but he promised to make a statement in Goldwater's behalf whenever Goldwater wished him to.[35] The nominee paid a courtesy call on Hoover again in early August.[36] Bonner Fellers later recalled that he had seen Hoover for the last time when he called on him while in New York to attend a Goldwater rally in Madison Square Garden shortly before Hoover's final attack. Fellers found the former president in his bathrobe, still determined to write another book. He recalled that Hoover "was strong for Goldwater. He didn't think that he was going to be elected, and I was so dumb that I thought he might be."[37]

As the "grand old man of the Grand Old Party" approached his ninetieth birthday in August, he received numerous tributes. Dr. Howard Rusk wrote in the *New York Times* of the inspiration Hoover had supplied for the creation of UNICEF and the support he had given that organization.[38] Again, Hoover was unable to hold his annual meeting with the press, but instead issued a birthday statement. He expressed optimism that American freedoms would continue to grow, including those that were not granted specifically by law— including the freedom to choose one's own method of livelihood, to buy or not to buy, and to venture into new pursuits and to protect one's success. He concluded: "In short we have freedom of choice. And the product of our freedom is the stimulation of our energies, initiative, ingenuity and creative faculties." He again deplored the rise in crime and juvenile delinquency and the denial in some parts of the country of "an equal chance to our Negro population." But he suggested that the 19 million American blacks probably owned more automobiles than the 220 million Russians and 200 million African blacks combined.[39]

A week later Congressman Craig Hosmer suggested the former president as a candidate for the 1965 Nobel Peace Prize, noting that under the terms of Dr. Alfred Nobel's will members of Congress were eligible to recommend living persons for the award.[40] This initiative led to numerous letters written in the final months of Hoover's life by congressmen, senators, academics, and others supporting him for the award.[41] Unfortunately, Hoover's death ended his candidacy for an award that would so fittingly have crowned his many humanitarian efforts.

For as long as he could, Herbert Hoover labored at his magnum opus. Ben Moreel later recalled that "his consuming ambition in those days and in his last years was to finish this one book on Communism." According to Moreel: "He told me that that was the one thing he wanted to do before he died."[42] Hoover used to tell his friends, according to Joseph F. Binns: " 'You know, I don't have too much time to finish what I'm doing,' but he would continue to work and his work became almost the center of of his life." He consented to fewer and fewer appointments in the final months of his life in order to devote his time to the book.[43]

Neil McNeil recalled that Hoover had used every resource to put together the story of what had happened to American foreign policy as a result of the diplomatic recognition of the Soviet Union by the United States in 1933, using the research staff of the Hoover Institution and combing through thousands of documents from all over the world. McNeil added that Hoover's son, as under secretary of state in the Eisenhower administration, had been able to gather materials for his father from the archives of the State Department, and that the former president had also drawn upon his acquaintanceship with world statesmen and the diaries and correspondence of prominent Americans. By McNeil's account, Hoover had completed two and one-half of the projected three volumes, working virtually down to the day that he died. A number of people were entrusted with reading and commenting on the work, and the staff at the Hoover Institution was given the task of checking the accuracy of what he had written. He wanted the book published regardless of the consequences and costs because he considered it, said McNeil, "a public duty." However, some close friends of the former president, as well as members of his family, opposed publication on the grounds that it might diminish Hoover's image and reopen old sores and attacks upon him.[44]

On October 3, 1964, Barry Goldwater wrote Hoover to thank him for his support in the campaign. He told the elder statesman: "This campaign will chart the course of conservatism in America for years to come, and I am counting on your continued efforts to help make it a success."[45] But Hoover was not to participate in the campaign, nor was he to live long enough to witness the defeat of the first Republican candidate since his own race in 1932 who embodied the principles he believed in. At 3:55 P.M. on Saturday, October 17, 1964, the cancer in his system launched its final assault and the aged statesman was soon in critical condition. On October 20, at 11:35 A.M., Herbert Hoover died.[46]

The body of the former president lay in state first at St. Bartholomew's Episcopal Church in New York City, where an estimated 17,500 persons paid their last respects to him on the first day. On October 22 the political campaign ceased for a day as the presidential and vice-presidential candidates of both parties flew to New York to attend the funeral services. Also on hand were Bernard Baruch, James Farley, Mrs. Joseph Kennedy, Mr. and Mrs. Richard Nixon, Robert Kennedy, John Connally, Mayor Robert Wagner, as well as other leaders of American life. The large and elaborate St. Bartholomew's Church was a marked contrast to the small, plain Friends' meeting house in West Branch where Hoover had worshipped as a child.[47] But the simplicity of the service was closer to that of his youth.

The casket was then transported to Washington, D.C., by train, and covered the four blocks from Union Station to the Capitol on a caisson drawn by seven horses. To the sound of a dirge, the procession slowly made its way through a crowd four and five deep, while cannon executed a 21-gun salute and 48 jet fighters streaked overhead in groups of three. In the Capitol the former president lay in state on the same catafalque on which Presidents Lincoln and Kennedy had rested.[48] The end of Hoover's long journey came where it had begun over 90 years before, when his casket was flown to Cedar Rapids, Iowa, whence it was taken to West Branch for a simple burial service on October 25. Five thousand mourners met the plane in Cedar Rapids, and 75,000 were on hand for the burial service.[49]

With the transfer of Mrs. Hoover's casket from her burial site at Stanford University to West Branch, Herbert and Lou Henry Hoover now rest atop a grassy knoll overlooking the area where the young Herbert lived and played. Visiting the knoll, sheltered by a half-circle of pines, and the two plain, flat marble slabs covering their graves, a visitor on a summer's morning can glimpse rabbits and squirrels frolicking in the spacious and well-manicured park. A short distance away, a stream of visitors can be seen sightseeing amidst the buildings of Hoover's youth—the two room cabin in which he was born, the blacksmith shop in which his father labored, the meeting house in which the family worshipped—and entering the Hoover Museum to acquaint or reacquaint themselves with the accomplishments of a remarkable man. And in the rear of the one-story limestone museum, scholars labor at the desks of the Hoover Presidential Library, sifting through the materials of a busy life.

The magnum opus on which Hoover labored for over twenty years of his life, and which he thought so important that he drove himself to complete it in the final months of his life, has never been published. This last "will and testament" to the American people is still under lock and key.[50] But Herbert Clark Hoover, son of a small-town Iowa blacksmith, was himself an American "magnum opus," and an "American epic."

14

Conclusion

n the 31 years after he left the presidency, Herbert Hoover suffered his share of defeats. He was denied the Republican nomination in 1936 and 1940 and saw it go, instead, to men whose ideals he found alien to his own concept of traditional Republican liberalism. He lost in his attempt to keep the United States out of World War II, and failed in his efforts to relieve hunger in wartime Europe. After the war, he was unsuccessful in his opposition to renewed American commitments to the ground defense of Europe. Even the election of a Republican president in 1952, and again in 1956, after twenty years of Democratic dominance of the White House was, in its own way, a source of disappointment for Hoover, since Eisenhower's domestic policies represented too great a compromise with the New Deal to suit him. But Hoover also picked up some victories along the way—more than most men are granted. His campaign to put the Republican party on the side of American participation in the United Nations organization was successful, and his achievements as head of the Famine Emergency Committee and chairman of the two Hoover commissions are undeniable. There would be a secure place for Herbert Hoover in American history even if it were based only upon these contributions.

Even without such contributions, however, it would be difficult to ignore Hoover during these three decades because of the force of the ideas that he represented. Above all others, Hoover's was the voice of what came to be identified as American conservatism, although for Hoover it was the only true liberalism. He nurtured it through a trying period, even while he harbored a profound fear that the United States had already deviated too far from its traditional values to ever turn back. But he was a fighter, and he made few concessions to the changes that he saw taking place around him during those three decades. Throughout the period, there was in Hoover's positions on the issues a remarkable consistency whatever the time and the situation.

In economic policy, Hoover never strayed from his conviction that the best economic system is that of a free enterprise economy properly regulated, but not regimented, to prevent abuses. He came to this view from many conclusions, not only relating to the efficiency of private enterprise and its potential for providing growth and prosperity, but, far more importantly, from a deep conviction that the other freedoms of American life—political, religious, intellectual, and all others—were inextricably bound up with economic freedom. Critics of such a philosophy have pointed to the willingness of businessmen to advocate such a view for less than laudable ends, but this misuse does not, in itself, disprove the validity of the philosophy. It is noteworthy that Hoover adhered to this view at the same time that he harbored profound suspicions of big business and was determined that the destiny of America not be placed in its hands. In his view, big businessmen frequently were incapable of seeing beyond their own narrow interests—property rights—to envision the broader scope of American life into which big business must fit itself. It was not, in his view, property rights that were fundamentally important, but the indispensable foundation that they provided for all of the other rights essential to a free society. Free enterprise, then, was an indispensable part of the organism of freedom, but it could not be allowed unlimited growth until like a cancer it devoured and destroyed the organism itself.

Hoover viewed state and local governmental action as the first level of problem solving when private interests were incapable of a solution. The federal government's role should be limited to dealing with those problems that private interests and state and local governments were incapable of solving. Even then the federal government should seek to bring about solutions through voluntary cooperation rather than compulsion. Unfortunately, this view, too, could be advocated for malevolent ends, which tended to discredit it. The advocacy of "states' rights" during these years was too often a cloak for the protection of racist policies. Yet, like the misuse of the concept of free enterprise, such abuses of the limited government concept could discredit it only with those who refused to recognize the far greater dangers that were potential in the centralization of power.

In international relations, Hoover was an internationalist in the sense of advocating international cooperation to solve world problems and preserve peace. He was one of the leading Republican supporters of the League of Nations in 1919–20, and he was committed to American entry into a world institution after World War II. But he did not believe that the United States should intervene in the wars of other nations unless it could be clearly demonstrated that the interests of the United States were directly threatened. Nor did he wish to see the United States follow policies that might lead to its involvement in such wars. He abhorred the role of "world policeman" for the United States, not only because of the economic strains it would pose for the nation, but because he feared it would lead to mistrust and antagonism on the part of other countries toward the United States.

Hoover's views were expressed with greatest force during the two decades of Democratic presidents. Predictably, he opposed the New Deal with its rapid growth in the size of the federal government, its unbalanced budgets, and its intrusion into virtually every aspect of American life, including the entry of the government into competition with private enterprise. Throughout the Roosevelt years he spoke out against these tendencies in American government, and with the advent of the Hoover commissions under Truman and Eisenhower, he sought to roll back the size and activities of the federal government by the recommendations of the commissions. Continually, Hoover deplored the baneful effects of increasing government size and spending in fueling inflation, and the paralysis that such free-spending government policies and intervention in the free-enterprise system were causing in American business and industry. He saw a vicious cycle developing. The policies of the federal government stifled business and brought economic hardship. This, in turn, resulted in demands for further governmental action, which led to more worsening of the economy. The cycle could only lead eventually, in Hoover's view, to the collapse of the free-enterprise system altogether, its replacement with something akin either to fascism or socialism, and the eventual loss of American liberties with the demise of economic freedom. The only way to break the cycle was to restore the federal government to its rightful role only of "policeman" in the economic affairs of the country.

What particularly disturbed Hoover during the New Deal years was the suspicion that such a situation was not being created by well-intentioned incompetence, but by design. He was convinced that some of those advising Roosevelt were intent on remaking American life along collectivist lines under the direction of centralized planning in Washington. Such centralized planning was in Hoover's eyes incompatible with democracy. His suspicions led him to worry not only about the effects of the "emergency" policies on the American system, but also over the prospect that these "emergency" policies were intended by some, at least, to become a permanent part of American life.

It was this prospect that contributed to Hoover's opposition to American entry into World War II. Recalling the expansion of the powers of the federal government and the loss of civil liberties that accompanied American entry into World War I, he worried that the New Dealers would use American participation in World War II for further expansion of the federal government's role in American life and, unlike Wilson, would not easily surrender their new powers once the war was ended. But Hoover's opposition to intervention was based on other grounds, as well. In his view, such conflagrations as that which broke out in Europe in 1939 were endemic to that part of the world and the United States would only waste its youth and its resources by involvement in them. World War I had already demonstrated the folly in the American delusion that it could bring permanent peace to Europe. Germany represented no threat to the United States, and wise diplomacy could avoid a confrontation with Japan. Hoover saw clearly that the only beneficiary of American intervention against Germany and Japan would be expansion of communism, which he viewed as a far greater threat to world peace and American security than Germany and Japan.

When intervention came, despite his attempts to prevent it, Hoover turned to planning for the peace, concerned that another such peace treaty as that written in the heat of the emotions of war at Versailles should be avoided and that a permanent basis for postwar peace should be created. Here he was more successful. His proposals for peacemaking were largely followed, and he was influential in building a consensus within the Republican party in favor of American participation in the United Nations organization. When the predicted communist expansion took place in the midst and aftermath of the war, however, the United Nations proved powerless to stop it. America's European allies likewise showed no disposition to make the sacrifices necessary to put up an effective defense. Burdened already with the enormous expense of aiding the world in recovering from the war, the nation could not, in Hoover's view, undertake the costs of defending the world by itself. He counseled against the commitment of American ground troops to the defense of Europe until the nations there showed a greater willingness to defend themselves, and advocated, instead, the reliance of the United States on air and sea power for defense against the Soviet Union. His policies were rejected by the Truman administration, but heavily influenced the American defense posture under Eisenhower.

In most of the great issues of the Democratic decades Hoover was on the losing side, even when his was a popular position. In too many histories of the period it is blandly assumed that the losing side was also the wrong side. But Hoover was confident that his positions on the issues would be vindicated in the future and that history would eventually regard him in a more favorable light. Whether one agrees with it or not, it is impossible to deny that what Hoover predicted is taking place. Clearly, the principles espoused by Herbert Hoover have experienced a renaissance in the late 1970s and early 1980s. The problems that Hoover warned of during the three decades after he left the presidency were perceived by only a minority of Americans then, but they are real to more of his countrymen today. His concerns with the effects of government deficits, inflation, the growth of bureaucracy, waste in government, centralization of power in Washington at the expense of state and local and individual initiative, the growth of power in the presidency at the expense of the legislative branch, the rise in welfare costs, the loss of morality in government, the stultifying effects on economic growth of government over-regulation of business, the loss of individual liberty, and the pernicious effects on America and its image in the world produced by the role of self-appointed international policeman have all increasingly become the concerns of Americans since the 1960s. As Hoover feared, the overcommitment of American funds to the rehabilitation and defense of the world since World War II has taken its toll. While foreign factories were modernized, sometimes at American expense, the crushing tax load and inflation slowed similar modernization in the United States. By the 1970s many American industrial products were no longer competitive even in the American market, and the nation groaned under an enormous trade deficit and saw jobs lost to workers in factories in foreign lands. Government over-regulation and tax policies, combined with inflation, continued to stifle private enterprise. In large part the scenario has played itself out exactly as Hoover predicted that it would.

Herbert Hoover harbored little hope that a nation, once it embarked upon such policies as those of the New Deal, could ever right itself. A nation of consumers, workers, farmers, businessmen, and welfare recipients, once grown dependent upon a powerful federal government would not, he believed, ever recover the stamina to wean itself. But the public philosophy preached by Herbert Hoover grows more attractive to a significantly increasing number of people as the problems of the 1970s and 1980s bring the legacy of the New Deal increasingly into question. The "weaning of America" that he hoped for may yet take place.

Notes

ABBREVIATIONS USED IN THE NOTES

FEC   Famine Emergency Committee Papers, Hoover Institution on War, Revolution and Peace

HP-HI   Hoover Papers, Hoover Institution on War, Revolution and Peace

HP-PPI   Hoover Papers, Post-Presidential Individual Files, Hoover Presidential Library

HP-PPS Hoover Papers, Post-Presidential Subject Files, Hoover Presidential Library

NCFSD National Committee, Food for the Small Democracies Papers, Hoover Institution on War, Revolution and Peace

PREFACE

1. Eugene Lyons, *Our Unknown Ex-President: A Portrait of Herbert Hoover* (Garden City, 1949), p. 1.
2. Carl N. Degler, "The Ordeal of Herbert Hoover," *The Yale Review* 52 (Summer 1963): 563.
3. William Appleman Williams, *The Contours of American History* (New York, 1973), p. 426.

4. George T. Mazuzan, "Herbert Clark Hoover, 1874–1933: A Comment on His Early Death," *Herbert Hoover Reassessed*, Senate Document 96–63 (Washington, D.C., 1981), pp. 223–26.

INTRODUCTION

1. Rexford G. Tugwell, "The Protagonists: Roosevelt and Hoover," *Antioch Review* 13 (December 1953): 442.
2. *Washington Post*, June 2, 1934.

CHAPTER 1

1. Rexford G. Tugwell, "The Protagonists: Roosevelt and Hoover," *Antioch Review* 13 (December 1953): 419.
2. Edgar Rickard Diary, March 3, 1933, Hoover Presidential Library.
3. Ibid, March 5, 1933.
4. *Baltimore Sun*, March 4 and 6, 1933.
5. Statement of March 6, 1933, in Public Statements, 1933, Hoover Papers, Hoover Presidential Library.
6. *Baltimore Sun*, March 8, 1933.
7. Hoover to Reed, March 10, 1933, HP-PPI.
8. *New York Times*, March 22, 1933.
9. Mark Sullivan to Robinson, November 21, 1932, Mark Sullivan Papers, Hoover Institution on War, Revolution and Peace.
10. Sullivan to Robinson, January 26, 1933, ibid.
11. Hoover to Walter Brown, January 27, 1933, HP-PPI.
12. Edgar Rickard Diary, March 15, 1933.
13. See, for example, O'Laughlin to Hoover, March 8, 1933, John Callan O'Laughlin Papers, Library of Congress.
14. Edgar Rickard Diary, April 6, 1933.
15. O'Laughlin to Hoover, February 2, 1933, and Hoover to O'Laughlin, February 3, 1933, O'Laughlin Papers.
16. Akerson to Hoover, March 22, 1933, HP-PPI.
17. Harry Chandler (*Los Angeles Times*) to Hoover, April 6, 1933, ibid.
18. Hoover to Walter Brown, March 25, 1933, ibid.
19. Hoover to Knox, April 5, 1933, ibid.
20. Hoover to O'Laughlin, April 6, 1933, O'Laughlin Papers.
21. Hoover to Walter Hope, April 6, 1933, HP-PPI.
22. Hoover to Mark Sullivan, April 10, 1933, Sullivan Papers.

23. Hoover to Walter Brown, April 26, 1933, HP-PPI.
24. Hoover to Simeon Fess, April 27, 1933, ibid.
25. Hoover to Mark Sullivan, July 5, 1933, Sullivan Papers.
26. Hoover to Franklin Fort, September 3, 1933, HP-PPI.
27. Hoover to Paul Wooton, September 9, 1933, ibid.
28. Hoover to Cleveland Newton, November 13, 1933, ibid.
29. Hoover to Hope, August 9, 1933, ibid.
30. Hoover to O'Laughlin, August 22, 1933, O'Laughlin Papers.
31. Hoover to O'Laughlin, April 19, 1933, ibid.
32. Hoover to George Akerson, September 9, 1933, George Akerson Papers, Hoover Institution on War, Revolution and Peace.
33. Hoover to Walter Brown, April 25, 1933, Walter Brown Papers, Ohio Historical Center.
34. Hoover to O'Laughlin, April 28, 1933, O'Laughlin Papers.
35. Hoover to William S. Bennet, May 5, 1933, HP-PPI.
36. Hoover to Raymond Benjamin, April 24, 1933, ibid.
37. O'Laughlin to Hoover, April 24, 1933, O'Laughlin Papers.
38. Hoover to J. R. Nutt, April 29, 1933, HP-PPI.
39. Vandenberg to Hoover, April 2, 1933, HPHI.
40. Hoover to Fess, May 9, 1933, HP-PPI.
41. Hoover to Brown, April 4, 1933, Brown Papers.
42. Hoover to John J. Watson, June 13, 1933, HP-PPI.
43. Hoover to Crowther, June 19, 1933, ibid.
44. Hoover to Lorimer, June 1, 1933, ibid.
45. See, for example, O'Laughlin to Hoover, June 10, 1933, O'Laughlin Papers.
46. O'Laughlin to Hoover, June 17, 1933, ibid.
47. O'Laughlin to Hoover, June 26, 1933, ibid.
48. O'Laughlin to Hoover, July 3, 1933, ibid.
49. Hoover to O'Laughlin, July 4, 1933, ibid.
50. Hoover to Everett Sanders, July 5, 1933, HP-PPI.
51. O'Laughlin to Hoover, April 7, 1933, and Hoover to O'Laughlin, April 10, 1933, O'Laughlin Papers.
52. O'Laughlin to Hoover, April 26, 1933, ibid.
53. Hoover to O'Laughlin, April 29, 1933, ibid.
54. Hoover to O'Laughlin, May 9, 1933, ibid.
55. O'Laughlin to Hoover, May 13, 1933, ibid.
56. O'Laughlin to Hoover, May 17, 1933, ibid.
57. Hoover to Brown, May 17, 1933, Brown Papers.
58. Brown to Hoover, May 23, 1933, and Hoover to Brown, May 29, 1933, ibid.
59. O'Laughlin to Hoover, June 10, 1933, O'Laughlin Papers.

60. O'Laughlin to Hoover, June 17, 1933, and June 20, 1933, and Hoover to O'Laughlin, July 4, 1933, ibid.
61. Brown to Hoover, June 22, 1933, HP-PPI.
62. Brown to Hoover, March 29, 1933, Brown Papers.
63. O'Laughlin to Hoover, May 6, 1933, O'Laughlin Papers.
64. Brown to Hoover, May 16, 1933, Brown Papers.
65. Mills to William Breed, June 6, 1933, Ogden Mills Papers, Library of Congress.
66. Brown to Hoover, June 22, 1933, HP-PPI.
67. O'Laughlin to Hoover, July 3, 1933, O'Laughlin Papers.
68. O'Laughlin to Hoover, July 21, 1933, ibid.
69. O'Laughlin to Hoover, August 18, 1933, ibid.
70. Hoover to O'Laughlin, August 22, 1933, ibid.; Hoover to Sanders, September 2, 1933, and Hoover to J. R. Nutt, September 2, 1933, HP-PPI.
71. Hoover to Gallagher, October 4, 1933, HP-PPI.
72. Hoover to Brown, October 22, 1933, Brown Papers.
73. See, for example, Hoover to Arch Shaw, September 3, 1933, and other correspondence between Hoover and Shaw in the Shaw file, HP-PPI.
74. O'Laughlin to Hoover, October 9, 1933, O'Laughlin Papers.
75. O'Laughlin to Hoover, October 10, 1933, ibid.
76. Brown to Hoover, October 10, 1933, Brown Papers.
77. Hoover to O'Laughlin, October 12, 1933, O'Laughlin Papers.
78. Draft statement with Hoover to O'Laughlin, October 12, 1933, ibid.
79. Hoover to Brown, October 22, 1933, Brown Papers.
80. Hoover to Reed, October 23, 1933, and Hoover to Walter Brown, October 23, 1933, HP-PPI.
81. Hoover to Fess, October 23, 1933, ibid.
82. Hoover to O'Laughlin, October 24, 1933, O'Laughlin Papers.
83. O'Laughlin to Hoover, October 24, 1933, ibid.
84. Hoover to Raymond Benjamin, October 14, 1933, HP-PPI.
85. Fess to Hoover, November 20, 1933, ibid.
86. O'Laughlin to Hoover, November 12, 1933, O'Laughlin Papers.
87. Hoover to Charles Scott, November 27, 1933, Charles Scott Papers, Kansas Historical Society.
88. Hoover to Reed, November 15, 1933, HP-PPI.
89. Brown to Hoover, November 29, 1933, ibid.
90. Hoover to Raymond Benjamin, November 14, 1933, and Hoover to Wilbur Matson, December 5, 1933, ibid.
91. Hoover to Brown, December 5, 1933, ibid.
92. Hoover to Fess, December 9, 1933, ibid.

93. Brown to Hoover, October 10, 1933, and Hoover to Brown, October 22, 1933, ibid.

94. Coleman to Hoover, January 10, 1934, Arch Coleman Papers, Hoover Institution on War, Revolution and Peace.

95. U.S., Congress, Senate, *Congressional Record*, 1934, p. 1821 (copy in Hoover Papers).

96. Hoover to Snell, telegram, February 2, 1934, HP-PPI.

97. "Book Manuscript Material—MEMOIRS V. III The Aftermath—1950 Printed Edition," p. 209, Hoover Papers.

98. Hoover to Russell Doubleday, September 15, 1933, HP-PPI.

99. Hoover to Whiting Williams, October 23, 1933, ibid.

100. Hoover to Hunt, September 14, 1933, ibid.

101. Hoover to Lane, January 31, 1934, ibid.

102. Hoover to O'Laughlin, January 29, 1934, O'Laughlin Papers.

103. Hoover to Wheeler, April 25, 1934, HP-PPI.

104. Hoover to Sullivan, February 3, 1934, Sullivan Papers.

105. Hoover to Will Irwin, February 16, 1934, Will Irwin Papers, Hoover Institution on War, Revolution and Peace.

106. Castle to Hoover, April 30, 1934, and Hoover to Castle, May 8, 1934, HP-PPI. The Cheka had been a Russian secret police.

107. Hoover to Ashmun Brown, March 13, 1934, ibid.

108. O'Laughlin to Hoover, February 27, 1934, O'Laughlin Papers,

109. Hoover to Hyde, March 5, 1934, HP-PPI.

110. O'Laughlin to Hoover, January 26, 1934, O'Laughlin Papers.

111. Hoover to O'Laughlin, January 29, 1934, HP-PPI. Edge was supported by Daniel Reed and George Moses, but was willing to stand for the office only if it would not mean a fight. See memorandum of October 30, 1933, in Edge file, HP-PPI.

112. See, for example, O'Laughlin to Hoover, July 14, 1933, O'Laughlin Papers.

113. O'Laughlin to Hoover, February 10, 1934, ibid.

114. Hoover to O'Laughlin, March 4, 1934, ibid.

115. See Arch Shaw to Hoover, May 21, 1934, and Hoover to Harrison Spangler, May 23, 1934, HP-PPI.

116. Hoover to Creager, May 23, 1934, ibid.

117. Spangler to Hoover, May 12, 1934, ibid.

118. Minutes of the Republican National Committee meeting, June 5, 1934, Republican National Headquarters.

119. Report of the continuation of the Republican National Committee meeting, June 6, 1934, Republican National Headquarters.

120. Ibid.

121. *New York Times*, June 7, 1934; *New York Herald Tribune*, June 7, 1934.

122. *Baltimore Sun*, June 7, 1934.

123. Report of the continuation of the Republican National Committee meeting, June 6, 1934, Republican National Headquarters.

124. Hoover to Fletcher, telegram, June 6, 1934, HP-PPI.

125. Creager to Hoover, telegram, June 6, 1934, ibid.

126. Hoover to Creager, June 8, 1934, ibid.

127. *Baltimore Sun*, June 7, 1934.

128. *New York Herald Tribune*, June 7, 1934.

129. Sullivan to Hoover, May 21, 1934, Sullivan Papers; Edgar Rickard Diary, April 29, 1934, June 19, 1934, and June 21, 1934.

130. Hoover to Gertrude Lane, July 9, 1934, HP-PPI.

131. Hoover to Austin, August 10, 1934. ibid.

132. Hoover to O'Laughlin, August 11, 1934, O'Laughlin Papers.

133. Hoover to Akerson, August 14, 1934, HP-PPI.

134. Hoover to White, July 31, 1934, William Allen White Papers, Library of Congress.

135. The articles appeared in *Saturday Evening Post* on September 8 and 15, 1934.

136. Herbert Hoover, *The Challenge to Liberty* (New York, 1934), pp. 202–3.

137. Hoover to Henry Allen, September 17, 1934, HP-PPI.

138. White to Book-of-the-Month-Club, telegram, August 15, 1934, White Papers.

139. Hoover to White, August 23, 1934, ibid.

140. *New York Herald Tribune*, September 5, 1934.

141. *The Nation*, October 17, 1934, p. 456.

142. *New York Times*, September 30, 1934.

143. *Saturday Review*, October 6, 1934, p. 155.

144. Durant to Hoover, October 8, 1934, HP-PPI.

145. Frank to Hoover, October 23, 1934, ibid.

146. O'Laughlin to Hoover, September 6, 1934, O'Laughlin Papers.

147. *Washington Post*, September 28, 1934.

148. Hoover to L. Ward Bannister, August 7, 1934, HP-PPI.

149. Hoover to Arthur Ballantine, August 23, 1934, ibid.

150. Hoover to Ashmun Brown, October 17, 1934, ibid.

151. The correspondence files of the Hoover papers contain numerous thank-you letters for gifts of the book; on the circulation see "Book Manuscript Material—Memoirs V. III The Aftermath—1950 printed edition," p. 211, Hoover Papers.

152. *United States News*, September 10, 1934.

153. Chadwick Hall, "America's Conservative Revolution," *Antioch Review* (June 1955): 204.

154. A description of the Bohemian Club encampment is in the Edgar Rickard Diary, July 19, 1947, to August 2, 1947.

155. *Washington Post*, July 29, 1934.

156. George Wolfskill, *The Revolt of the Conservatives* (Boston, 1962), pp. 20–25.

157. Hoover to O'Laughlin, September 6, 1934, O'Laughlin Papers.

158. Hoover to Sullivan, September 1, 1934, HP-PPI.

159. Hoover to Castle, August 31, 1934, ibid.

160. Hoover to Ballantine, August 23, 1934, ibid.

161. Hoover to Mills, August 24, 1934, ibid.

162. Fletcher to Hoover, August 31, 1934, ibid.

163. Hoover to Shaw, September 7, 1934, ibid.

164. Hoover to Patrick Hurley, September 11, 1934, ibid.

165. Hoover to Allen, October 17, 1934, ibid.

166. Borah to Mark Requa, William Borah Papers, Library of Congress.

167. Snell to Hoover, October 17, 1934, HP-PPI.

168. Dickinson to Hoover, November 1, 1934, ibid.

169. Mark Sullivan to Hoover, October 18, 1934, HPHI.

170. Hoover to White, October 29, 1934, HP-PPI.

171. Hoover to Ashmun Brown, November 9, 1934, ibid.

172. See, for example, Henry Allen to Hoover, November 6, 1933, and George Akerson to Hoover, November 21, 1933, both ibid., and Julius Klein to Hoover, November 16, 1933, Julius Klein Papers, Hoover Institution on War, Revolution and Peace.

173. Schall to Hoover, November 22, 1933, and Arch Shaw to Hoover, June 6, 1934, both HP-PPI, and Mark Sullivan to Hoover, April 30, 1934, Sullivan Papers.

174. Hoover to Hyde, November 23, 1934, HP-PPI.

175. Hoover to Theodore Joslin, January 2, 1935, ibid.

176. Hoover to Franklin Fort, November 17, 1934, ibid.

177. James Farley to Franklin D. Roosevelt, August 1, 1935, transmitting account by a student named Grey of Hoover's comments of January 19, 1935, in Roosevelt Papers, PPF-820, Roosevelt Presidential Library; copy in Hoover Presidential Library.

178. Hoover to Charles Hilles, October 19, 1934, HP-PPI.

179. William Starr Myers Diary, January 8, 1935, Hoover Institution on War, Revolution and Peace.

180. Hoover to White, January 12, 1935, White Papers.

181. Edgar Rickard Diary, February 7, 1935.

182. O'Laughlin to Hoover, February 16, 1935, O'Laughlin Papers.

183. Edgar Rickard Diary, February 11, 1935.

184. Ibid., February 14, 1935.

185. Ibid., February 11, 1935.

186. Ibid., March 4, 1935; Hoover to Roy Howard, February 27, 1935, HP-PPI. The United Press at first thought it was a prankster using Hoover's name and wired Tucson to verify that it came from Hoover. He sent the wire collect, and it cost United Press $19.10.

187. Statement of February 20, 1935, in Public Statements, 1935, Hoover Papers.

188. *New York Times*, February 21, 1935.

189. *New York Herald Tribune*, February 22, 1935.

190. *New York Times*, February 22, 1935.

191. Hoover to Hyde, February 25, 1935, HP-PPI.

192. D. M. Reynolds to Paul Sexson, telegram, March 20, 1935, ibid.

193. Reprinted in Herbert Hoover, *Addresses Upon the American Road, 1933–38* (New York, 1938), pp. 40–44.

194. *New York Herald Tribune*, March 24, 1935.

195. Letter from M. L. Bullard, March 27, 1935, ibid.

CHAPTER 2

1. Hoover to Hope, January 14, 1935, HP-PPI.

2. Hoover to White, February 25, 1935, White Papers.

3. Hoover to Hyde, March 25, 1935, HP-PPI.

4. Hoover to John Cowles, March 19, 1935, and Hoover to Orville Bullington, March 28, 1935, ibid.

5. Hoover to Allen, April 22, 1935, and Hoover to A. H. Kirchhofer, April 22, 1935, ibid.

6. Hoover to Ashmun Brown, April 27, 1935, ibid.

7. Spangler to Hoover, January 24, 1935; Spangler to Frank Knox, March 31, 1935; Spangler to Hoover, March 26, 1935; and Hoover to Spangler, March 29, 1935; all in ibid.

8. Harry M. Morris, "The GOP in a Minority Role, 1933–38" (Ph.D. diss., University of Iowa, 1960), pp. 110–11.

9. Hoover to White, May 10, 1935, White Papers.

10. Hoover to Spangler, May 10, 1935; Hyde to Hoover, May 10, 1935; and Spangler to Hoover, May 13, 1935; all in HP-PPI.

11. White to Frank Knox, June 26, 1935, White Papers.

12. Morris, "The GOP in a Minority Role," pp. 113–14.

13. Hoover to Robert Simmons, June 20, 1935, and Hoover to R. B. Creager, June 21, 1935, both in HP-PPI.

14. Hoover to Walter W. Head, May 15, 1935, ibid.

15. Newton to Hoover, June 13, 1935, ibid.
16. Edgar Rickard Diary, April 17, 1935.
17. Ibid., June 9, 1935, to June 12, 1935.
18. Hoover to Knox, April 29, 1935, HP-PPI.
19. Hoover to O'Laughlin, April 27, 1935, O'Laughlin Papers.
20. Reprinted in Hoover, *Addresses Upon the American Road, 1933–38*, pp. 45–47.
21. Statement of May 24, 1935, in Public Statements, 1935, Hoover Papers.
22. Hoover to O'Laughlin, May 20, 1935, O'Laughlin Papers.
23. Hoover to Bullington, June 20, 1935, HP-PPI.
24. Interview with Alf Landon by the author, August 17, 1977.
25. Landon to Hoover, February 22, 1935, HP-PPI.
26. Landon to Hoover, telegram, July 5, 1935, ibid.
27. White to Hoover, July 15, 1935, White Papers.
28. White to Hoover, July 24, 1935, ibid.
29. See, for example, Edgar Rickard Diary, July 30, 1935.
30. Knox to Spargo, September 6, 1935, John Spargo Papers, University of Vermont.
31. White to Walter Newton, June 26, 1935, White Papers.
32. Edgar Rickard Diary, August 12, 1935, through August 15, 1935.
33. Ibid., August 8, 1935, and August 16, 1935.
34. See, for example, ibid., August 30, 1935; also see Walter Newton to Larry Richey, April 20, 1935, and Hoover to Newton, June 20, 1935, both in HP-PPI.
35. Edgar Rickard Diary, October, 9, 1935.
36. D. M. Reynolds to Hoover, May 1, 1935, HP-PPI.
37. Memorandum of phone conversation with Hoover of May 6, 1935, in Sullivan Papers.
38. D. M. Reynolds memorandum of June 24, 1935, in HP-PPI.
39. See, for example, Edmond E. Lincoln to Hoover, June 24, 1935, and Hoover to Walter Brown, June 26, 1935, HP-PPI, as well as Hoover to Brown, September 10, 1935, Brown Papers.
40. See, for example, Goodrich to Hoover, September 23, 1935, HP-PPI.
41. Reprinted in Hoover, *Addresses Upon the American Road, 1933–38*, pp. 63-74.
42. Ibid.
43. Edgar Rickard Diary, November 13, 1935.
44. Smith to Hoover, October 16, 1935, HP-PPI.
45. Hoover to Rickard, October 19, 1935, ibid.
46. Edgar Rickard Diary, November 13, 1935.

47. Reprinted in Hoover, *Addresses Upon the American Road, 1933–38*, pp. 75–86.
48. Ibid.
49. Gross to Hoover, December 3, 1935, HP-PPI.
50. Hoover to Walter Brown, November 27, 1935, and Hoover to Styles Bridges, November 5, 1935, ibid.
51. Hilles to Fletcher, November 18, 1935, copy in ibid.
52. Brown to Hoover, November 20, 1935, Brown Papers.
53. *New York Times*, November 30, 1935.
54. O'Laughlin to Hoover, November 30, 1935, O'Laughlin Papers.
55. Hoover to O'Laughlin, December 4, 1935, ibid.; also Hoover to Scott, December 7, 1935, Scott Papers.
56. Reprinted in Hoover, *Addresses Upon the American Road, 1933–38*, pp. 87–100.
57. Ibid.
58. Ibid.
59. Ibid.
60. See Ben Allen folder, HP-PPI.
61. Hoover to William Gross, December 22, 1935, ibid.
62. Hoover to Newton, December 22, 1935, ibid.
63. Hoover to George Getz, telegram, December 22, 1935, ibid.
64. Reprinted in Hoover, *Addresses Upon the American Road, 1933–38*, pp. 101–13.
65. Ibid.
66. Hoover to Raymond G. Barnett, December 23, 1935, HP-PPI.
67. Hoover to Creager, January 19, 1936, ibid.
68. Hoover to O'Laughlin, January 24, 1936, O'Laughlin Papers.
69. Hoover to Henry F. Misselwitz, January 21, 1936, HP-PPI.
70. Hoover to Alan Fox, January 24, 1936, ibid.
71. Hoover to James P. Goodrich, January 25, 1936, HPHI.
72. Edgar Rickard Diary, November 27, 1935, and December 4, 1935.
73. Hoover to Hope, November 27, 1935, HP-PPI.
74. See, for example, Newton to Hoover, January 6, 1936, ibid.
75. Edgar Rickard Diary, January 10, 1936.
76. Robert G. Simmons to Hoover, January 30, 1936, HP-PPI.
77. Hoover to Jones, January 29, 1936, ibid.
78. See Hoover to Hyde, January 27, 1936, and Chandler to Hoover, January 28, 1936, ibid.
79. Hoover to Chandler, February 1, 1936, ibid.
80. Alan Fox to Hoover, February 4, 1936, ibid.

81. Hoover to Fox, February 11, 1936, ibid.

82. See, for example, Walter Newton to Hoover, January 22, 1936; Hoover to Newton, January 24, 1936; Newton to Hoover, January 28, 1936; Newton to Hoover, January 30, 1936; and Newton to Hoover, February 17, 1936; ibid.

83. Reprinted in Hoover, *Addresses Upon the American Road, 1933–38*, pp. 126–41.

84. Edgar Rickard Diary, February 26, 1936.

85. D. M. Reynolds to Hoover, February 5, 1936, HP-PPI.

86. Hoover to Edwin Hanak, February 6, 1936, ibid.

87. Reprinted in Hoover, *Addresses Upon the American Road, 1933–38*, pp. 126–41.

88. Ibid.

89. Ibid.

90. Coleman to Newton, February 27, 1936, copy in HP-PPI.

91. Newton to Larry Richey, March 18, 1936, ibid.

92. Edgar Rickard Diary, March 11, 1936.

93. Newton to Hoover, March 19, 1936, HP-PPI.

94. Vandenberg to Allison Reppy, March 23, 1936, copy in ibid.

95. Donald R. McCoy, *Landon of Kansas* (Lincoln, 1966), pp. 245–46.

96. Edgar Rickard Diary, March 18, 1936.

97. Ibid., March 27, 1936.

98. Reprinted in Hoover, *Addresses Upon the American Road, 1933–38*, pp. 142–48.

99. See, for example, O'Laughlin to Hoover, April 4, 1936, O'Laughlin Papers.

100. Fox to Hoover, March 31, 1936, HP-PPI.

101. Fox to Hoover, April 17, 1936, ibid.

102. Hoover to Fox, April 22, 1936, ibid.

103. Hoover to Spargo, May 4, 1936, ibid.

104. See, for example, Hoover to Dorothy Thompson, April 10, 1936, ibid.

105. Hoover to Ballard Dunn, April 18, 1936, ibid.

106. Hoover to Chauncey McCormick, April 22, 1936, ibid.

107. Fox to Hoover, April 23, 1936, ibid.

108. Hoover to Fox, April 27, 1936, ibid.

109. Fox to Hoover, May 1, 1936, ibid.

110. Edgar Rickard Diary, May 6, 1936; O'Laughlin to Hoover, May 11, 1936, O'Laughlin Papers.

111. Reprinted in Hoover, *Addresses Upon the American Road, 1933–38*, pp. 159–72.

112. Edgar Rickard Diary, May 12, 1936.

113. Ibid., May 13, 1936.

114. Miles W. Jones to Hoover, May 18, 1936, HP-PPI.

115. Morris, "The GOP in a Minority Role, 1933–38," p. 163; George Henry Lobdell, Jr., "A Biography of Frank Knox" (Ph.D. diss., University of Illinois, 1954), pp. 263–64, 266, 274.

116. "Book Manuscript Material—MEMOIRS V. III The Aftermath—1950 Printed Edition," p. 261, Hoover Papers.

117. Statement of May 18, 1936, in Public Statements, 1936, ibid.

118. See, for example, O'Laughlin to Ruth Simms, May 19, 1936, and O'Laughlin to Hoover, May 21, 1936, in O'Laughlin Papers; Fox to Hoover, May 25, 1936, HP-PPI.

119. Hoover to Fort, May 26, 1936, HP-PPI.

120. "Book Manuscript Material—MEMOIRS V. III The Aftermath—1950 Printed Edition," p. 262, Hoover Papers.

121. Hoover to Fox, June 4, 1936, HP-PPI.

122. O'Laughlin to General Douglas MacArthur, May 23, 1936, O'Laughlin Papers.

123. O'Laughlin to Hoover, June 2, 1936, ibid.

124. Edgar Rickard Diary, June 9, 1936, and June 11, 1936.

125. Ibid, June 11, 1936.

126. Reprinted in Hoover, *Addresses Upon the American Road, 1933–38*, pp. 173–83.

127. George H. Mayer, *The Republican Party* (New York, 1967), p. 441.

128. Chester Rowell to Myrtle, June 11, 1936, Rowell Papers, University of California at Berkeley.

129. Mayer, *The Republican Party*, p. 441.

130. Rowell to Myrtle, June 11, 1936, Rowell Papers.

131. Mayer, *The Republican Party*, p. 441.

132. Rowell to Myrtle, June 11, 1936, Rowell Papers.

133. Ibid.

134. Ibid.

135. Edgar Rickard Diary, June 9, 1936, to June 11, 1936; see also Rickard to Mills, June 13, 1936, copy in Spargo Papers.

136. Morris, "The GOP in a Minority Role, 1933–38," p. 163.

137. Hoover to White, June 22, 1936, HP-PPI.

138. "Book Manuscript Material—MEMOIRS V. III The Aftermath—1950 Printed Edition," p. 260.

139. Ibid., pp. 270–71.

140. Reprinted in Hoover, *Addresses Upon the American Road, 1933–38*, pp. 184–85.

141. "Book Manuscript Material—MEMOIRS V. III The Aftermath—1950 Printed Edition," p. 271, Hoover Papers; see also McCoy, *Landon of Kansas*, p. 257.

142. Senator Walcott to Hoover, telegram, June 11, 1936, HP-PPI.

143. Edgar Rickard Diary, June 12, 1936.

144. Miles W. Jones to Larry Richey, June 18, 1936, HP-PPI.

145. See, for example, Albert Mattei to Hoover, June 14, 1936, ibid.

146. Hoover to William D. Mitchell, June 22, 1936, ibid.

147. Edgar Rickard Diary, August 14, 1936.

148. Hoover to Chandler, June 23, 1936, HP-PPI.

149. Hoover to Brown, June 23, 1936, Brown Papers.

150. Hoover to Hamilton, June 24, 1936, copy in ibid.

151. Hoover to O. Glenn Saxon, July 1, 1936, HP-PPI.

152. Hoover to Shaw, July 9, 1936, ibid.

153. Saxon to Hoover, July 9, 1936, ibid.

154. Hoover to Shaw, July 9, 1936, ibid.

155. O'Laughlin to Hoover, July 11, 1936, O'Laughlin Papers.

156. Hoover to O'Laughlin, July 14, 1936, ibid.

157. Hoover to Hyde, July 17, 1936, ibid.

158. Charles Taft to Robert A. Taft, July 28, 1936, Robert A. Taft Papers, Library of Congress.

159. Robert A. Taft to Charles Taft, July 30, 1936, ibid.

160. Landon to Hoover, August 7, 1936, Alf M. Landon Papers, Kansas Historical Society.

161. Hoover to Newton, August 15, 1936, HP-PPI.

162. Hoover to Shaw, August 18, 1936, ibid.

163. Hoover to Bullington, July 9, 1936, ibid.

164. Transcript of a telephone conversation between Landon and Hoover, September 2, 1936, ibid.

165. Hoover to Landon, September 2, 1936, Landon Papers.

166. Edgar Rickard Diary, September 4, 1936.

167. Ibid., September 9 and 17, 1936.

168. Newton to Hoover, September 26, 1936, HP-PPI.

169. Edgar Rickard Diary, September 28, 1936.

170. McCoy, *Landon of Kansas*, p. 309.

171. Ibid.; interview with Alf Landon by the author, August 17, 1977.

172. Edgar Rickard Diary, October 5, 1936.

173. Reprinted in Hoover, *Addresses Upon the American Road, 1933–38*, pp. 201–15.

174. Ibid.

175. Reprinted in ibid., pp. 216–27.

176. Ibid.

177. "Book Manuscript Material—MEMOIRS V. III The Aftermath—1950 Printed Edition," p. 281, Hoover Papers.

178. See, for example, Harold L. Ickes, *The Secret Diary of Harold L. Ickes* (New York, 1953), vol. l, p. 641.

179. Raymond Moley, *27 Masters of Politics* (Westport, 1972), pp. 26–27.

180. Ickes, *The Secret Diary*, vol. 1, p. 639.

181. Bascom N. Timmons, *Garner of Texas* (New York, 1948), p. 208.

182. Hoover to Ogden Mills, November 4, 1936, HP-PPI.

CHAPTER 3

1. Spangler to Hoover, November 19, 1936, HP-PPI; John D. M. Hamilton oral history, Hoover Presidential Library.

2. Edgar Rickard Diary, November 30, 1936.

3. Hoover to Ogden Mills, November 4, 1936, and Hoover to Walter Newton, January 9, 1937, HP-PPI.

4. Hoover to Robert Simms family, November 30, 1936, ibid.

5. William Starr Myers Diary, December 4, 1936.

6. Hoover to Arthur Hyde, January 1, 1937, HP-PPI.

7. Hyde to Hoover, January 9, 1937, ibid.

8. Arch Shaw to Hoover, telegram, January 5, 1937, ibid.

9. Hoover to William Allen White, January 9, 1937, White Papers.

10. Landon to Richard Lloyd Jones, January 7, 1937, Landon Papers.

11. Landon to William Allen White, January 8, 1937, White Papers.

12. Lowden to Landon, January 27, 1937, Landon Papers.

13. Lowden to Arch Shaw, telegram, January 22, 1937, HP-PPI.

14. Hyde to Shaw, January 21, 1937, ibid.

15. Shaw to Hoover, undated, but sometime in January 1937, ibid.

16. Edgar Rickard Diary, February 5, 1937.

17. Arthur Sears Henning to Hoover, February 1, 1937, HP-PPI.

18. Edgar Rickard Diary, February 7, 1937.

19. See, for example, Rickard to the *Christian Science Monitor*, October 15, 1937, copy in Spargo Papers, and Hoover to John Bricker, March 12, 1937, HP-PPI.

20. Baxter to Hoover, February 9, 1937, and Bricker to Hoover, February 24, 1937, HP-PPI.

21. Karl A. Lamb, "The Opposition Party as Secret Agent: Republicans and the Court Fight, 1937," *Papers of the Michigan Academy of Science, Arts, and Letters* 46 (1961): 540–41.

22. John D. M. Hamilton oral history, Hoover Presidential Library.

23. Reprinted in Herbert Hoover, *Addresses Upon the American Road, 1933–38* (New York, 1938), p. 228.

24. Edgar Rickard Diary, February 11, 1937.
25. Ibid., February 9, 1937.
26. Mark Sullivan to Hoover, February 12, 1937, Sullivan Papers.
27. Reprinted in Hoover, *Addresses Upon the American Road, 1933–38*, pp. 229–36.
28. Edgar Rickard Diary, February 24, 1937.
29. Mark Sullivan to Hoover, February 24, 1937, Sullivan Papers.
30. O'Laughlin to Hoover, February 23, 1937, O'Laughlin Papers.
31. O'Laughlin to Hoover, February 22, 1937, ibid.
32. See, for example, Hoover to Bricker, February 24, 1937, HP-PPI.
33. Landon to John Lambert, February 24, 1937, Landon Papers; Hoover to Charles B. Goodspeed, February 25, 1937, HP-PPI.
34. Hoover to O'Laughlin, February 26, 1937, O'Laughlin Papers.
35. William Starr Myers Diary, March 1, 1937, and March 2, 1937.
36. Ibid., March 10, 1937.
37. Landon to Amos Pinchot, March 11, 1937, Landon Papers.
38. Larry Richey to George Getz, March 15, 1937, HP-PPI; Rickard Diary, April 12, 1937.
39. Hoover to Arch Shaw, telegram, March 26, 1937, ibid.
40. Hamilton oral history, Hoover Presidential Library.
41. Edgar Rickard Diary, April 18, 1937.
42. Ibid, April 19, 1937.
43. Hoover to Hamilton, April 23, 1937, HP-PPI.
44. Edgar Rickard Diary, April 28, 1937.
45. Hamilton oral history, Hoover Presidential Library.
46. Edgar Rickard Diary, May 2, 1937.
47. Hyde to Spargo, May 3, 1937, Spargo Papers.
48. William Starr Myers Diary, May 18, 1937.
49. Hyde to Spargo, May 10, 1937, Spargo Papers.
50. Edgar Rickard Diary, May 10, 1937.
51. Landon to William Hard, May 10, 1937, Landon Papers.
52. Hard to Landon, May 10, 1937, ibid.
53. Edgar Rickard Diary, May 12, 1937.
54. Hyde to Lester Dickinson, May 10, 1937, copy in HP-PPI.
55. Hoover to Jacob Allen, May 20, 1937, ibid.
56. Hoover to Henry Robinson, May 24, 1937, ibid.
57. Edgar Rickard Diary, May 15, 1937.
58. Ibid., May 19, 1937.
59. Hard to Landon, May 11, 1937, Landon Papers.
60. Reppy to Spargo, May 24, 1937, HP-PPI.

61. Spargo to Reppy, June 7, 1937, ibid.
62. Hyde to Spargo, June 14, 1937, ibid.
63. See Samuel Crowther to Hoover, May 22, 1937, and Bricker to Hoover, June 1, 1937, ibid.
64. Edgar Rickard Diary, May 27, 1937.
65. Ibid., June 1, 1937.
66. Ogden Mills to Landon, June 11, 1937, Landon Papers.
67. Hard to Hoover, telegram, June 11, 1937, HP-PPI.
68. Hoover to Hard, June 21, 1937, ibid.
69. Clipping from the *New York Daily Mirror*, June 25, 1937, in ibid.
70. Sullivan to Hoover, June 28, 1937, Sullivan Papers.
71. Spargo to Hyde, June 26, 1937, HP-PPI.
72. Spangler to Hoover, August 13, 1937, ibid.
73. Rickard to Bernice Miller (Hoover's secretary), August 16, 1937, ibid.; see also Edgar Rickard Diary, July 28, 1937.
74. Reprinted in Hoover, *Addresses Upon the American Road, 1933–38*, pp. 243–63.
75. Ibid.
76. See, for example, Hoover to A. H. Kirchhofer, August 21, 1937, HP-PPI.
77. See, for example, Hoover to Robert D. Blue, August 21, 1937, ibid.
78. See, for example, O. Glenn Saxon to Hoover, July 7, 1937, ibid.
79. Landon to Mossman, August 10, 1937, Landon Papers.
80. Capper to Landon, August 13, 1937, ibid.
81. Landon to Capper, August 17, 1937, ibid.
82. Snell to Hoover, August 9, 1937, HP-PPI.
83. Roger T. Johnson, "Charles L. McNary and the Republican Party During Prosperity and Depression" (Ph.D. diss., University of Wisconsin, 1967), p. 248.
84. Hoover to Robert Simmons, August 24, 1937, HP-PPI.
85. Press Statement of August 20, 1937, in Public Statements, 1937, Hoover Papers.
86. Hoover to Spangler, August 21, 1937, HP-PPI.
87. Hoover to Jacob Allen, August 21, 1937, ibid.
88. Ibid.
89. Hyde to Spargo, August 16, 1937, and Spargo to Jay N. Tittemore, August 26, 1937, Spargo Papers.
90. Hoover to Robert Simmons, August 24, 1937, HP-PPI.
91. Hoover to John Bricker, August 24, 1937, ibid.
92. Spangler to Hoover, August 25, 1937, ibid.
93. Hoover to Spangler, August 28, 1937, ibid.

94. See, for example, Hoover to Jacob Allen, August 23, 1937, ibid.

95. Hoover to Hard, August 24, 1937, and to Arthur Ballantine, August 28, 1937, ibid.

96. Hoover to Spangler, August 28, 1937, ibid.

97. Hoover to Rowell, September 8, 1937, ibid.

98. Landon to Sterling Morton, September 2, 1937, ibid.

99. Landon to C. M. Harger, September 2, 1937, ibid.

100. Saxon to Hoover, September 7, 1937, HP-PPI.

101. Knox to Hoover, September 13, 1937, ibid.

102. Spangler to Hoover, September 15, 1937, ibid.

103. *New York Times*, September 13, 1937.

104. Edgar Rickard Diary, September 13, 1937.

105. Ibid.

106. Hoover to Frank O. Horton, September 4, 1937, HP-PPI.

107. Landon to Hard, September 13, 1937, Landon Papers.

108. Knox to Hoover, September 13, 1937, HP-PPI, ibid.

109. Hadley Cantril, *Public Opinion, 1935–1946* (Westport, 1951), pp. 749–50.

110. Clipping from *Washington Post*, September 19, 1937, Hoover Papers.

111. Jacob Allen to Spangler, September 21, 1937, HP-PPI.

112. Edgar Rickard Diary, September 20, 1937.

113. Press statement of Spangler, September 23, 1937, in "Republican Policy Committee," HP-PPS.

114. *New York Times*, September 23, 1937.

115. Ibid., September 24, 1937.

116. Edgar Rickard Diary, September 25, 1937, and September 28, 1937.

117. Clipping from *Cleveland News*, September 30, 1937, in "Republican Policy Committee," HP-PPS.

118. See, for example, *New York Times*, September 26, 1937.

119. Clipping from *Baltimore Sun*, September 28, 1937, in "Republican Policy Committee," HP-PPS.

120. Jacob Allen to D. M. Reynolds, October 1, 1937, HP-PPI.

121. William T. Hutchinson, *Lowden of Illinois* (Chicago, 1957), vol. 2, p. 725.

122. Hoover to Hamilton, October 5, 1937, HP-PPI.

123. Landon to Senator John Townsend, Jr., October 6, 1937, Landon Papers.

124. See, for example, Landon to Knox, October 14, 1937, and Landon to Vandenberg, October 14, 1937, ibid.

125. According to Hoover to Arch Shaw, October 8, 1937, HP-PPI.

126. Hoover to Lowden, October 8, 1937, and Lowden to Hoover, October 11, 1937, ibid.

127. Spangler to Hoover, October 9, 1937, ibid.

128. Landon to Harold Johnson, October 14, 1937, and Landon to James L. Wright, October 25, 1937, Landon Papers.

129. Landon to Richard Lloyd Jones, October 21, 1937, ibid.

130. Hoover to Don Berry, October 25, 1937, ibid.

131. Hoover to James Howell, October 6, 1937, HP-PPI.

132. Hoover to Wilbur, October 6, 1937, Ray Lyman Wilbur Papers, Hoover Institution on War, Revolution and Peace.

133. Hyde to Spargo, August 23, 1937, Spargo Papers.

134. Edgar Rickard Diary, October 9, 1937.

135. Ibid.

136. William Starr Myers Diary, October 12, 1937.

137. See *New York Times*, October 13, 1937.

138. Ibid., October 14, 1937.

139. Landon to Vandenberg, October 14, 1937, Landon Papers.

140. Donald R. McCoy, *Landon of Kansas* (Lincoln, 1966), p. 370; Spangler to Hoover, October 18, 1937, HP-PPI.

141. *New York Times*, October 21, 1937; see also the issue of October 24, 1937.

142. *Time*, November 1, 1937, p. 20.

143. Hoover to Spangler, telegram, October 23, 1937, Harrison Spangler Papers, Hoover Presidential Library.

144. Reprinted in Hoover, *Addresses Upon the American Road, 1933–38*, pp. 264–75.

145. *New York Times*, October 27, 1937.

146. Edgar Rickard Diary, October 27, 1937.

147. Carter to Hoover, October 27, 1937, HP-PPI.

148. Hoover to Carter, October 28, 1937, ibid.

149. For the earlier difficulty with Landon, see Hamilton to Landon, November 1, 1937, Landon Papers.

150. Hamilton to Landon, November 2, 1937, ibid.

151. Rickard to Spargo, October 29, 1937, Spargo Papers; Edgar Rickard Diary, November 3, 1937; Landon to Joseph Martin, October 15, 1937, and Landon to Frank Altschul, November 5, 1937, Landon Papers.

152. "An Abstract of the Stenographic Report of a Meeting of the Republican National Committee Held at Chicago, November 5, 1937," Republican National Headquarters.

153. Ibid.

154. McCoy, *Landon of Kansas*, p. 373.

155. *New York Times*, November 6, 1937.

156. Hoover to Frank Knox, November 6, 1937, HP-PPI.

157. Knox to Hoover, November 9, 1937, ibid.

158. Spargo to Reppy, November 8, 1937, ibid.

159. Spargo to Reppy, November 27, 1937, ibid.

160. See, for example, Hoover to Spangler, November 11, 1937, ibid.; Landon to Henry Fletcher, November 16, 1937, Landon Papers.

161. See, for example, Hoover to Spangler, December 2, 1937, and December 9, 1937, HP-PPI; Fletcher to Landon, November 23, 1937, and January 31, 1938, and Landon to Fletcher, February 1, 1938, Landon Papers.

162. Reprinted in Hoover, *Addresses Upon the American Road, 1933–38*, pp. 276–80.

163. Ibid., pp. 281–86.

164. Reppy to Spargo, November 23, 1937, and Spargo to Reppy, November 27, 1937, HP-PPI.

165. Edgar Rickard Diary, November 26, 1937.

166. Hoover to Spargo, December 10, 1937, HP-PPI.

167. Kenneth D. Roose, "The Recession of 1937–38," *Journal of Political Economy* 56 (1948): 241.

168. Reprinted in Hoover, *Addresses Upon the American Road, 1933–38*, pp. 287–99.

169. Ibid.

170. *San Francisco Chronicle*, December 18, 1937.

171. D. M. Reynolds to Hoover, December 20, 1937, HP-PPI.

172. See, for example, Hulbert Taft to Landon, December 22, 1937, Landon Papers.

173. Hoover to Colby, December 23, 1937, HP-PPI.

174. Hoover to Lane, December 15, 1937, ibid.

175. For example, Shaw to Hoover, December 28, 1937, ibid.

176. For example, Hoover to H. Alexander Smith, December 28, 1937, HPHI.

177. Hoover to Smith, January 3, 1938, ibid.

178. Hoover to Smith, January 11, 1938, ibid.

179. Reprinted in Hoover, *Addresses Upon the American Road, 1933–38*, pp. 300–308.

180. Ibid.

181. Fish to Hoover, telegram, January 17, 1938, HP-PPI.

182. Hoover to John Hartigan, September 19, 1935, ibid.

183. Edgar Rickard Diary, November 12, 1936.

184. Ibid., December 7, 1936.

185. Hoover to Verne Marshall, January 20, 1938, HP-PPI.

186. Hoover to Smith, January 25, 1938, HPHI.

187. Snell to Hoover, January 27, 1938, HP-PPI.

188. Fletcher to Landon, January 31, 1938, Landon Papers.

189. Hoover to H. Alexander Smith, February 28, 1938, HPHI.

190. "Interview by the London Press with Hoover, March 18, 1938," Public Statements, 1938, Hoover Papers.

191. Accounts of the trip are given in Suda Bane, "Mr. Hoover's European Trip, 1938," and Perrin Galpin, "Through Europe with Mr. Hoover," both unpublished, in HP-PPS.

192. Reprinted in Hoover, *Addresses Upon the American Road, 1933–38*, pp. 309–24.

193. Ibid.

194. Hoover to Ditter, telegram, April 1, 1938, HP-PPI.

195. "Press Interview in Chicago, April 4, 1938," Public Statements, 1938, Hoover Papers.

196. "Press Interview in San Francisco, April 7, 1938," ibid.

197. William E. Leuchtenburg, *Franklin D. Roosevelt and the New Deal* (New York, 1963), p. 279.

198. Hoover to Snell, April 10, 1938, HP-PPI.

199. Hoover to Castle, April 9, 1938, ibid.

200. Reprinted in Hoover, *Addresses Upon the American Road, 1933–38*, pp. 325–44.

201. Hoover to Wilson, April 25, 1938, Hugh Wilson Papers, Hoover Presidential Library.

202. Wilson to Hoover, May 11, 1938, ibid.

203. Reppy to Hoover, April 5, 1938, HP-PPI.

204. White to Hoover, April 4, 1938, White Papers.

205. Clapper to White, April 11, 1938, ibid.

206. Reprinted in Hoover, *Addresses Upon the American Road, 1933–38*, pp. 335–42.

207. Ibid., pp. 343–54.

208. For example, H. Alexander Smith to Hoover, June 9, 1938, HPHI.

209. Frank to Hoover, telegram, June 20, 1938, HP-PPI.

210. Hoover to H. Alexander Smith, June 26, 1938, HPHI; Hoover to Frank, June 26, 1938, HP-PPI.

211. Smith to Hoover, July 5, 1938, HPHI.

212. Hoover to Mussatti and others, July 27, 1938, HP-PPI.

213. See, for example, William Gross to Hoover, August 5, 1938, ibid.

214. A copy of the declaration is in "Campaign, 1938–39," HP-PPS.

215. H. Alexander Smith to Hoover, August 15, 1938, HPHI, and Arch Shaw to Hoover, August 26, 1938, HP-PPI.

216. Rowell to Hoover, August 14, 1938, HP-PPI.

217. Hoover to William Gross, August 11, 1938, ibid.

218. Hoover to Arch Shaw, August 15, 1938, ibid.

219. Hoover to Shaw, August 27, 1938, ibid.

220. Hoover to Sullivan, July 16, 1938, Sullivan Papers.

221. Hoover to Spargo, August 11, 1938, Spargo Papers.

222. Spargo to Hoover, August 31, 1938, ibid.

223. Address of August 6, 1938, in Public Statements, 1938, Hoover Papers.

224. Will Irwin, "Herbert Hoover Tells 'What America Must Do Next,' " article for *American Magazine*, July 16, 1938, in Public Statements, 1938, ibid.

225. Hoover to Paul Sexson, August 11, 1938, HP-PPI.

226. Hoover to Chandler, August 24, 1938, ibid.

227. Reprinted in Herbert Hoover, *Further Addresses Upon the American Road, 1938–40* (New York, 1940), pp. 3–20.

228. Ibid., pp. 21–38.

229. Ibid., pp. 39–57.

230. Ibid.

231. Ibid., pp. 85–92.

232. See John B. Canning to Hoover, October 21, 1938, HP-PPI.

233. Hoover to Sanborn Young, September 3, 1938, ibid.

234. Hoover to Paul Smith, telegram, October 29, 1938, and Wilbur to Hoover, October 31, 1938, ibid.

235. Hoover to Bernice Miller, telegram, November 4, 1938, ibid.

236. For example, Landon to Don Berry, November 16, 1938, Landon Papers.

237. For example, Will Irwin to Hoover, November 12, 1938, and Hoover to Irwin, November 16, 1938, HP-PPI.

CHAPTER 4

1. Hoover to Miles Jones, November 15, 1938, HP-PPI.

2. Press statement of November 9, 1938, Public Statements, 1938, Hoover Papers.

3. Hoover to William Honnold, November 12, 1938, HP-PPI.

4. Mencken to White, November 23, 1938, White Papers.

5. Hoover to Will Irwin, November 16, 1938, Irwin Papers.

6. Julius Klein to Hoover, November 14, 1938, Klein Papers.

7. For Hoover's attempts to reestablish relations with Landon see Castle to Hoover, October 18, 1938, and Hoover to Castle, October 19, 1938, HP-PPI.

8. Edgar Rickard Diary, October 27, 1938.

9. Strauss to Hoover, December 23, 1938, HP-PPI.

10. Hoover to Walter Lichtenstein, October 3, 1938, ibid.

11. Reprinted in Herbert Hoover, *Further Addresses Upon the American Road, 1938–40* (New York, 1940), pp. 93–103.

12. Ibid.
13. Chandler to Hoover, February 7, 1939, HP-PPI.
14. Libby to Hoover, telegram, February 13, 1939, ibid.
15. See Hoover to Castle, December 12, 1938, and Castle to Hoover, December 12, 1938, ibid.
16. Congressman W. G. Andrews to Hoover, January 23, 1939, ibid.
17. Bridges to Hoover, February 18, 1939, ibid.
18. Quoted in Everett Colby to Hoover, February 23, 1939, ibid.
19. Hoover to O'Laughlin, March 25, 1939, O'Laughlin Papers.
20. Hoover to O'Laughlin, April 14, 1939, ibid.
21. Hoover to Myers, December 28, 1938, HP-PPI.
22. James Selvage to Hoover, January 24, 1939, ibid.
23. Reprinted in Hoover, *Further Addresses Upon the American Road, 1938–40*, pp. 58–68.
24. Edgar Rickard Diary, February 22, 1939.
25. Landon to John Henry, August 28, 1939, Landon Papers.
26. Hoover to Dewey, March 10, 1939, HP-PPI; Donald R. McCoy, *Landon of Kansas* (Lincoln, 1966), pp. 417–18.
27. For Simpson's activities, see Judith Stein, "The Impact of the New Deal on New York Politics: Kenneth Simpson and the Republican Party," *The New York Historical Society Quarterly* 56 (January 1972): 29–53; McCoy, *Landon of Kansas*, p. 401.
28. Dewey to White, July 1, 1939, and White to Dewey, July 5, 1939, White Papers.
29. Jacob Allen to Ben Allen, January 22, 1939, HP-PPI.
30. Mott to Hoover, February 23, 1939, ibid.
31. Hoover to Hyde, telegram, March 11, 1939, ibid.
32. Ben Allen to James Selvage, April 11, 1939, ibid.
33. Edgar Rickard Diary, December 15, 1938; Mallon to Selvage, April 7, 1939, HP-PPI.
34. Selvage to Mallon, April 8, 1939, HP-PPI.
35. Hoover to Wilbur D. Matson, April 11, 1939, ibid.
36. Spangler to Hoover, April 17, 1939, and Hoover to Spangler, April 19, 1939, ibid.
37. See, for example, Rowell to Hoover, January 10, 1939, and August 2, 1939, and Hoover to Rowell, November 11, 1939, ibid.
38. Hoover to James Goodrich, April 25, 1939, ibid.
39. See, for example, Will Loomis to Justus F. Craemer, May 22, 1939, copy in ibid.
40. Hoover to Wesley Stout, March 18, 1939, ibid.
41. Reprinted in Hoover, *Further Addresses Upon the American Road, 1938–40*, pp. 104–115.

42. Ibid.

43. Edgar Rickard Diary, May 31, 1939.

44. Ben Allen to James Selvage, April 11, 1939, HP-PPI; Frank Fetzer to Ben Allen, June 12, 21, and 27, 1939, Ben Allen Papers, Hoover Institution on War, Revolution and Peace.

45. Hoover to Campbell, June 24, 1939, and Campbell to Hoover, June 30, 1939, HP-PPI.

46. Hoover to Moore, August 28, 1939, ibid.

47. Reprinted in Hoover, *Further Addresses Upon the American Road, 1938–40*, pp. 197–207.

48. Ibid., pp. 208–14.

49. Edgar Rickard Diary, June 5, 1939; Hoover to Mark Sullivan, June 21, 1939, Sullivan Papers.

50. Hoover to Reppy, June 23, 1939, HP-PPI.

51. Edgar Rickard Diary, June 7, 1939.

52. Ibid., May 17 and 23, 1939.

53. Ibid., July 30, 1939.

54. Hoover to Hogan, July 31, 1939, HP-PPI.

55. Hogan to Ben Allen, telegram, August 4, 1939, ibid.

56. Hoover to Ashmun Brown, August 11, 1939, ibid.

57. Reprinted in Hoover, *Further Addresses Upon the American Road, 1938–40*, pp. 116–28.

58. Hoover to Getrude Lane, June 27, 1939, HP-PPI.

59. Reprinted in Hoover, *Further Addresses Upon the American Road, 1938–40*, pp. 129–38.

60. Durant to Hoover, July 6, 1939, HP-PPI.

61. O'Laughlin to Hoover, July 8, 1939, O'Laughlin Papers.

62. See, for example, Hoover to Senator Capper, July 14, 1939, HP-PPI.

63. Hoover to O'Laughlin, July 18, 1939, O'Laughlin Papers.

64. Paul Shoup to Hoover, July 24, 1939, HP-PPI.

65. Hoover to Shoup, July 31, 1939, ibid.

66. Hoover to O'Laughlin, August 28, 1939, O'Laughlin Papers.

67. Statement of September 1, 1939, Public Statements, 1939, Hoover Papers.

68. Hoover to O'Laughlin, August 7, 1939, O'Laughlin Papers.

69. "Bart" to "Dave," August 24, 1939, Robert A. Taft Papers.

70. Nathan MacChesney to Frank Knox, August 11, 1939, MacChesney Papers, Hoover Presidential Library.

71. Hoover to Boake Carter, August 16, 1939, and Hoover to Frank Kent and O'Laughlin, August 16, 1939, all in HP-PPI.

72. Kent to Hoover, August 31. 1939, ibid.

73. Hoover to Kent, August 27, 1939, ibid.

74. Hoover to Newton, September 3, 1939, ibid.
75. Simmons to Hoover, August 18, 1939, ibid.
76. Selvage to Hoover, August 22, 1939, ibid.
77. Hoover to Selvage, August 27, 1939, ibid.
78. Hoover to Simmons, August 28, 1939, ibid.
79. Edgar Rickard Diary, September 13, 1939, through September 15, 1939.
80. Ibid., September 14, and 19, 1939; that the suggestion originated with Roosevelt is clear, but that Hoover's interpretation of its motive was correct is not. See Harold L. Ickes, *The Secret Diary of Harold L. Ickes* (New York, 1954), vol. 3, p. 9.
81. Edgar Rickard Diary, September 21, 1939.
82. Gross to Hoover, September 9, 1939, HP-PPI.
83. John Henry to Landon, September 8, 1939, Landon Papers.
84. Hoover to Castle, September 14, 1939, HP-PPI.
85. Ibid.
86. Hoover to O'Laughlin, September 4, 1939, O'Laughlin Papers.
87. Jacob Allen to Ben Allen, September 11, 1939, HP-PPI.
88. Jacob Allen to Hoover, September 20, 1939, ibid.
89. Hoover to Allen, September 16, 1939, ibid.
90. Ibid.
91. Jacob Allen to Hoover, September 20, 1939, ibid.
92. Hoover to Allen, September 29, 1939, ibid.
93. Edgar Rickard Diary, October 4, 1939.
94. For this description of Robinson, see *New York Times,* October 8, 1932.
95. See Mattei to Hoover, May 9, 1938, and articles of incorporation for Constitutional Publications, Inc., therein, HP-PPI. Robinson had died in 1937.
96. See, for example, Hoover to Kellogg, January 7, 1942, ibid.
97. See Hoover to James Howell, September 7, 1939, Howell to Hoover, September 12, 1939, and Hoover to Howell, September 14, 1939, ibid.
98. George H. Lobdell, Jr., "A Biography of Frank Knox" (Ph.D. diss., University of Illinois, 1954), pp. 301–3; Steven M. Mark, "An American Interventionist: Frank Knox and United States Foreign Relations" (Ph.D. diss., University of Maryland, 1977), pp. 215–17.
99. Hoover to Tobey, September 27, 1939, HP-PPI.
100. Hoover to Tobey, another letter of September 27. 1939, ibid.
101. For the story of Hoover's World War II–related relief activities, see Herbert Hoover, *An American Epic* (Chicago, 1964), vol. 4, pp. 1–97.
102. See, for example, Frank Kent to Hoover, September 7, 1939, HP-PPI; Edgar Rickard Diary, September 20, 1939.
103. Hoover to Herter, September 14, 1939, HP-PPI.

104. Reprinted in Hoover, *Further Addresses Upon the American Road, 1938–40*, pp. 139–57.

105. Interview of October 3, 1939, with Roy Howard, in Public Statements, 1939, Hoover Papers.

106. Hoover to Leland W. Cutler, October 5, 1939, HP-PPI.

107. Edgar Rickard Diary, October 7, 1939.

108. Ibid., October 10, 1939.

109. See, for example, William Gross to Hoover, October 5, 1939, HP-PPI.

110. Bridges to Hoover, October 10, 1939, ibid.

111. Hoover to Bridges, October 11, 1939, ibid.

112. Memorandum on neutrality bill, October 11, 1939, in Public Statements, 1939, Hoover Papers.

113. Newsreel re embargo repeal, October 11, 1939, ibid.

114. White to Hoover, October 11, 1939, White Papers.

115. Vandenberg to MacChesney, October 19, 1939, MacChesney Papers.

116. Hoover to Vandenberg, October 12, 1939, HP-PPI.

117. Vandenberg to Hoover, October 13, 1939, ibid.

118. O'Laughlin to Hoover, October 14, 1939, O'Laughlin Papers; Edgar Rickard Diary, October 13, 1939.

119. MacChesney to Vandenberg, October 16, 1939, MacChesney Papers.

120. Edgar Rickard Diary, October 16, 1939; Hoover to Gross, telegram, October 17, 1939, HP-PPI.

121. Hoover to Vandenberg, October 17, 1939, HP-PPI.

122. Neutrality bill broadcast, October 20, 1939, Public Statements, 1939, Hoover Papers.

123. Edgar Rickard Diary, October 19, 1939.

124. William Gross to Hoover, October 20, 1939, HP-PPI.

125. Hoover to Gross, October 21, 1939, ibid.

126. Edgar Rickard Diary, October 23, 1939; Hoover to O'Laughlin, October 23, 1939, O'Laughlin Papers.

127. Edgar Rickard Diary, October 23, 1939.

128. Hoover to Shaw, October 28, 1939, HP-PPI.

129. Knox to White, October 27, 1939, White Papers.

130. Shaw to Hoover, October 30, 1939, HP-PPI.

131. Landon to White, October 30, 1939, White Papers.

132. Landon to White, November 2, 1939, ibid.

133. McCoy, *Landon of Kansas*, p. 419.

134. William P. Langer and S. Everett Gleason, *The Challenge to Isolation: The World Crisis of 1937–1940 and American Foreign Policy* (New York, 1952), pp. 230–31.

135. Vandenberg to Hoover, November 6, 1939, HP-PPI.
136. Hoover to O'Laughlin, November 6, 1939, O'Laughlin Papers.
137. Hoover to Vandenberg, November 7, 1939, HP-PPI.
138. Hoover to O'Laughlin, November 22, 1939, O'Laughlin Papers.
139. Edgar Rickard Diary, October 6, 1939.
140. Fox to Hoover, October 31, 1939, HP-PPI.
141. Fox to Larry Richey, November 3, 1939, ibid.
142. Fox to Hoover, November 26, 1939, ibid.
143. Hoover to Fox, December 27, 1939, ibid.
144. Willard to Hoover, November 3, 1939, and Hoover to Willard, November 19, 1939, ibid.
145. L. O. Hartman to Hoover, November 20, 1939, ibid.
146. Hoover to Hartman, November 26, 1939, ibid.
147. Davis to Hoover, November 23, 1939, ibid.
148. In "Peace Proposal" file, HP-PPS.
149. Hoover to Kenneth Simpson, December 3, 1939, HP-PPI.
150. Hoover to Rickard, December 5, 1939, NCFSD.
151. Interview with *Editor and Publisher*, December 23, 1939, Public Statements, 1939, Hoover Papers.
152. Edgar Rickard Diary, December 16, 1939.
153. Ibid., December 31, 1939.
154. Ibid., January 3, 1940.

CHAPTER 5

1. See, for example, Hyde to Hoover, December 15, 1939, HP-PPI.
2. See, for example, MacChesney to Monte Appel, December 15, 1939, and Appel to MacChesney, December 16, 1939, MacChesney Papers.
3. Hoover to Kirchhofer, January 1, 1940, HP-PPI.
4. Taft to Hoover, January 25, 1940, ibid.
5. William P. Langer and S. Everett Gleason, *The Challenge to Isolation: The World Crisis of 1937–1940 and American Foreign Policy* (New York, 1952), pp. 337–38.
6. Edgar Rickard Diary, February 4, 1940.
7. Fox to Hoover, February 1, 1940, HP-PPI.
8. Fox to Hoover, February 8, 1940, ibid.
9. Results of Lewis Strauss polls, February 14, 1940, and Queens postcard poll, February 14, 1940, both in "Campaign, 1940," HP-PPS.
10. Gross to Hoover, February 16, 1940, HP-PPI.
11. Edgar Rickard Diary, February 22, 1940.

12. Reprinted in Herbert Hoover, *Further Addresses Upon the American Road, 1938–40* (New York, 1940), pp. 69–81.
13. Hoover to Sewell Avery, November 4, 1939, HP-PPI.
14. Jacob Allen to Hoover, December 15, 1939, ibid.
15. Allen to Hoover, telegram, December 16, 1939, ibid.
16. Allen to Hoover, December 18, 1939, ibid.
17. Mott to Hoover, January 23, 1940, Jacob Allen to Hoover, January 23, 1940, Mott to Hoover, February 5, 1940, ibid.
18. Hoover to Mott, February 8, 1940, ibid.
19. Harold Jones to David Ingalls, February 15, 1940, Taft Papers.
20. Undated memo, David Ingalls to John Henry, ibid.
21. See, for example, Hoover to Herbert Clark, February 7, 1940, and Hoover to Robert Simmons, telegram, February 17, 1940, HP-PPI.
22. Hoover to Arch Shaw, February 19, 1940, ibid.
23. Hoover to Gross, February 19, 1940, ibid.
24. *Washington Evening Star*, February 29, 1940.
25. Edgar Rickard Diary, February 29, 1940.
26. Ibid., March 21, 1940.
27. Hoover to Rickard, April 2, 1940, NCFSD.
28. Edgar Rickard Diary, March 10, 1940.
29. Fox to Hoover, March 4, 1940, HP-PPI.
30. Fox to Hoover, March 25, 1940, ibid.
31. See, for example, W. B. Daugherty to Hoover, March 27, 1940, and Thomas Campbell to Hoover, April 5, 1940, ibid.
32. Edgar Rickard Diary, April 9, 1940.
33. Hoover to Ross Laird, April 13, 1940, HP-PPI.
34. Hoover to Ben Allen, April 13, 1940, Ben Allen Papers; memorandum for Allen, April 22, 1940, HP-PPI.
35. Victoria Allen to Hoover, May 6, 1940, ibid.
36. Memorandum for Ben Allen, April 22, 1940, ibid.
37. H. Alexander Smith to Hoover, May 8, 1940, HPHI.
38. William Starr Myers to Hoover, April 9, 1940, HP-PPI.
39. Edgar Rickard Diary, April 12 and 15, 1940.
40. Ibid., April 17, 1940.
41. Hoover to Hyde, April 15, 1940, HP-PPI.
42. Selvage to Gross, April 19, 1940, copy in ibid.
43. Rickard to Spargo, April 22, 1940, Spargo Papers.
44. Bullington to Larry Richey, May 30, 1940, HP-PPI.
45. Note of April 27, 1940, in "Campaign, 1940," HP-PPS.
46. Note of April 25, 1940, concerning telephone conversation with Bricker, ibid.

47. Calvin Zimmerman to Hoover, April 27, 1940, HP-PPI.
48. Edgar Rickard Diary, April 30, 1940.
49. Memoranda of April 28 and 29, 1940, in O'Laughlin Papers.
50. Vandenberg to O'Laughlin, April 29, 1940, and O'Laughlin to Hoover, April 30, 1940, ibid.
51. Reprinted in Hoover, *Further Addresses Upon the American Road, 1938–40*, pp. 158–71.
52. Vandenberg to Hoover, April 23, 1940, HP-PPI.
53. Hoover to Vandenberg, April 24, 1940, ibid.
54. See, for example, Vandenberg to Hoover, April 25, 1940, ibid.
55. Edgar Rickard Diary, May 3, 6, 9, and 11, 1940.
56. Laird to Herbert Clark, May 19, 1940, HP-PPI.
57. Laird to Richey, May 24, 1940, ibid.
58. Edgar Rickard Diary, May 14, 16, and 20, 1940.
59. Hoover to John Brown, May 4, 1940, HP-PPI.
60. See, for example, Paul Shoup to Hoover, May 4, 1940, ibid.
61. Hoover to Newton, May 11, 1940, ibid.
62. Edgar Rickard Diary, May 26, 1940.
63. Ibid., May 29, 1940.
64. Sullivan to Hoover, May 2, 1940, HP-PPI.
65. Hoover to Sullivan, May 3, 1940, ibid.
66. Hoover to John Brown, May 4, 1940, ibid.
67. Arthur B. Dunne to Taft, May 24, 1940, Taft Papers.
68. See, for example, Laird to Richey, May 28, 1940, concerning Oregon, HP-PPI.
69. Taft to Arthur B. Dunne, May 31, 1940, Taft Papers.
70. Brochure in "Food for the Small Democracies," HP-PPS.
71. See, for example, memoranda of telephone conversations between Hoover and Norman Davis of the Red Cross, ibid.
72. Kellogg to Hoover, July 25, 1940, and Hoover to Kellogg, July 29, 1940, HP-PPI.
73. Press statement of May 17, 1940, in Public Statements, 1940, Hoover Papers.
74. Hoover to Martin, May 17, 1940, HP-PPI.
75. Statement of May 29, 1940, in Public Statements, 1940, Hoover Papers.
76. Pamphlet, "Political Outlook for 1940," by Opinion Research Corporation, May 21, 1940, in "Campaign 1940," HP-PPS.
77. Edgar Rickard Diary, June 3, 1940.
78. Ibid., June 4, 1940.
79. Ibid., June 6 and 7, 1940.

80. Ibid., June 10, 1940.

81. Ibid., June 11, 1940.

82. Miles W. Jones to Hoover, June 8 and 14, 1940, HP-PPI.

83. Hoover to Bricker, June 7, 1940, ibid.

84. "The Nine Horsemen and America," in *Liberty Magazine*, June 5, 1940, Public Statements, 1940, Hoover Papers.

85. Mundt to Hoover, June 8, 1940, HP-PPI.

86. *San Francisco Chronicle*, June 26, 1940.

87. *New York Times*, June 14, 1940.

88. Ibid., June 18, 1940.

89. Ibid., June 19, 1940.

90. Richey to Tobey, telegram, May 20, 1940, and Charles W. Tobey, Jr., to Hoover, May 23, 1940, HP-PPI.

91. Hoover to Tobey, May 24, 1940, ibid.

92. *New York Times*, June 21, 1940.

93. Ibid.

94. Press release of June 21, 1940, Public Statements, 1940, Hoover Papers.

95. Hoover to Robert Simmons, June 7, 1940, HP-PPI.

96. Simmons to Hoover, June 7, 1940, ibid.

97. Hoover to Simmons, June 11, 1940, ibid.

98. Herter to Richey, June 11, 1940, ibid.

99. Queeny to Hoover, June 13, 1940, ibid.

100. Edgar Rickard Diary, June 21, 1940.

101. See, for example, Charles Hebberd to Hoover, June 5, 1940, and Hebberd to Richey, June 15, 1940, HP-PPI.

102. Carlyle S. Littleton to Hoover, June 21, 1940, ibid.

103. Memorandum for Hoover, June 21, 1940, in Perrin Galpin Papers, Hoover Institution on War, Revolution and Peace.

104. *New York Times*, June 13, 16, and 18, 1940.

105. Ibid., June 18, 1940.

106. Ibid., June 19, 1940.

107. Ibid., June 20, 1940.

108. Ibid., June 23, 1940.

109. Ibid., June 25, 1940.

110. Interview with Samuel F. Pryor by the author, July 9, 1980. Pryor's reference to television is correct, since the 1940 GOP convention was the first political event ever telecast. See *New York Times*, June 22, 1940.

111. In Public Statements, 1940, Hoover Papers.

112. Ibid.

113. *New York Times*, June 26, 1940.

114. Ibid.

115. Ibid.

116. James P. Selvage oral history, Hoover Presidential Library.

117. Edgar Rickard Diary, June 28, 1940.

118. Interview with Samuel F. Pryor, July 9, 1980, by the author. Pryor also denied any involvement in the "packing" of the galleries with Willkie supporters.

119. *New York Times*, June 26, 1940.

120. Ibid., June 27, 1940. George Mayer has described this as "an extreme anti-war plank," but it was no more so than the plank in the Democrats' own platform. George H. Mayer, "The Republican Party, 1932–1952," in Arthur M. Schlesinger, Jr., ed., *History of U.S. Political Parties* (New York, 1973), vol. 3, p. 2279. The Democratic platform is given on pp. 2032–2033 of the same volume.

121. In Public Statements, 1940, Hoover Papers.

122. *New York Times*, June 27, 1940.

123. Edgar Rickard Diary, June 26 and 27, 1940.

124. Ibid., June 27, 1940.

125. *New York Times*, June 28, 1940.

126. Ibid.

127. Dewey oral history, Hoover Presidential Library.

128. Edgar Rickard Diary, June 28, 1940.

129. Fox to Hoover, August 6, 1940, HP-PPI.

130. Edgar Rickard Diary, June 28, 1940.

131. John D. M. Hamilton oral history, Hoover Presidential Library.

132. McCoy, *Landon of Kansas*, p. 443.

133. Edgar Rickard Diary, June 29, 1940.

134. Brown to Hoover, July 1, 1940, HP-PPI.

135. Mott to Hoover, July 11, 1940, ibid.

136. *New York Times*, June 28, 1940.

137. Ibid., July 1, 1940.

138. Hoover to Dewey, July 17, 1940, HP-PPI.

139. Edgar Rickard Diary, July 1, 1940.

140. H. Alexander Smith to Hoover, July 12, 1940, HPHI; Simmons to Hoover, July 1, 1940, HP-PPI.

141. See, for example, Hoover to Justus Craemer, July 17, 1940, HP-PPI. The reference is to Leon Blum, premier of the leftist popular front regime that governed France in 1936 and 1937.

142. Hoover to Brown, July 26, 1940, ibid.

143. Memorandum of August 15, 1940, in O'Laughlin Papers.

144. Hoover to O'Laughlin, August 14, 1940, ibid.

145. Hoover to Gross, August 15, 1940, HP-PPI.

146. Hoover to James Wright, August 19, 1940, ibid.

147. Edgar Rickard Diary, August 24, 1940; Hoover to Saxon, August 24, 1940, HP-PPI.

148. Hoover to Newton, August 26, 1940, HP-PPI; Edgar Rickard Diary, September 11 and 12, 1940.

149. Hoover to Sam Crowther, August 27, 1940, HP-PPI.

150. White to Hoover, August 31, 1940, White Papers.

151. Hoover to O'Laughlin, August 5, 1940, O'Laughlin Papers.

152. Memorandum of August 15, 1940, in ibid.

153. Hoover to O'Laughlin, August 15, 1940, ibid.

154. Statement of September 4, 1940, in Public Statements, 1940, Hoover Papers.

155. Ibid.

156. *New York Times*, September 20, 1940.

157. Ibid., September 19, 1940.

158. Ibid., September 20, 1940.

159. Edgar Rickard Diary, September 20 and 28, 1940.

160. O'Laughlin to Hoover, September 27, 1940, O'Laughlin Papers.

161. Edgar Rickard Diary, September 28 and 29, 1940.

162. Hoover to Simmons, September 29, 1940, HP-PPI.

163. Edgar Rickard Diary, October 11, 1940; Hoover to Gross, October 7, 1940, HP-PPI.

164. Hoover to O'Laughlin, October 11, 1940, O'Laughlin Papers.

165. In Public Statements, 1940, Hoover Papers.

166. Ibid.

167. Hoover to O'Laughlin, October 30, 1940, O'Laughlin Papers.

168. In Public Statements, 1940, Hoover Papers.

169. Ibid.

170. Hoover to Hugh Gibson, October 4, 1940, NCFSD.

171. Edgar Rickard Diary, August 20, 1940.

172. White to Hoover, October 24, 1940, White Papers.

173. Hoover to Kenneth Wherry, November 4, 1940, HP-PPI.

174. Edgar Rickard Diary, November 6, 1940.

175. Hoover to Mrs. Harold Brunson, November 7, 1940, HP-PPI.

176. Hoover to Gross, November 7, 1940, ibid.

177. Hoover to John Quinn, November 7, 1940, ibid.

178. Hoover to Sullivan, November 9, 1940, Sullivan Papers.

CHAPTER 6

1. Hoover to Hyde, November 19, 1940, NCFSD.
2. Hoover to Hendrik W. Van Loon, November 19, 1940, ibid.
3. Hoover to Bison, November 29, 1940, ibid.
4. See folders of correspondence for November and December, 1940, ibid.
5. Hoover to O'Laughlin, telegram, December 3, 1940, and O'Laughlin to Hoover, December 5, 1940, O'Laughlin Papers.
6. Hoover to Castle, December 20, 1940, NCFSD.
7. "Memorandum of a meeting with Ambassador Joseph Kennedy, November 22, 1940," Kennedy file, HP-PPI.
8. Hoover to Stuart, December 6, 1940, ibid.
9. Hoover to Taft, January 6, 1941, ibid.
10. Reprinted in Herbert Hoover, *Addresses Upon the American Road, 1940–41* (New York, 1941), p.63.
11. Hoover to Bloom, January 15, 1941, HP-PPI; also reprinted in ibid., pp. 63–64.
12. Hoover to Taft, January 6, 1941, HP-PPI.
13. Hoover to Newton, January 25, 1941, ibid.
14. Robert Wood to Hoover, telegram, January 11, 1941, Robert Wood Papers, Hoover Presidential Library; R. Douglas Stuart to Hoover, January 13, 1941, HP-PPI.
15. Hoover to Wood, January 14, 1941, Wood Papers.
16. Donald R. McCoy, *Landon of Kansas* (Lincoln, 1966), pp. 456–57; see also Burton K. Wheeler to Landon, telegram, January 13, 1941, Landon Papers.
17. Clapper to Landon, January 16, 1941, Landon Papers.
18. Landon to Clapper, January 20, 1941, ibid.
19. Spargo to Hoover, January 16, 1941, Spargo Papers.
20. Hoover to Vandenberg, January 24, 1941, HPHI.
21. Vandenberg to Hoover, January 27, 1941, ibid.
22. Hoover to O'Laughlin, January 26, 1941, O'Laughlin Papers.
23. Gross to Hoover, telegram, November 8, 1940, HP-PPI.
24. Statement of November 11, 1940, in Public Statements, 1940, Hoover Papers.
25. Ben Allen to Hoover, November 13, 1940, HP-PPI.
26. Hoover to Gross, November 17, 1940, ibid.
27. Kenneth Wherry to Hoover, November 19, 1940, ibid.
28. Herbert Clark to Hoover, November 26, 1940, and Hoover to Clark, November 28, 1940, ibid.
29. See, for example, Senator Capper to Landon, January 23, 1941, and February 1, 1941, Landon Papers.
30. See, for example, Julius Klein to Hoover, January 29, 1941, and Klein to Hoover, February 1, 1941, with clippings, HP-PPI.

31. Landon to Capper, January 4, 1941, Landon Papers.

32. Taft to Landon, telegram, February 5, 1941, and Landon to Taft, telegram, February 8, 1941, ibid.

33. See, for example, Hoover to O'Laughlin, February 2, 1941, and O'Laughlin to Hoover, February 3, 1941, O'Laughlin Papers.

34. See, for example, Hoover to Taft, February 18, 1941, HP-PPI.

35. Edgar Rickard Diary, January 30, 1941.

36. Hoover to O'Laughlin, February 18, 1941, O'Laughlin Papers.

37. Hoover to Castle, March 1, 1941, William R. Castle Papers, Hoover Presidential Library.

38. *United States Statutes at Large*, 77th Congress, 1st sess., vol. 55, part 1, pp. 31–33.

39. Memorandum from William H. Tuck to Hoover, January 24, 1941, William H. Tuck Papers, Hoover Institution on War, Revolution and Peace.

40. Hoover to Van Loon, February 21, 1941, NCFSD.

41. Hoover memorandum, February 21, 1941, ibid.

42. Hoover to O'Laughlin, February 23, 1941, O'Laughlin Papers.

43. O'Laughlin to Hoover, February 24, 1941, ibid.

44. Reprinted in Hoover, *Addresses Upon the American Road, 1940–41*, pp. 147–55.

45. "Memorandum of a Meeting with Hull at 9:30 on February 28, 1941," Hull file, HP-PPI.

46. Edgar Rickard Diary, February 28, 1941.

47. Robert L. Bliss to Hoover, March 5, 1941, HP-PPI.

48. Edgar Rickard Diary, March 7, 1941.

49. Reprinted in Hoover, *Addresses Upon the American Road, 1940–41*, pp. 156–61.

50. Edgar Rickard Diary, March 25, 1941.

51. Hoover memorandum of March 26, 1941, in NCFSD.

52. Hoover to Hull, March 27, 1941, ibid.

53. Edgar Rickard Diary, March 28, 1941.

54. Ibid., March 31, 1941, and April 10, 1941.

55. Ibid., April 25, 1941.

56. Hoover to O'Laughlin, March 9, 1941, O'Laughlin Papers.

57. Landon to Franklyn Waltman, March 21, 1941, Landon Papers.

58. Castle to Hoover, March 19, 1941, Castle Papers.

59. Hoover to Castle, March 20, 1941, ibid.

60. Reprinted in Hoover, *Addresses Upon the American Road, 1940–41*, pp. 66–76.

61. Hoover to Crowther, April 1, 1941, HP-PPI.

62. Jay Darling to Mark Sullivan, April 2, 1941, ibid.

63. Hoover to Ben Allen, April 2, 1941, ibid.
64. Hoover to Hyde, April 5, 1941, ibid.
65. Draft letter by Hoover, April 7, 1941, in O'Laughlin Papers.
66. Hoover to O'Laughlin, April 7, 1941, ibid.
67. "A Survey of the American Scene Today," undated memorandum by Hoover in ibid.
68. Hoover to Tobey, May 9, 1941, HP-PPI.
69. Reprinted in Hoover, *Addresses Upon the American Road, 1940–41*, pp. 77–86.
70. Hoover to Dawes, May 1, 1941, and Dawes to Hoover, May 12, 1941, HP-PPI.
71. Wiley to Hoover, May 13, 1941, ibid.
72. Moley to Hoover, May 17, 1941, ibid.
73. Wood to Hoover, May 26, 1941, ibid.
74. *New York Times*, June 23, 1941; the *Wall Street Journal* of June 25, 1941, expressed similar sentiments in describing the Russo–German conflict as between "Tweedledum and Tweedledee."
75. "Broadcast by Robert A. Taft over CBS, 6–25–1941," in Taft file, HP-PPI.
76. Reprinted in Hoover, *Addresses Upon the American Road, 1940–41*, pp. 87–102.
77. A memorandum of the conversation is in "Book Manuscript Material— MEMOIRS V. III Sixth Edition—1949 (Post–Volume 3)," pp. 95–96.
78. Hoover to O'Laughlin, June 26, 1941, O'Laughlin Papers.
79. Hoover to Hyde, June 6, 1941, HP-PPI.
80. William H. Tuck to Hugh Gibson, April 14, 1941, Tuck Papers.
81. Hoover to Bellamy, May 2, 1941, and to Ben Allen, June 4, 1941, HP-PPI.
82. Hoover to Hull, June 3, 1941, NCFSD.
83. Hull to Hoover, June 28, 1941, HP-PPI.
84. Paul D. Boone to Landon, May 28, 1941, Landon Papers.
85. Knox to Landon, "received June 11, 1941," ibid.
86. Landon to Knox, June 16, 1941, ibid.
87. Hoover to Landon, June 27, 1941, HP-PPI.
88. Hutchins to Hoover, June 29, 1941, ibid.
89. Landon to Moley, July 1, 1941, Raymond Moley Papers, Hoover Institution on War, Revolution and Peace; Landon to Cliff Stratton, July 1, 1941, Landon Papers; Hoover to Landon, July 1, 1941, Kennedy to Hoover, July 1, 1941, and Hutchins to Hoover, telegram, July 1, 1941, HP-PPI.
90. Landon to Hoover, July 7, 1941, HP-PPI.
91. Hoover to Hutchins, telegram, July 11, 1941, Hoover to Morley, telegram, July 11, 1941, Landon to Hoover, July 14, 1941, Hoover to Morley, telegram, July 18, 1941, ibid.

92. Morley to Landon, July 25, 1941, Landon Papers.
93. Landon to Hoover, July 26, 1941, and Kennedy to Hoover, telegram, July 29, 1941, HP-PPI.
94. Landon to Hoover, telegram, August 4, 1941, ibid.
95. *New York Times*, August 6, 1941.
96. Shaw to Hoover, telegram, June 30, 1941, HP-PPI.
97. Hoover to Fulton Lewis, Jr., July 1, 1941, ibid.
98. Taft to Hoover, July 3, 1941, ibid.
99. Edgar Rickard Diary, June 30, 1941.
100. Hoover to Carter, July 14, 1941, HP-PPI.
101. Hoover to Woodruff, July 13, 1941, ibid.
102. Hoover to Taft, July 14, 1941, Taft Papers.
103. Hoover to Ditter, July 14, 1941, HP-PPI.
104. Taft to Hoover, July 16, 1941, ibid.
105. Woodruff to Hoover, July 18, 1941, ibid.
106. Waltman to Landon, July 31, 1941, Landon Papers.
107. Robert Wood to Hoover, August 21, 1941, HP-PPI.
108. Willkie to White, August 29, 1941, and White to Willkie, September 4, 1941, White Papers.
109. "Broadcast of Sunday, July 20, 1941," Landon Papers.
110. In Hoover, *Addresses Upon the American Road, 1940–41*, p. 87.
111. Hoover to Landon, September 4, 1941, HP-PPI.
112. Hoover to Castle, July 23, 1941, ibid.
113. Hoover to Castle, September 4, 1941, ibid.
114. Reprinted in Hoover, *Addresses Upon the American Road, 1940–41*, pp. 103–14.
115. Hoover to Mott, September 12, 1941, HP-PPI.
116. Hoover to Joseph Scott, September 14, 1941, ibid.
117. Hoover to Charles Teague, September 22, 1941, Charles Teague Papers, Hoover Presidential Library.
118. Statement of October 1, 1941, in Public Statements, 1941, Hoover Papers.
119. Mundt to Hoover, October 20, 1941, HP-PPI.
120. Hoover to Mundt, October 21, 1941, ibid.
121. Hoover to Vandenberg, October 29, 1941, ibid.
122. Vandenberg to Hoover, October 31, 1941, ibid.
123. Hoover to Wesley W. Stout, telegram, September 17, 1941, HP-PPI.
124. In Public Statements, 1941, Hoover Papers.
125. Mundt to Hoover, October 30, 1941, HP-PPI.
126. Landon to Hoover, October 28, 1941, Landon Papers.
127. Hoover to Landon, November 1, 1941, ibid.

128. Julius Klein to Ernest Klein, November 3, 1941, Klein Papers.
129. Hoover to White, November 5, 1941, HP-PPI.
130. Hoover to Wood, November 12, 1941, ibid.
131. In Public Statements, 1941, Hoover Papers.
132. Hoover to O'Laughlin, February 8, 1938, O'Laughlin Papers.
133. Hoover to O'Laughlin, July 31, 1939, ibid.
134. Hoover to O'Laughlin, August 5, 1940, ibid.
135. Castle to Hoover, undated, but July 1941, HP-PPI.
136. Hoover to O'Laughlin, August 30, 1941, O'Laughlin Papers.
137. Hoover to Castle, September 4, 1941, HP-PPI.
138. Hoover to O'Laughlin, September 7, 1941, O'Laughlin Papers.
139. Hoover to O'Laughlin, November 16, 1941, ibid.
140. "Pearl Harbor—HH Diary of Events Around," entry for November 23, 1941, HP-PPS. See also, in the same file, memorandum of February 10, 1942, by Hoover.
141. Ibid., November 29, 1941.
142. Ibid., November 30, 1941, and December 1, 1941. According to Baruch's memoirs, it was Ray Moley who phoned him to arrange the meeting with Desvernine. See Bernard M. Baruch, *Baruch: The Public Years* (New York, 1960), pp. 288–91.
143. Ibid., December 2, 3, 4, and 5, 1941.
144. Castle to Hoover, November 2, 1949, HP-PPI.

CHAPTER 7

1. John D. M. Hamilton oral history, Hoover Presidential Library.
2. Hoover to Taft, December 8, 1941, HP-PPI.
3. Press statement of December 8, 1941, Public Statements, 1941, Hoover Papers.
4. Hoover to Boake Carter, December 11, 1941, HP-PPI.
5. Taft to Hoover, December 12, 1941, ibid.
6. Memorandum of April 26, 1945, in "Food—World Wars I & II, Food, Prices, Conserv. & Consumption," HP-PPS.
7. Hoover to Herbert Clark, December 19, 1941, and Hoover to Ruth Simms, December 18, 1941, HP-PPI.
8. Taft to Hoover, January 3, 1942, ibid.
9. Hoover to Wallace Meyer, November 21, 1941, ibid.
10. Whitney Darrow to Hoover, December 23, 1941, ibid.
11. Hoover to Darrow, December 26, 1941, ibid.
12. Hoover to Raymond Moley, January 17, 1942, ibid.
13. Hoover to Clarence Kelland, January 19, 1942, ibid.

14. Bowles to Hoover, September 17, 1941, ibid.

15. Bowles to Hoover, November 28, 1941, ibid.

16. Hoover to Kellogg, January 7, 1942, ibid.; Edgar Rickard Diary, December 30, 1941.

17. Hoover to Dulles, January 21, 1942, HP-PPI.

18. Dulles to Hoover, January 28, 1942, ibid.

19. Hoover to Dulles, February 2, 1942, ibid.

20. Hoover to Jones, February 18, 1942, ibid.

21. Hoover to Jones, February 26, 1942, ibid.

22. Hoover to O'Laughlin, February 24, 1942, O'Laughlin Papers.

23. Hoover to Landon, January 12, 1942, Landon Papers.

24. See, for example, Hoover to Landon, February 16, 1942, re Senator C. Wayland Brooks, ibid.

25. Hoover to O'Laughlin, February 23, 1942, O'Laughlin Papers.

26. Collady to Landon, February 25, 1942, Landon Papers.

27. Taft to Hoover, February 24, 1942, HP-PPI.

28. Landon to Taft, March 3, 1942, Landon Papers.

29. Landon to Hoover, March 7, 1942, ibid.

30. Ibid.

31. Hoover to Mrs. Ogden Reid, March 10, 1942, HP-PPI.

32. Hoover to Gibson, telegram, April 11, 1942, Hugh Gibson Papers, Hoover Institution on War, Revolution and Peace.

33. "Report of Committee on Resolutions," in Taft folder, HP-PPI.

34. Hoover to O'Laughlin, April 22, 1942, O'Laughlin Papers.

35. "Report of Committee on Resolutions," Taft folder, HP-PPI.

36. Reprinted in Herbert Hoover, *Addresses Upon the American Road, 1941–45* (New York, 1945) pp. 160–71.

37. Ibid.

38. Capper to Hoover, May 22, 1942, HP-PPI.

39. Taft to Hoover, May 15, 1942, ibid.

40. Hoover to Landon, May 29, 1942, Landon Papers.

41. Hoover to Landon, June 2, 1942, HP-PPI.

42. Landon to Hoover, June 2, 1942, and Hoover to Landon, June 5, 1942, Landon Papers.

43. Edgar Rickard Diary, April 26, 1942.

44. Ibid., May 2, 1942.

45. Hoover to O'Laughlin, June 5, 1942, O'Laughlin Papers.

46. "An Interesting Parallel," in Welles folder, HP-PPI.

47. Hoover to Wood, June 10, 1942, ibid.

48. Wood to Hoover, June 15, 1942, ibid.

49. Edgar Rickard Diary, June 23, 1942.

50. Ibid., June 24, 1942.
51. Ibid., July 9, 1942.
52. Hoover to Taft, July 9, 1942, HP-PPI.
53. Herbert Hoover and Hugh Gibson, *The Problems of Lasting Peace* (New York, 1942), passim.
54. Ibid.
55. Ibid.
56. Ibid.
57. See, for example, White to Capper, June 16, 1942, Arthur Capper Papers, Kansas State Historical Society, and White to James Wadsworth, June 16, 1942, White Papers.
58. White to Landon, July 10, 1942, White Papers.
59. Capper to White, June 26, 1942, Capper Papers.
60. Taft to Hoover, July 14, 1942, HP-PPI.
61. Hoover to Taft, July 19, 1942, ibid.
62. Hoover to Julius Klein, July 31, 1942, Klein Papers.
63. Stolz to Chauncey McCormick, May 26, 1942, HP-PPI.
64. Burton to Hoover, August 14, 1942, ibid., and Burton to Hugh Gibson, August 14, 1942, Gibson Papers.
65. Burton to Hoover, August 31, 1942, HP-PPI.
66. See, for example, Alonzo L. Baker to Hoover, November 11, 1942, ibid.
67. Edgar Rickard Diary, April 26, 1942.
68. Hoover to O'Laughlin, March 10, 1942, O'Laughlin Papers.
69. Hoover to O'Laughlin, March 30, 1942, ibid.
70. Hoover to O'Laughlin, April 10, 1942, ibid.
71. Hoover to Philip Bancroft, September 4, 1942, HP-PPI.
72. Hoover to O'Laughlin, May 5, 1942, O'Laughlin Papers.
73. Hoover to O'Laughlin, July 14, 1942, ibid.
74. Hoover to O'Laughlin, August 3, 1942, ibid.
75. Hoover to Shaw, September 12, 1942, HP-PPI.
76. Hoover to Sulzberger, September 12, 1942, ibid.
77. Landon to Hoover, October 13, 1942, Landon Papers.
78. Hoover to O'Laughlin, October 26, 1942, O'Laughlin Papers.
79. Press statement, November 4, 1942, Public Statements, 1942, Hoover Papers.
80. Hoover to Martin, November 6, 1942, HP-PPI.
81. Hoover to Simmons, November 9, 1942, ibid.
82. Hoover to Castle, December 1, 1942, ibid.
83. Edgar Rickard Diary, November 23 and 24, 1942.
84. Hoover to Lehman, November 24, 1942, HP-PPI.
85. Edgar Rickard Diary, November 25, 1942.

86. Ibid., December 3, 1942; Hoover to Lehman, November 25, 1942, HP-PPI.
87. Memorandum of December 3, 1942, in Lehman folder, HP-PPI.
88. *New York Times*, December 4, 1942.
89. Thomas to Hoover, November 27, 1943, HP-PPI.
90. Edgar Rickard Diary, November 5, 7, and 18, 1942.
91. White to Hoover, November 30, 1942, HP-PPI; Landon to White, November 30, 1942, White Papers.
92. Landon to White, November 30, 1942, White Papers.
93. Landon to William Castle, November 30, 1942, Landon Papers.
94. William Hutchinson to Landon, November 30, 1942, ibid.; Hoover to White, December 2, 1942, HP-PPI.
95. Hoover to Chauncey McCormick, November 10, 1942, NCFSD; Hoover to Schroeder, November 26, 1942, HP-PPI.
96. Chauncey McCormick to Hoover, November 20, 1942, and Hoover to Schroeder, November 26, 1942, HP-PPI.
97. Hutchinson to Landon, November 30, 1942, Landon Papers.
98. See Ellsworth Barnard, *Wendell Willkie, Fighter for Freedom* (Marquette, Michigan, 1966), pp. 382–84; Edgar Rickard Diary, December 11, 1942.
99. Walter Brown to Taft, December 9, 1942, Brown Papers.
100. Hoover to William Allen White, December 9, 1942, HP-PPI.
101. Hoover to Wilbur, December 13, 1942, Ray Lyman Wilbur Papers.
102. Barnard, *Wendell Willkie*, p. 384.
103. Both Hoover and Taft had supported American entry into the League of Nations after World War I.
104. Reprinted in Hoover, *Addresses Upon the American Road, 1941–45*, pp. 5–13.
105. Willkie to Hoover, telegram, December 17, 1942, HP-PPI.
106. Hoover to Willkie, December 20, 1942, ibid.
107. White to Landon, December 28, 1942, White Papers.
108. Hoover to Lippmann, December 23, 1942, HP-PPI.
109. Hoover to White, January 5, 1943, ibid.
110. White to Hoover, January 5, 1943, ibid.
111. Landon to Hoover, January 7, 1943, ibid.
112. Spangler to White, January 7, 1943, White Papers.
113. Edgar Rickard Diary, January 6, 1943.
114. Memorandum of January 8, 1943, in Halifax file, HP-PPI.
115. Ibid.
116. Edgar Rickard Diary, January 9, 1943.
117. Landon to Hoover, January 12, 1943, with memorandum, HP-PPI
118. Hoover to Landon, January 19, 1943, ibid.

119. Landon to Hoover, January 29, 1943, ibid.
120. Hoover to Martin, January 12, 1943, ibid.
121. Hugh Butler to Hoover, January 14 and 23, 1943, and telegram, January 30, 1943, ibid.; Edgar Rickard Diary, January 30, 1943.
122. Hoover to Castle, February 2, 1943, HP-PPI.
123. Castle to Hoover, February 10, 1943, ibid.
124. Martin to Hoover, January 15, 1943, ibid.
125. Hoover to Martin, January 18, 1943, ibid.
126. William A. Baker to Hoover, November 18, 1942, ibid.
127. Hoover to Castle, January 17, 1943, ibid.
128. Hoover to Martin, January 19, 1943, ibid.
129. "Civilian Organization in War," in Martin file, ibid.
130. Ibid.
131. Martin to Hoover, January 20, 1943, ibid.
132. See, for example, Hoover to Senator George Aiken, January 31, 1943, ibid.
133. Hoover to Butler, January 31, 1943, and Butler to Hoover, February 3, 1943, ibid.
134. Edgar Rickard Diary, February 3, 1943.
135. White to Hoover, February 4, 1943, HP-PPI.
136. *New York Times*, February 8, 1943.
137. Ibid., February 9, 1943.
138. Ibid.
139. Wickard to Hoover, telegram, February 6, 1943; and Hoover to Wickard, telegram, February 6, 1943; and Wickard to Hoover telegram (#2), February 6, 1943, HP-PPI.
140. See Taft to Hoover, February 7, 1943, and Hoover to Norman Thomas, February 15, 1943, ibid.
141. Edgar Rickard Diary, February 9, 1943.
142. *New York Times,* February 14, 1943.
143. Spangler to Landon, February 20, 1943, Landon Papers.
144. Spangler to Landon, February 26, 1943, ibid.
145. Hoover to Butler, February 25, 1943, and to Landon, February 25, 1943, HP-PPI.
146. Landon to Hoover, March 2, 1943, Landon Papers.
147. Butler to Hoover, March 2, 1943, HP-PPI.
148. White to McNary, March 18, 1943, also White to Stassen, March 18, 1943, White Papers.
149. Burton to Hoover, March 19, 1943, HP-PPI.
150. Harold H. Burton, "The Roads to Lasting Peace," *The Republican*, March 1943, with ibid.
151. Contained with ibid.

152. Marginalia on ibid.

153. Hoover to Burton, March 23, 1943, ibid.

154. Ibid.

155. Arthur H. Vandenberg, Jr., ed., *The Private Papers of Senator Vandenberg* (Boston, 1952), pp. 41–43, 47.

156. Hoover to White, March 23, 1943, HP-PPI.

157. White to Hoover, March 29, 1943, ibid.

158. *New York Times*, March 16, 1943.

159. Ibid., March 23, 1943.

160. Ibid., April 4, 1943.

161. Castle to Hoover, March 22, 1943, HP-PPI.

162. Bernice Miller to Castle, telegram, March 24, 1943, and Castle to Hoover, March 25, 1943, ibid.

163. Castle to Hoover, April 19, 1943, ibid.

164. Hoover to White, March 31, 1943, ibid.

165. White to [addressee not given], April 2, 1943, copy in White file, ibid.

166. Landon to Hoover, March 26, 1943, Landon Papers.

167. Hoover to Landon, March 29, 1943, ibid.

168. James L. Wright to Landon, March 25, 1943, ibid.

169. Landon to Wright, March 29, 1943, ibid.

170. Landon to Hoover, April 3, 1943, ibid.

171. For example, Hoover to John Spargo, April 6, 1943, Spargo Papers.

172. Hoover to Burton, April 5, 1943, HP-PPI.

173. White to Hoover, April 12, 1943, ibid.

174. Edgar Rickard Diary, April 13, 1943.

175. See Tobey to Hoover, April 21, 1943, Ferguson to Hoover, May 10, 1943, and Capper to Hoover, May 18, 1943, HP-PPI.

176. Wendell L. Willkie, *One World* (New York, 1943), pp. 85–87.

177. Ibid., pp. 177–78.

178. Landon to John O'Donnell, May 8, 1943, and John Henry to Landon, May 8, 1943, Landon Papers.

179. White to Landon, May 11, 1943, White Papers.

180. Hoover to Landon, telegram, May 15, 1943, Landon Papers.

181. White to Roger Straus, May 15, 1943, White Papers.

182. Spangler to Landon, May 29, 1943, Landon Papers.

183. For example, George H. Mayer, *The Republican Party* (New York, 1967), p. 462.

184. White to Spangler, April 6, 1943, White Papers.

185. See Landon to Hoover, June 8, 1943, and Landon to O'Donnell, May 8, 1943, Landon Papers.

186. Spangler to Austin, July 8, 1943, and Austin to Spangler, July 15, 1943, Warren Austin Papers, University of Vermont.

187. Edgar Rickard Diary, May 27, 1943, and June 17, 1943.

188. Hoover to Warren, June 7, 1943, HP-PPI.

189. Landon to Hoover, July 19, 1943, Landon Papers.

190. Hamilton to Hoover, July 21, 1943, HP-PPI.

191. James T. Patterson, *Mr. Republican: A Biography of Robert A. Taft* (Boston, 1972), pp. 268–69.

192. Reynolds to Hoover, July 28, 1943, and Reynolds to Hoover, August 3, 1943, HP-PPI.

193. Hoover to Michael Shannon, August 3, 1943, ibid.

194. Vandenberg, ed., *Private Papers*, p. 54.

195. Spangler to Austin, July 31, 1943, Austin Papers.

196. *New York Times*, June 11, 1943.

197. Davis to Hoover, June 12, 1943, HP-PPI.

198. Hoover to Davis, June 19, 1943, ibid.

199. Hoover to Sam D. Goza, July 15, 1943, ibid.

200. The letter is not in the Hoover Papers, but it is mentioned in Hoover to Kelland, July 21, 1943, and John Hamilton to Hoover, August 2, 1943, ibid.

201. Hoover to Kelland, July 21, 1943, ibid.

202. Hamilton to Hoover, August 2, 1943, ibid.

203. Hawkes to Hoover, August 12, 1943, ibid.

204. Smith to Austin, August 5, 1943, Austin Papers.

205. Draft of August 4, 1943, included with ibid.

206. Austin to Fred H. Howland, August 7, 1943, ibid.

207. Austin to Vandenberg, August 19, 1943, ibid.

208. Edgar Rickard Diary, August 24, 1943.

209. Hoover to Bricker, August 30, 1943, HP-PPI.

210. Ibid.

211. Hoover to Bricker, August 31, 1943, ibid.

212. Hoover to Vandenberg, August 31, 1943, and to Austin, same date, ibid.

213. Reprinted in Hoover, *Addresses Upon the American Road, 1941–45*, pp. 71–84.

214. Hoover to Shaw, telegram, September 8, 1943, HP-PPI.

215. Printed in *Tennessee Republican Age* (February/March 1944), pp. 16–18.

216. Robert A. Divine, *Second Chance: The Triumph of Internationalism in America During World War II* (New York, 1971), p. 132.

217. Hoover to William Allen White, September 16, 1943, HP-PPI.

218. Austin to Boyd Edwards, September 14, 1943, Austin Papers.

219. White to Hoover, September 20, 1943, HP-PPI.

CHAPTER 8

1. William Allen White to Hoover, September 20, 1943, HP-PPI.
2. Taft to Hoover, September 23, 1943, ibid.
3. Austin to Hoover, September 21, 1943, ibid.
4. Hoover to Austin, September 22, 1943, ibid.
5. Hoover to Taft, September 25, 1943, ibid.
6. Chauncey McCormick to Hoover, September 8, 1943, ibid.
7. Hoover to Taft, September 25, 1943, ibid.
8. O'Laughlin to Hoover, December 19, 1942, O'Laughlin Papers.
9. O'Laughlin to Hoover, September 17, 1943, ibid.
10. Hoover to Landon, September 20, 1943, HP-PPI.
11. Hoover to Clark, October 6, 1943, ibid.
12. Hoover to O'Laughlin, June 15, 1942, O'Laughlin Papers.
13. Frederick Libby to Hoover, April 29, 1943, HP-PPI.
14. Hoover to O'Laughlin, May 9, 1943, O'Laughlin Papers.
15. Landon to Frank Carlson, May 20, 1943, Landon Papers.
16. Walter Lippmann, *U.S. Foreign Policy: Shield of the Republic* (Boston, 1950), chapter 10.
17. George Holden Tinkham to Landon, August 21, 1943, Landon Papers.
18. Frank C. Hanighen to Landon, October 23, 1943, ibid.
19. Hoover to Landon, November 2, 1943, ibid.
20. Ibid.
21. O'Laughlin to Hoover, November 8, 1943, O'Laughlin Papers.
22. Taft to Hoover, November 9, 1943, HP-PPI.
23. Landon to Hoover, November 18, 1943, ibid.
24. Hoover to O'Laughlin, November 10, 1943, O'Laughlin Papers.
25. Hoover to Roy Howard, November 2, 1943, HP-PPI.
26. *New York Times*, November 11, 1943.
27. O'Laughlin to Hoover, December 3, 1943, O'Laughlin Papers.
28. Hoover to O'Laughlin, December 9, 1943, ibid.
29. Hoover to O'Laughlin, December 13, 1943, ibid.
30. Ibid.
31. O'Laughlin to Hoover, December 11, 1943, ibid.
32. Hoover to Martin, March 31, 1943, HP-PPI.
33. Martin to Hoover, April 1, 1943, ibid.
34. Hoover to Taft, April 7, 1943, ibid.
35. Hoover to Jenkins, June 3, 1943, and Jenkins to Hoover, June 5, 1943, ibid.
36. *New York Times*, June 9, 1943.

37. Ibid.
38. Hoover to Hyde, June 18, 1943, HP-PPI.
39. *New York Times*, September 16, 1943.
40. Jenkins to Hoover, September 27, 1943, HP-PPI.
41. Hoover to Jenkins, September 29, 1943, ibid.
42. Jenkins to Hoover, October 4, 1943, ibid.
43. Jenkins to Hoover, November 18, 1943, ibid.
44. Hoover to Mrs. H. H. Hamilton, March 25, 1943, NCFSD.
45. Gillette to Taft, April 23, 1943, Taft Papers.
46. Taft to Gibson, April 27, 1943, ibid.
47. Gibson to Taft, April 29, 1943, ibid.
48. Taft to Mrs. Philip E. Jacob, May 14, 1943, ibid.
49. See, for example, Hoover to Congressman Howard Buffett, May 7, 1943, and Paul Clapp to Hoover, telegram, May 18, 1943, NCFSD.
50. Hoover to Lehman, June 23, 1943, HP-PPI.
51. Ibid.
52. Gillette to Taft, October 6, 1943, Taft Papers.
53. E. Stanley Jones to Hoover, October 15, 1943, NCFSD.
54. Sayre to Senator Elbert Thomas, November 1, 1943, Taft Papers.
55. Thomas to Senator Elbert Thomas, November 2, 1943, copy in ibid.
56. Herbert Hoover, *An American Epic* (Chicago, 1964), vol. 4, pp. 96–97.
57. Roy E. Dunn to Hoover, September 6, 1943, HP-PPI.
58. Hoover to Dunn, September 9, 1943, ibid.
59. Hoover to Bricker, October 1, 1943, ibid.
60. Hoover to Dewey, October 15, 1943, ibid.
61. Dewey to Hoover, October 16, 1943, ibid.
62. Unsent letter from Hoover to Dewey, January 26, 1943, with notation that Hoover had phoned, instead, ibid.
63. Edgar Rickard Diary, January 7, 1944.
64. Kemper to Hoover, January 27, 1944, Gibson Papers.
65. Hoover to David Lawrence, November 1, 1943, HP-PPI.
66. Castle to Landon, January 31, 1944, Landon Papers.
67. Hoover to O'Laughlin, February 7, 1944, O'Laughlin Papers.
68. *New York Times*, February 3, 1944.
69. Hoover to Gibson, February 16, 1944, HP-PPI.
70. Hoover to Homer Mann, March 17, 1944, ibid.
71. Memorandum of March 19, 1944, in Dewey file, ibid.
72. Ibid.
73. See, for example, Hoover to Bricker, March 11, 1944, and April 12, 1944, ibid.; Edgar Rickard Diary, April 18, 1944.

74. Hoover to Landon, March 16, 1944, HP-PPI.
75. Landon to Frank Carlson, April 7, 1944, Landon Papers.
76. Hoover to Jones, April 13, 1944, HP-PPI.
77. Hoover to Dewey, April 5, 1944, ibid.
78. Hoover to Dewey, April 10, 1944, ibid.
79. A copy of the speech is in the Bricker file, ibid.
80. Hoover to Dewey, May 1, 1944, ibid.
81. Clarence F. Hewes to Landon, May 1, 1944, Landon Papers.
82. Wood to Vandenberg, May 2, 1944, Wood Papers.
83. Wood to Vandenberg, May 3, 1944, ibid.
84. For example, Gross to Hoover, May 12, 1944, HP-PPI.
85. Hoover to Gross, May 21, 1944, ibid.
86. Statement of May 25, 1944, Public Statements, 1944, Hoover Papers.
87. Edgar Rickard Diary, May 26, 1944.
88. Ibid., June 9 and 11, 1944.
89. Ibid., May 13, 1944 and June 13 and 23, 1944.
90. *New York Times*, June 28, 1943.
91. Ibid.
92. Ibid.
93. Ibid.
94. Ibid.
95. Ibid.
96. Ibid., June 27 and 28, 1944; according to Bricker, Hoover did not actually tell him to take the second spot, but did indicate that Dewey was sure to be nominated and, by implication, suggested that the best Bricker could hope for was the second spot on the ticket. Interview with John Bricker by the author, May 21, 1980.
97. Ibid., June 30, 1944.
98. Hoover to Michael Shannon, July 5, 1944, HP-PPI.
99. Hoover to Bricker, July 7, 1944, ibid.
100. Memorandum with ibid.
101. Dewey to Hoover, July 18, 1944, ibid.
102. Hoover to Hamilton, July 12, 1944, ibid.
103. Brownell to Hoover, August 17, 1944, ibid.
104. Edgar Rickard Diary, September 13, 1944.
105. Hoover to Simms, September 7, 1944, HP-PPI.
106. Edgar Rickard Diary, September 21, 1944.
107. Ibid., September 22, 1944.
108. Ibid., September 26, 1944.
109. Hoover to Simmons, September 21, 1944, HP-PPI.

110. Edgar Rickard Diary, September 29, 1944.
111. Ibid., November 6, 1944.
112. Hoover to William Barrett, August 4, 1944, HP-PPI.
113. Public Statements, 1944, Hoover Papers.
114. Edgar Rickard Diary, October 10, 1944; Frank E. Mason oral history, Hoover Presidential Library.
115. Edgar Rickard Diary, November 8, 1944.
116. Hoover to Castle, November 17, 1944, HP-PPI.
117. Hoover to Homer Mann, November 20, 1944, ibid.
118. Albert C. Wedemeyer oral history, Hoover Presidential Library.
119. Edgar Rickard Diary, December 5, 1944.
120. Hoover to O'Laughlin, December 18, 1944, O'Laughlin Papers.
121. Hoover to Wilbur, January 28, 1945, HP-PPI.
122. Public Statements, 1945, Hoover Papers.
123. Hoover to Wilbur, February 15, 1945, Ray Lyman Wilbur Papers.
124. Castle to Hoover, February 16, 1945, HP-PPI.
125. Hoover to Landon, February 18, 1945, ibid.
126. Hoover to Castle, February 18, 1945, ibid.
127. Castle to Hoover, February 26, 1945, ibid.
128. Public Statements, 1945, Hoover Papers.
129. Stettinius to Hoover, telegram, April 20, 1945, HP-PPI.
130. Hoover to Lewis Strauss, April 23, 1945, ibid.
131. Hoover to Stettinius, telegram, April 23, 1945, ibid.
132. Felix Morley, *For the Record* (South Bend, 1979), p. 416.
133. Edgar Rickard Diary, April 14, 1945.
134. Ibid., April 16, 1945.
135. Hoover to Hyde, April 23, 1945, HP-PPI.
136. Hyde to Hoover, April 27, 1945, ibid.
137. Hoover to May Leavitt, April 24, 1945, May Hoover Leavitt Papers, Hoover Presidential Library.
138. See John Coulter to Hoover, May 20, 1944; Bernice Miller to Hanighen, May 30, 1944; Hoover to Hanighen, February 28, 1945; and Bernice Miller to Hanighen, April 7, 1945, HP-PPI.
139. Hoover to Edgar Queeny, November 29, 1944, Henry Regnery to Hoover, March 2, 1945, and Bernice Miller to Regnery, April 7, 1945, ibid.
140. Edgar Rickard Diary, April 17, 1945.
141. Reprinted in Hoover, *Addresses Upon the American Road, 1941–45*, pp. 111–23.
142. Ibid.
143. Ibid.

144. Undated memorandum of April 1945, in Stimson file, HP-PPI.

145. Tobey to Hoover, April 19, 1945, ibid.

146. Memorandum of a conversation with Brewster, dated April 28, 1945, in Brewster file, ibid.

147. Donald R. McCoy, "Herbert Hoover and Foreign Policy, 1939–1945," *Herbert Hoover Reassessed*, Senate Document 96–63 (Washington, D.C., 1981), p. 416.

148. Edgar Rickard Diary, May 13, 1945.

149. Ibid., May 14, 1945.

150. Memorandum of May 15, 1945, in Kennedy file, HP-PPI.

151. Memorandum of May 15, 1945, in Stimson file, ibid.

152. Ibid.

153. Memorandum of May 23, 1945, in Public Statements, 1945, Hoover Papers; Edgar Rickard's diary gives the date of this meeting as May 24, 1945.

154. Edgar Rickard Diary, May 24, 1945.

155. Truman to Hoover, May 24, 1945, HP-PPI.

156. Edgar Rickard Diary, May 26, 1945.

157. Ibid., May 27, 1945.

158. Memorandum of May 28, 1945, in Truman file, HP-PPI.

159. Ibid.

160. Ibid.

161. Edgar Rickard Diary, May 30, 1945.

162. Castle to Hoover, June 2, 1945, HP-PPI.

163. Shaw to Hoover, May 28, 1945, ibid.

164. Memorandum of May 30, 1945, in Public Statements, 1945, Hoover Papers.

165. Hoover to Truman, May 30, 1945, ibid.

166. Truman to Hoover, June 1, 1945, ibid.

167. Hoover to O'Laughlin, June 8, 1945, O'Laughlin Papers.

168. O'Laughlin to Hoover, June 9, 1945, ibid.

169. Hoover to Knowland, June 12, 1945, HP-PPI.

170. Jenkins to Hoover, June 11, 1945, ibid.

171. Hoover to Jenkins, June 20, 1945, ibid.

172. Ibid.

173. Raymond L. Buell, et al. to Hoover, July 8, 1945, and Christopher T. Emmet, Jr., to Hoover, telegram, July 18, 1945, ibid.

174. Reprinted in Hoover, *Addresses Upon the American Road, 1941–45*, pp. 137–43.

175. Ibid.

176. Edgar Rickard Diary, January 13, 1945.

177. O'Laughlin to Hoover, August 9, 1945, and August 11, 1945, O'Laughlin Papers.

178. Edgar Rickard Diary, August 9 and 10, 1945; see, for example, Edgar Queeny to Warren, telegram, August 9, 1945; Selvage to Hoover, August 9, 1945; Arnold Stifel to Hoover, August 9, 1945; John Bricker to Warren, telegram, August 13, 1945; copies or originals in HP-PPI.

179. Hoover to Stifel, August 17, 1945, and Hoover to Selvage, August 17, 1945, ibid.

180. In Public Statements, 1945, Hoover Papers.

CHAPTER 9

1. In Public Statements, 1945, Hoover Papers.

2. Ibid.

3. Hoover to Jenkins, September 11, 1945, HP-PPI.

4. Hoover to Edgar Queeny, June 16, 1945; Hoover to Robert Wood, June 16, 1945; Regnery to Hoover, June 16, 1945, and June 18, 1945; and Henry Allen to Hoover, August 2, 1945; all in ibid.

5. Hoover to Jeremiah Milbank, April 24, 1945, ibid.

6. Hoover to Taft, September 1, 1945, ibid.

7. Eberstadt to Hoover, August 20, 1945, ibid.

8. Hoover to Eberstadt, September 19, 1945, ibid.

9. In Public Statements, 1945, Hoover Papers.

10. Jenkins to Hoover, November 6, 1945, HP-PPI.

11. Jenkins to Hoover, November 24, 1945, ibid.

12. R. G. A. Jackson to Hoover, November 27, 1945, ibid.

13. Hoover to Jackson, December 2, 1945, ibid.

14. Jackson to Hoover, December 8, 1945, ibid.

15. Hoover to Will Shafroth, December 29, 1945, ibid.

16. Hoover to Bricker, October 12, 1945, ibid.

17. Edgar Rickard Diary, November 14, 1945.

18. Hoover to Christopher T. Emmet, Jr., November 13, 1945, HP-PPI.

19. Edgar Rickard Diary, review of the year 1945.

20. With Hoover to Kelland, January 30, 1945, HP-PPI.

21. In Public Statements, 1946, Hoover Papers.

22. Bernice Miller to O'Laughlin, February 9, 1946, O'Laughlin Papers.

23. Hoover to Fulbright, February 8, 1946, HP-PPI.

24. Fulbright to Hoover, February 11, 1946, ibid.

25. See, for example, Willy Brandt to Bernice Miller, February 13, 1946, Allen Hoover Papers, Hoover Presidential Library.

26. In Public Statements, 1946, Hoover Papers.

27. "Memorandum of a Telephone Conversation, February 25, 1946," in FEC.
28. Hoover to Anderson, February 26, 1946, ibid.
29. *New York Times*, March 1, 1946.
30. Gibson to wife, February 28, 1946, Gibson Papers.
31. *New York Times*, March 2, 1946.
32. Gibson to wife, March 3, 1946, Gibson Papers.
33. Edgar Rickard Diary, March 2, 1946.
34. Gibson to wife, March 5, 1946, Gibson Papers.
35. Irwin to Hoover, March 11, 1946, FEC.
36. Edgar Rickard Diary, March 13, 1946.
37. Gibson to wife, March 13, 1946, Gibson Papers.
38. Hoover to Anderson, March 15, 1946, FEC.
39. Lewis to Hoover, March 15, 1946, ibid.
40. Milton O. Gustafson, "Congress and Foreign Aid: The First Phase, UN-RRA, 1943–1947" (Ph.D. diss., University of Nebraska, 1966), pp. 240–41.
41. *New York Times*, March 15, 1946.
42. Ibid., March 16, 1946.
43. Ibid., March 17, 1946.
44. Ibid., March 22, 1946.
45. Ibid., March 27, 1946, and March 29, 1946.
46. Edgar Rickard Diary, April 16, 1946.
47. Gibson to wife, April 20, 1946, Gibson Papers.
48. *New York Times*, April 20, 1946.
49. Ibid., May 11, 1946.
50. Edgar Rickard Diary, May 12, 1946.
51. Hoover, et al., to Truman, May 13, 1946, HP-PPI.
52. *New York Times*, May 11, 1946.
53. See, for example, *New York Sun*, May 13, 1946; *New York Daily Mirror*, May 14, 1946; *New York Daily News*, May 14, 1946.
54. Truman to Hoover, May 15, 1946, HP-PPI.
55. Edgar Rickard Diary, May 15, 1946.
56. Memorandum, May 16, 1946, Truman file, HP-PPI.
57. Edgar Rickard Diary, May 18, 1946.
58. *Columbus Evening Despatch*, May 27, 1946.
59. *New York Herald Tribune*, June 20, 1946.
60. Edgar Rickard Diary, June 21, 1946.
61. Hoover to Ed Anthony, June 25, 1946, FEC.
62. Reprinted in Herbert Hoover, *Addresses Upon the American Road, 1945–48* (New York, 1948), pp. 259–66.
63. Ibid.

64. Chester Davis to Hoover, July 12, 1946, FEC.
65. Hoover to Davis, July 16, 1946, ibid.
66. Hoover to O'Laughlin, December 31, 1945, O'Laughlin Papers.
67. Hoover to Bricker, August 17, 1946, HP-PPI.
68. Hoover to Wilbur Matson, October 10, 1946, ibid.
69. Hoover to MacArthur, October 17, 1946, ibid.
70. MacArthur to Hoover, October 31, 1946, ibid.
71. *New York Times*, August 13, 1946.
72. Ibid., August 27, 1946.
73. Ibid., September 11, 1946.
74. Ibid., August 31, 1946.
75. Ibid., September 24, 1946.
76. Ibid., November 6, 1946.
77. Ibid., November 7, 1946.
78. In Public Statements, 1946, Hoover Papers.
79. Davis to Hoover, November 26, 1946, FEC.
80. Hoover to Davis, December 3, 1946, ibid.
81. Hoover to Truman, December 3, 1946, HP-PPI.
82. Edgar Rickard Diary, December 11, 1946.
83. Hoover to Taft, December 21, 1946, HP-PPI.
84. In Public Statements, 1946, Hoover Papers.
85. Edgar Rickard Diary, January 16, 1947.
86. Truman to Hoover, January 18, 1947, FEC.
87. Hoover to Truman, telegram and letter, January 19, 1947, ibid.
88. Memorandum, January 22, 1947, Truman file, HP-PPI.
89. Frank E. Mason oral history, Hoover Presidential Library.
90. Edgar Rickard Diary, February 23, 1947.
91. Reprinted in Hoover, *Addresses Upon the American Road, 1945–48*, pp. 83–97.
92. Ibid.
93. Lucius Clay, *Decision in Germany* (Garden City, 1950), p. 156.
94. Charles Eaton to Hoover, February 24, 1947, HP-PPI; Edgar Rickard Diary, March 1, 1947.
95. Edgar Rickard Diary, March 2, 1947.
96. Ibid., March 21, 1947.
97. Hoover to C. Tyler Wood, March 29, 1947, HP-PPI.
98. Vandenberg to Hoover, April 22, 1947, ibid.
99. Draper to Hoover, April 25, 1947, ibid.
100. Hoover to Patterson, May 7, 1947, ibid.

101. Hoover to Marshall, May 12, 1947, ibid.
102. Marshall to Hoover, May 15, 1947, ibid.
103. Hoover to O'Laughlin, September 25, 1945, O'Laughlin Papers.
104. Hoover to George Bender, telegram and letter, October 1, 1945, HP-PPI.
105. Truman to Hoover, October 11, 1945, ibid.
106. Hoover to Brown, February 1, 1947, ibid.
107. Brown to Hoover, February 4, 1947, ibid.
108. Reprinted in Hoover, *Addresses Upon the American Road, 1945–48*, pp. 3–13.
109. Ibid.
110. Ibid.
111. Edgar Rickard Diary, May 22, 1947.
112. Hoover to Taber, May 26, 1947, HP-PPI.
113. Ibid.
114. Edgar Rickard Diary, May 29, 1947.
115. O'Laughlin to Hoover, June 3, 1947, O'Laughlin Papers.
116. R. B. Patterson to Hoover, June 13, 1947, HP-PPI.
117. Senator Styles Bridges to Hoover, undated, but sometime in May 1947, ibid.
118. Hoover to Bridges, June 15, 1947, ibid.
119. Bridges to Hoover, June 20, 1947, ibid.
120. Taft to "Julius," June 16, 1947, Taft Papers.
121. Hoover to O'Laughlin, June 16, 1947, O'Laughlin Papers.
122. Hoover to O'Laughlin, June 23, 1947, ibid.
123. Hoover to Baruch, with memorandum, June 29, 1947, HP-PPI.
124. Hoover to Baruch, with memorandum, July 3, 1947, ibid.
125. Ibid.
126. Hoover to Baruch, July 4, 1947, ibid.
127. Hoover to Taft, June 24, 1947, ibid.
128. Taft to Hoover, July 11, 1947, ibid.
129. Hoover to Taft, July 16, 1947, ibid.
130. Hoover to O'Laughlin, July 23, 1947, O'Laughlin Papers.
131. Taft to Hoover, August 13, 1947, HP-PPI.
132. Gibson to Hoover, July 29, 1947, Gibson Papers.
133. Hoover to Ray Lyman Wilbur, October 2, 1947, Wilbur Papers.
134. Edgar Rickard Diary, September 2, 1947.
135. Reprinted in Hoover, *Addresses Upon the American Road, 1945–48*, pp. 306–10.
136. Press statement, September 20, 1947, Public Statements, 1947, Hoover Papers.

137. Fellers to Hoover, September 3, 1947, HP-PPI.
138. Hoover to Fellers, September 5, 1947, and Taft to Hoover, October 11, 1947, ibid.
139. Hoover to Herter, October 30, 1947, ibid.
140. Ibid.
141. Stimson to Hoover, telegram, November 4, 1947, ibid.
142. Hoover to Stimson, November 7, 1947, ibid.
143. Stimson to Hoover, November 12, 1947, ibid.
144. Landon to Hoover, November 11, 1947, Landon Papers.
145. Hoover to Landon, November 20, 1947, ibid.
146. Landon to Hoover, November 24, 1947, ibid.
147. *New York Times*, April 8, 1946.
148. Ibid., September 12, 1947.
149. Edgar Rickard Diary, October 23, 1947.
150. Ibid., October 30, 1947.
151. Ibid., November 13, 1947.
152. Ibid., December 18, 1947.
153. *New York Times*, August 10, 1947.
154. Ibid., November 21, 1947.
155. Ibid., September 30, 1947.
156. Vandenberg to Hoover, December 20, 1947, HP-PPI.
157. Hoover to Vandenberg, December 24, 1947, ibid.
158. Vandenberg to Hoover, December 30, 1947, and Hoover to Vandenberg, January 2, 1948, ibid.
159. Vandenberg to Hoover, January 5, 1948, ibid.
160. Reprinted in Hoover, *Addresses Upon the American Road, 1945–48*, pp. 120–30.
161. Ibid.
162. Ibid.
163. Edgar Rickard Diary, January 23, 1948.
164. Ibid., February 9, 1948.
165. Ibid., February 29, 1948.
166. O'Laughlin to Hoover, March 2, 1945, O'Laughlin Papers.
167. Hoover to O'Laughlin, March 3, 1948, ibid.
168. Hoover to O'Laughlin, telegram, March 4, 1948, and O'Laughlin to Hoover, telegram, March 4, 1948, HP-PPI.
169. Reprinted in Hoover, *Addresses Upon the American Road, 1945–48*, pp. 131–37.
170. Hoover to Baruch, March 24, 1948, HP-PPI.
171. Edgar Rickard Diary, March 8, 1948.

172. Ibid., March 9, 1948.

173. Ibid., March 19, 1948.

174. Taft to Royal Moore, March 26, 1948, Taft Papers.

175. Hoover to Smith, March 30, 1948, HP-PPI.

176. Stassen to Hoover, telegram, May 28, 1947, and June 11, 1947; Hoover to Stassen, June 13, 1947, ibid.

177. Stassen to Hoover, April 14, 1948, ibid.

178. Brown to Hoover, telegram, May 6, 1948, ibid.

179. Herbert Hoover, "Remarks at the Bohemian Grove Encampment, August 1, 1953," Public Statements, 1953, Hoover Papers. In his talk, Hoover described this as having happened at the 1944 convention, but as Taft was not a candidate in 1944, and as the meetings with Taft and Dewey that he described were held in 1948, it is clear that it was the 1948 convention that he was describing.

180. Hoover, *Addresses Upon the American Road, 1945–48*, pp. 67–73.

181. Brownell to Hoover, July 24, 1948, HP-PPI.

182. Hoover to Brownell, August 2, 1948, ibid.

183. Hoover to Gibson, August 12, 1948, Gibson Papers.

184. Hoover to Robert Simmons, September 2, 1948, HP-PPI.

185. Hoover to Mark Sullivan, September 6, 1948, ibid.

186. O'Laughlin to Hoover, September 17, 1948, O'Laughlin Papers.

187. Hoover to O'Laughlin, September 20, 1948, ibid.

188. O'Laughlin to Hoover, September 22, 1948, ibid.

189. Edgar Rickard Diary, May 15, 1948.

190. Hoover to Dewey, July 2, 1948, HP-PPI.

191. Hoover to *Newsweek*, September 20, 1948; Hoover to Dewey, September 20, 1948; and Dewey to Hoover, October 4, 1948, ibid.

192. Edgar Rickard Diary, September 21, 1948.

193. Ibid., September 30, 1948.

194. Ibid., September 9, 1948.

195. Ibid., October 9, 1948.

196. Public Statements, 1948, Hoover Papers.

CHAPTER 10

1. Edgar Rickard Diary, November 2, 1948.

2. Hoover to Shaw, November 28, 1942, HP-PPI.

3. See, for example, Henry L. Stimson to Hoover, November 22, 1948, and Hoover to Stimson, November 30, 1948, ibid., and Hoover's testimony before a subcommittee of the Senate Committee on Post Office and Civil Service, December 13 and 14, 1948, in Public Statements, 1948, Hoover Papers; Edgar Rickard Diary, November 13, 1948.

4. Edgar Rickard Diary, December 4, 1948.

5. *New York Times*, February 8, 11, and 15, 1949.

6. Ibid., February 18, 22, and 23, 1949.

7. Ibid., February 25, 1949, March 1, 3, 4, 8, and 11, 1949.

8. Ibid., March 12, 13, 14, and 15, 1949.

9. Ibid., March 22 and 26, 1949.

10. No adequate study of either of the Hoover Commissions has yet been made. The complete report of the first commission was published by McGraw-Hill, *The Hoover Commission Report* (New York, no date). A short summary and analysis is in *The Hoover Report: Half a Loaf*, Public Affairs Institute Occasional Papers #3 (Washington, D.C., 1949). See also Jewel L. Prestage, "The Status of the First Hoover Commission Report: An Analysis of the Roles of the President and Congress" (Ph.D. diss., University of Iowa, 1954).

11. Memorandum of telephone call, February 6, 1949, Truman file, HP-PPI.

12. Memorandum of February 9, 1949, ibid.

13. Truman to Hoover, February 11, 1949, ibid.

14. Hoover to Truman, February 14, 1949, ibid.

15. Truman to Hoover, February 16, 1949, ibid.

16. Memo, April 7, 1949, Truman file, ibid.

17. Edgar Rickard Diary, January 28, 1949.

18. Ibid., March 19, 1949.

19. Ibid., April 9, 1949.

20. Ibid., February 10, 1949.

21. Ibid., April 22, 1949.

22. Hoover to Doughton, April 25, 1949, HP-PPI.

23. Hoover to Kean, May 7, 1949, ibid.

24. Enclosed with Bernice Miller to William I. Nichols, May 19, 1949, ibid.; it appeared in *This Week* magazine, October 9, 1949.

25. Hoover to Samuel K. McConnell, Jr., June 22, 1949, ibid.

26. Hoover to Dewey, July 6, 1949, ibid.

27. Dewey to Hoover, July 18, 1949, and Hoover to Dewey, July 26, 1949, ibid.

28. Edgar Rickard Diary, December 9, 1949; the unpublished drafts are in the Hoover Papers.

29. Hoover to Knowland, December 31, 1949, HP-PPI.

30. Knowland to Hoover, January 3, 1950, ibid.

31. Taft to Fletcher, January 9, 1950, Taft Papers.

32. Hoover to Knowland, January 20, 1950, HP-PPI.

33. Hoover to Hurley, February 2, 1950, ibid.

34. Knowland to Hoover, March 29, 1950, enclosing a copy of letter to Acheson, ibid.

35. Acheson to Knowland, April 6, 1950, copy in ibid.
36. Edgar Rickard Diary, December 14, 1949.
37. Johnson to Hoover, October 19, 1949, HP-PPI.
38. Frank Pace, Jr., to Hoover, January 6, 1950, ibid.
39. Hoover to Pace, January 9, 1950, ibid.
40. Hoover to Nixon, January 22, 1950, ibid.
41. Edgar Rickard Diary, April 8, 1950.
42. Hoover to Wherry, May 6, 1950, with memorandum, HP-PPI.
43. Ibid.
44. Statement of June 28, 1950, in Public Statements, 1950, Hoover Papers.
45. Hoover to Truman, July 1, 1950, HP-PPI.
46. Truman to Hoover, July 3, 1950, ibid.
47. Ferguson to Hoover, July 17, 1950, ibid.
48. Hoover to Ferguson, July 20, 1950, ibid.
49. In Public Statements, 1950, Hoover Papers.
50. Hoover to Taft, August 13, 1950, HP-PPI.
51. Hoover to Hughston M. McBain, September 8, 1950, ibid.
52. Hoover to Guy D. Gabrielson, September 28, 1950, ibid.
53. Hoover to Edgar Rickard, October 13, 1950, ibid.
54. Hoover to Stassen, October 18, 1950, ibid.
55. Public Statements, 1950, Hoover Papers.
56. Truman to Hoover, November 25, 1950, HP-PPI.
57. Hoover to Truman, November 26, 1950, ibid.
58. Reprinted in *Congressional Record*, December 18, 1950, p. A8235.
59. Clipping in "For. Pol., Opposition," HP-PPS.
60. Hoover to Raymond Moley, December 1950, Moley Papers, Hoover Presidential Library.
61. Hoover to Taft, December 18, 1950, Taft Papers.
62. Hoover to Neil MacNeil, December 19, 1950, HP-PPI.
63. Public Statements, 1950, Hoover Papers.
64. *San Francisco Examiner*, December 21, 1950.
65. Arthur Kemp to Hoover, undated but December 1950 or January 1951, HP-PPI.
66. *New York Herald Tribune*, December 22, 1950.
67. Quoted in ibid.
68. Hoover to Smith, December 27, 1950, HP-PPI.
69. Nixon to Hoover, December 22, 1950, ibid.
70. Moley to Hoover, December 21, 1950, ibid.
71. Morley to Hoover, December 17, 1950, Morley Papers.

72. Landon to Hoover, December 26, 1950, HP-PPI.

73. Dulles to Taft, December 29, 1950, with copy of Dulles to Hoover, December 18, 1950, in Taft Papers.

74. *Houston Post*, January 1, 1951.

75. *New York Times*, January 3, 1951.

76. "The Safety of the Nation," in Taft Papers.

77. Taft to Ethan Shepley, January 8, 1951, ibid.

78. Hoover to Edward Anthony (*Collier's*), January 8, 1951, and Hoover to Anthony, January 11, 1951, both in HP-PPI.

79. Knowland to Hoover, January 9, 1951, and Hoover to Knowland, January 11, 1951, ibid.

80. Taft to A. G. Spieker, January 13, 1951, Taft Papers.

81. Transcript of the forum in Foreign Policy file, HP-PPS.

82. Stassen to Hoover, January 16, 1951, enclosing copy of Stassen to *New York Herald Tribune* of same date, HP-PPI.

83. See, for example, Karl Mundt to Hoover, January 19, 1951, ibid.

84. "Possibilities in Reply Speech," in "Foreign Policy, Opposition," HP-PPS.

85. Hoover to Wedemeyer, December 31, 1950, HP-PPI.

86. See, for example, Hoover to Felix Morley, January 24, 1951, and Morley to Hoover, January 26, 1951, Morley Papers.

87. *New York Herald Tribune*, January 28, 1951.

88. Public Statements, 1951, Hoover Papers.

89. Ibid.

90. Fellers, "The Real Deterrent," *Human Events*, January 24, 1951.

91. For background on de Seversky I have used Vernon C. Bottenfield, "Defense, Power and Victory Through the Air: Major Alexander P. De Seversky's Impact upon America's Military Posture" (senior thesis, University of Hawaii at Hilo, 1980).

92. Press statement in de Seversky file, HP-PPI.

93. Wherry to Hoover, February 6, 1951, ibid.

94. "Defense of Europe," Public Statements, 1951, Hoover Papers.

95. Fellers to Hoover, February 27, 1951, HP-PPI.

96. De Seversky to Hoover, March 19, 1951, ibid.

97. Hoover to Fulton Lewis, Jr., March 4, 1951, ibid.

98. Taft to Hoover, March 5, 1951, Taft Papers.

99. Memorandum of telephone call, February 21, 1951, Brown folder, HP-PPI.

100. *New York Times*, March 14, 1951.

101. Wesley A. D'Ewart to Hoover, March 21, 1951, HP-PPI.

102. Hoover to William Jenner, March 22, 1951, ibid.

103. Fellers to Hoover, March 29, 1951, ibid.

104. James T. Patterson, *Mr. Republican: A Biography of Robert A. Taft* (Boston, 1972), pp. 480–81.

105. *Human Events*, January 17, 1951.

106. Joan Hoff Wilson, "Herbert Hoover Reassessed," *Herbert Hoover Reassessed*, Senate Document 96–63 (Washington, D.C., 1981), p. 112.

107. For Truman's account of the affair, see Harry S. Truman, *Years of Trial and Hope* (Garden City, 1956), pp. 438–50.

108. Bonner Fellers oral history, Hoover Presidential Library.

109. Memorandum, April 13, 1951, MacArthur file, HP-PPI.

110. Richard E. Berlin oral history, Hoover Presidential Library.

111. Memorandum, April 14, 1951, MacArthur file, HP-PPI.

112. Memorandum, April 15, 1951, ibid.

113. Richard E. Berlin oral history, Hoover Presidential Library.

114. Bonner Fellers oral history, ibid.

115. Hoover to Shaw, May 26, 1951, HP-PPI.

116. Hoover to Ferguson, June 25, 1951, ibid.

117. Ferguson to Hoover, June 29, 1951, and August 8, 1951, with enclosure, ibid.

118. Hoover to Ferguson, September 3, 1951, ibid.

119. In Public Statements, 1951, Hoover Papers.

120. *New York Times*, August 31, 1951.

121. Ibid., November 6, 1951.

122. Ibid., December 30, 1951.

123. Morley to Hoover, October 9, 1951, and Hoover to Morley, October 13, 1951, Morley Papers.

124. Morley to Hoover, October 15, 1951, ibid.

125. Felix Morley to the author, July 18, 1980.

126. *New York Times*, January 16, 1952.

127. Public Statements, 1952, Hoover Papers.

128. *New York Times*, February 8, 1952.

129. Included in Bernice Miller to Bonner Fellers, January 29, 1952, HP-PPI.

130. Taft to Hoover, February 5, 1952, Taft Papers.

131. *New York Times*, February 5, 1952.

132. Fellers to Hoover, January 30, 1952, HP-PPI.

133. Arthur Bliss Lane to Hoover, January 23, 1952, ibid.

134. Hoover to Lane, January 26, 1952, ibid.

135. Hoover to Hulett C. Merritt, December 31, 1951, ibid.

136. Hoover to Wilbur Matson, April 24, 1952, ibid.

137. Morley to Hoover, October 12, 1951, Morley Papers.

138. John D. M. Hamilton oral history, Hoover Presidential Library.

139. See Hoover to Lodge, telegram, June 26, 1952; Lodge to Hoover, June 26, 1952; and Hoover to Lodge, June 29, 1952, HP-PPI.

140. John D. M. Hamilton oral history, Hoover Presidential Library.

141. De Seversky to Hoover, July 1, 1952, HP-PPI.

142. De Seversky, "An Airman's Plea to all Republican Delegates," with ibid.

143. Hoover to de Seversky, July 3, 1952, ibid.

144. Public Statements, 1952, Hoover Papers.

145. Hoover to Gabrielson, telegram, July 3, 1952, HP-PPI; the statement is in Public Statements, 1952, Hoover Papers.

146. Patterson, *Mr. Republican*, pp. 554–55.

147. Albert C. Wedemeyer oral history, Hoover Presidential Library.

148. In Public Statements, 1952, Hoover Papers.

149. Hoover to Taft, July 11, 1952, HP-PPI.

150. Taft to Hoover, July 17, 1952, ibid.

151. Hoover to Gabrielson, July 23, 1952, ibid.

152. Gabrielson to Hoover, August 1, 1952, ibid.

153. Hoover to Dirksen, July 23, 1952, ibid.

154. Taft to Robert Wood, August 8, 1952, Wood Papers.

155. Eisenhower to Hoover, telegram, July 29, 1952, HP-PPI.

156. Hoover to Eisenhower, telegram, July 31, 1952, ibid.

157. Patterson, *Mr. Republican*, pp. 576–78.

158. Press release, September 25, 1952, Nixon file, HP-PPI.

159. Hoover to Wedemeyer, October 7, 1952, ibid.

160. Bonner Fellers oral history, Hoover Presidential Library.

161. Eisenhower to Hoover, telegram, October 7, 1952, HP-PPI.

162. Hoover to Eisenhower, telegram, October 8, 1952, ibid.

163. Public Statements, 1952, Hoover Papers.

164. Ibid.

165. Joseph N. Pew, Jr., to Hoover, November 6, 1952, HP-PPI.

166. Hoover to Eisenhower, October 21, 1952, ibid.

167. Hoover to Eisenhower, November 17, 1952, ibid.

168. Hoover to Clarence Kelland, October 22, 1952, ibid.

169. Interview with Clare Boothe Luce by the author, August 12, 1980.

CHAPTER 11

1. Hoover to Joseph N. Pew, Jr., November 10, 1952, HP-PPI.

2. Martin to Hoover, November 7, 1952, ibid.

3. Walter E. Ditmars to Hoover, November 8, 1952, ibid.

4. Hope to Hoover, April 13, 1953, ibid.

5. Albert C. Wedemeyer oral history, Hoover Presidential Library.

6. Hoover to Kelland, November 18, 1952, HP-PPI.

7. *New York Times*, December 24, 1952.

8. Ibid., January 7, 1953.

9. Hoover to Admiral William V. Pratt, March 9, 1953, HP-PPI.

10. Ferdinand Eberstadt to Hoover, March 13, 1953, ibid.

11. Eisenhower to Hoover, March 16, 1953, ibid.

12. Hoover to Joseph Dodge, March 24, 1953, ibid.

13. Hoover to Dodge, March 18 and 24, 1953, ibid.

14. Hoover to Dodge, April 10, 1953, ibid.

15. *New York Times*, April 12, 1953.

16. Hoover to Sam McKelvie, April 20, 1953, HP-PPI.

17. *New York Times*, April 17, 1953.

18. Thomas to Hoover, April 13, 1953, HP-PPI.

19. Hoover to Thomas, April 14, 1953, ibid.

20. According to Felix Morley, the only "officials" he knew of Hoover having shown the proposal was his former under secretary of state, William R. Castle. Morley to the author, July 29, 1980.

21. Draft form letter of March 19, 1953, Wedemeyer file, HP-PPI.

22. Wedemeyer to Hoover, March 21, 1953, ibid.

23. Hoover to Wedemeyer, March 23, 1953, ibid.

24. *New York Times*, April 19, 1953.

25. Hoover to McKelvie, April 20, 1953, HP-PPI.

26. Fellers to Hoover, May 10, 1953, ibid.

27. Hoover to Admiral W. V. Pratt, May 21, 1953, ibid.; on the adoption by the British of an emphasis on airpower see Bonner Fellers, *Wings for Peace* (Chicago, 1953), pp. 73–74.

28. Hoover to Eberstadt, May 28, 1953, HP-PPI.

29. Robert J. Huckshorn, "Congressional Reaction to the Second Hoover Commission" (Ph.D. diss., University of Iowa, 1957), p. 19.

30. Hoover to Brown, June 5, 1953, Clarence Brown Papers.

31. Hoover to Strauss, with memorandum, June 9, 1953, HP-PPI.

32. Hoover to Welker, June 18, 1953, ibid.

33. Eisenhower to Hoover, July 13, 1953, ibid.

34. Huckshorn, "Congressional Reaction," pp. 21–22.

35. Public Statements, 1953, Hoover Papers.

36. "Remarks at Bohemian Grove Encampment," August 1, 1953, ibid.

37. Hoover to Moley, August 6, 1953, Raymond Moley Papers.

38. Hoover to Leonard Hall, telegram, August 27, 1953, HP-PPI.

39. *New York Times,* July 28, 1953.
40. Public Statements, 1953, Hoover Papers.
41. Huckshorn, "Congressional Reaction," p. 25.
42. *New York Times,* September 30, 1953.
43. Huckshorn, "Congressional Reaction," p. 52.
44. Brown to Hoover, August 27, 1953, Clarence Brown Papers.
45. *New York Times,* November 13, 1953.
46. Ibid., November 16, 1953.
47. Hoover to Gibson, December 19, 1953, Hugh Gibson Papers.
48. Hoover to Wilbur Matson, December 27, 1953, HP-PPI.
49. Hoover to Gibson, January 24, 1954, Gibson Papers.
50. Knowland to Hoover, May 4, 1950, with copy of Knowland, et al., to Truman, May 2, 1950, HP-PPI.
51. Hoover to Knowland, May 6, 1950, ibid.
52. Knowland to Hoover, May 8, 1950, ibid.
53. Hoover to Walter Judd, September 17, 1953, ibid.
54. Grew, Edison, and Judd to Hoover, October 12, 1953, ibid.
55. The statement, of January 15, 1954, is with Hoover to Edison, January 15, 1954, ibid.
56. Landon to Felix Morley, November 24, 1953, Morley Papers.
57. *Newsweek,* March 29, 1954.
58. *New York Times,* January 24, 1954.
59. Ibid., March 11, 1954.
60. Hoover to Wiley, with memorandum, April 20, 1954, HP-PPI.
61. Ibid.
62. Memo of June 25, 1954, gift of Mrs. Kenneth C. Batchelder, "Foreign Policy," HP-PPS.
63. *New York Times,* June 25, 1954.
64. Ibid., August 11, 1954.
65. "Our Present Foreign Situation," memorandum of September 4, 1954, in "For. Policy—unpublished memo by HH," HP-PPS.
66. Ibid.
67. Ibid.
68. Ibid.
69. Ibid.
70. Eisenhower to Hoover, telegram, August 2, 1954, Hoover to Eisenhower, telegram, August 4, 1954, and Eisenhower to Hoover, August 6, 1954, HP-PPI.
71. In Public Statements, 1954, Hoover Papers.
72. Ibid.
73. *New York Times,* October 13 and 31, 1954.

74. Hoover to Kelland, November 19, 1954, HP-PPI.

75. *New York Times*, November 23, 1954.

76. Ibid., November 24, 1954.

77. Ibid., November 25, 1954.

78. Ibid., November 27, 1954.

79. Eisenhower to Hoover, December 2, 1954, HP-PPI.

80. *New York Times*, February 14, 1955.

81. Ibid., February 21, 1955.

82. Ibid., February 28, 1955.

83. Hoover to Kelland, March 7, 1955, HP-PPI.

84. *New York Times*, March 14, 1955.

85. Ibid., April 4, 1955.

86. Ibid., April 11, 1955.

87. Ibid., April 18, 1955.

88. Testimony of April 21, 1955, in Public Statements, 1955, Hoover Papers.

89. *New York Times*, April 22, 1955.

90. Ibid., April 25, 1955.

91. Ibid., May 16, 1955.

92. Ibid., May 5, 1955.

93. Ibid., May 20, 1955.

94. Ibid., May 26, 1955.

95. Ibid., June 1, 1955.

96. Ibid., June 6, 1955.

97. Ibid., June 11, 1955.

98. Ibid., June 14, 1955.

99. Ibid., June 20, 1955.

100. Ibid., June 25, 1955.

101. Ibid., June 26, 1955.

102. Ibid., June 27, 1955.

103. Ibid., June 30, 1955.

104. Ibid., July 1, 1955.

105. Ibid.; press release of June 30, 1955, in Hoover Commission Papers, Hoover Institution on War, Revolution and Peace.

106. Hoover to Brown, July 6, 1955, Clarence Brown Papers.

107. Brown to Hoover, July 8, 1955, ibid.

108. Hoover to Dewey, July 14, 1955, HP-PPI.

109. Hoover to Dodge, July 15, 1955, ibid.

110. "Government Is Too Big," *U. S. News and World Report*, August 5, 1955, pp. 48–56.

111. Press release of August 16, 1955, Public Statements, 1955, Hoover Papers.

112. Herbert Brownell oral history, Hoover Presidential Library.
113. Hoover to Lawrence E. Spivak, September 12, 1955, HP-PPI.
114. Spivak to Hoover, November 7, 1955, ibid.
115. Quoted in Spivak to Hoover, January 13, 1956, ibid.
116. For material on the Citizens Committee for the Hoover Report, see William Hallam Tuck Papers—Citizens' Committee for the Hoover Report, Hoover Presidential Library.
117. *New York Times*, July 9, 1955.
118. Ibid., July 26, 1955.
119. In Hoover, *Addresses Upon the American Road, 1955–60* (Caldwell, Idaho, 1961), pp. 79–85.
120. Hoover to Richard Lloyd Jones, January 11, 1956, HP-PPI.
121. Hoover to Farley, March 27, 1954, ibid.
122. *New York Times*, October 14, 1955, and November 1, 1955.
123. Ibid., November 12, 1955.
124. Hoover to Matson, December 20, 1955.

CHAPTER 12

1. Memorandum in "U. S. Commission on Organization of Govt. Adm. V. P.—Documents re 'Double Cross,' " in HP-PPS.
2. *New York Times*, January 16, 1956.
3. In Herbert Hoover, *Addresses Upon the American Road, 1955–60* (Caldwell, Idaho, 1961), pp. 16–26.
4. George H. Quinion to Hoover, March 10, 1956, and Hoover to Quinion, March 13, 1956, HP-PPI.
5. Hoover to Knowland, telegram, May 16, 1956, and Knowland to Hoover, May 17, 1956, ibid.
6. Bernice Miller to Loretta Camp, undated, 1956, and Camp to Miller, June 1, 1956, ibid.
7. Hoover to Hall, June 15, 1956, ibid.
8. Eisenhower to Hoover, July 2, 1956, ibid.
9. Hoover to Matson, July 17, 1956, ibid.
10. Hoover to Eisenhower, August 14, 1956, ibid.
11. Herbert Hoover, "Speech at the Bohemian Grove, July 28, 1956," Public Statements, 1956, Hoover Papers.
12. *New York Times*, August 10, 1956.
13. A copy is in Hoover to Melvin R. Laird, March 16, 1962, HP-PPI.
14. In Hoover, *Addresses Upon the American Road, 1955–60*, pp. 93–98.
15. Hoover to Robert Kennedy, February 19, 1954, HP-PPI.

16. Hoover to Joseph Kennedy, September 19, 1956, ibid.

17. Kennedy to Hoover, October 31, 1956, ibid.

18. L. Richard Guylay to Hoover, October 15, 1956, ibid.

19. William S. Raws to Hoover, telegram, October 18, 1956, ibid.

20. Hoover to Raws, telegram, October 21, 1956, ibid.

21. In Hoover, *Addresses Upon the American Road, 1955–60*, pp. 101–3.

22. Report of December 7, 1956, in First Aid for Hungary Papers, Hoover Institution on War, Revolution and Peace.

23. Perrin Galpin to W. Hallam Tuck, December 12, 1956, ibid.

24. Hoover to Eckardt, February 12, 1957, and memorandum from Galpin to Hoover, February 14, 1957, ibid.

25. Thomas S. Gordon to Hoover, telegram, January 3, 1957, HP-PPI.

26. Hoover to Gordon, telegram, January 6, 1957, ibid.

27. Hoover to Pratt, November 18, 1955, ibid.

28. Hoover to Gordon, telegram, January 6, 1957, ibid.

29. Hoover to Wiley, January 24, 1957, ibid.

30. See Kennedy to Hoover, April 23, 1957, and Brown to Hoover, September 4, 1957, ibid.

31. *New York Times*, July 7, 1957.

32. Hoover to Matson, December 23, 1957, HP-PPI.

33. Bernice Miller to Hugo Meier, February 1, 1958, ibid.

34. Herbert Hoover, *The Ordeal of Woodrow Wilson* (New York, 1958), p. vii.

35. Quoted in *Book Review Digest, 1958* (New York, 1959), p. 537.

36. Ibid., p. 538.

37. Kefauver to Hoover, January 10, 1958, HP-PPI.

38. Hoover to Kefauver, January 20, 1958, ibid.

39. *New York Times*, May 6, 1958.

40. Ibid., February 28, 1958.

41. Ibid., February 10, 1958.

42. Eisenhower to Hoover, June 11, 1958, HP-PPI.

43. Memo of telephone conversation, April 11, 1958, Eisenhower file, ibid.

44. *New York Times*, May 6, 1958.

45. Ibid., May 21, 1958.

46. Ibid., July 5, 1958.

47. Ibid., July 6, 1958.

48. Hoover to Eisenhower, July 7, 1958, HP-PPI.

49. *New York Times*, July 7, 1958.

50. Ibid., August 10, 1958.

51. Clarence Brown to Hoover, August 15, 1958, HP-PPI.

52. *New York Times*, October 30, 1958.

53. *Newsweek*, October 23, 1958.
54. *New York Times*, November 2, 1958.
55. Hoover to Gibson, May 10, 1953, Gibson Papers.
56. Hoover to David Lawrence, September 3, 1957, HP-PPI.
57. Hoover to Kelland, November 10, 1958, ibid.
58. Hoover to Matson, December 19, 1958, ibid.
59. Press release, July 15, 1958, Public Statements, 1958, Hoover Papers.
60. Public Statements, 1959, ibid.
61. Hoover to Berlin, September 6, 1959, HP-PPI.
62. Hoover to Donald G. Brownlow, January 2, 1960, ibid.
63. In Hoover, *Addresses Upon the American Road, 1955–60*, pp. 66–75.
64. Ibid., p. 389.
65. *New York Times*, August 10, 1959.
66. In Hoover, *Addresses Upon the American Road, 1955–60*, pp. 141–48.
67. In Public Statements, 1959, Hoover Papers.
68. Ben Moreel to Bernice Miller, December 1, 1959, and Hoover to Moreel, December 11, 1959, HP-PPI.
69. *New York Times*, February 14, 1960.
70. Hoover to Brown, March 7, 1960, HP-PPI.
71. Hoover to Henry Hazlitt, March 27, 1960, ibid.
72. Hoover to General Wilton B. Persons, April 7, 1960, ibid.
73. Thruston B. Morton to Hoover, June 17, 1960, ibid.
74. Hoover to Morton, June 22, 1960, ibid.
75. Morton to Hoover, June 23, 1960, and Hoover to Nichols, June 29, 1960, ibid.
76. Hoover to Hurley, July 8, 1960, ibid.
77. John D. M. Hamilton oral history, Hoover Presidential Library.
78. *New York Times*, May 14, 1960.
79. Ibid., June 16, 1960.
80. In Hoover, *Addresses Upon the American Road, 1955–60*, pp. 156–61.
81. Hoover to Roy Roberts, July 30, 1960, HP-PPI.
82. *New York Times*, July 25 and 27, 1960.
83. Public Statements, 1960, Hoover Papers.
84. *New York Times*, August 10, 1960.
85. Neil McNeil and Walter Trohan oral histories, Hoover Presidential Library.
86. "The Great Debate," memorandum in Nixon file, HP-PPI.
87. Neil McNeil oral history; *New York Times*, October 22, 1960.
88. *New York Times*, October 22, 1960.
89. Hoover to Thruston Morton, September 15, 1960, with enclosures, HP-PPI.
90. Hoover to William E. Lamb, October 12, 1960, ibid.

91. For Nixon's account, see Richard M. Nixon, *Six Crises* (Garden City, 1962), pp. 403–10; Hoover also told his close friend Neil McNeil that Kennedy's overture was by phone. See McNeil oral history, Hoover Presidential Library.

92. Neil McNeil oral history, Hoover Presidential Library; Hoover was apparently disturbed to find that the details of his involvement in the meeting had been leaked to the press, and he traced the leak to the Nixon "camp." See memorandum in Nixon file, HP-PPI.

93. Hoover to Ben Moreel, November 19, 1960, HP-PPI.

94. Hoover to Hook, December 20, 1960, ibid.

95. Hoover to Kennedy, telegram, January 19, 1961, ibid.

96. *New York Times*, January 12, 1961.

97. Kennedy to Hoover, telegram, March 2, 1961, and Hoover to Kennedy, March 4, 1961, HP-PPI; see also *New York Times*, March 11, 1961.

98. Bernice Miller to T. J. Reardon, Jr., April 25, 1961, HP-PPI.

99. Hoover to McGovern, April 25, 1961, ibid.

100. *New York Times*, April 29, 1961.

101. Memorandum of April 28, 1961, in Kennedy file, HP-PPI; see also Kennedy to Hoover, May 8, 1961, HP-PPI.

102. *New York Times*, May 5, 1961.

103. Hoover to David Packard, June 16, 1961, HP-PPI.

104. Saul Pett to Hoover, June 13, 1961, ibid.

105. William Lamb to Hoover, June 9, 1961, ibid.

106. Hoover to Lamb, June 13, 1961, ibid.

107. *New York Times*, June 28, 1961.

108. Ibid., July 23, 1961.

109. Hoover to Kennedy, June 16, 1961, HP-PPI.

110. Kennedy to Hoover, August 9, 1961, ibid.

111. Note of January 12, 1962, in Kennedy file, HP-PPI; Hoover to Kennedy, February 3, 1962, ibid.

112. *New York Times*, August 19, 1961.

113. Marvin Libman to Hoover, September 7, 1961, and Hoover to Libman, September 14, 1961, telegram, HP-PPI.

114. In Public Statements, 1961, Hoover Papers.

115. Hoover to Packard, March 6, 1962, HP-PPI.

116. Bernice Miller to Packard, January 2, 1962, ibid.

117. Bernice Miller to Hugo Meier, February 19, 1962, ibid.

118. *New York Times*, January 30, 1962.

119. Public Statements, 1962, Hoover Papers.

120. Hoover to Goldwater, March 11, 1962, HP-PPI.

121. *New York Times*, March 4, 1962.

122. Ibid., June 6, 1962.
123. Ibid., July 24, 1962.
124. Ibid., August 11, 1962.
125. Ibid., August 20, 1962.
126. Ibid., August 23, 1962.
127. The *New York Times* has extensive coverage of Hoover's illness from August 21, 1962, to September 5, 1962.

CHAPTER 13

1. Hoover to David Packard, October 8, 1962, HP-PPI.
2. *New York Times*, October 29, 1963.
3. Hoover to Truman, December 19, 1962, HPHI.
4. Hoover to Clarence B. Kelland, January 31, 1963, Kelland Papers, Hoover Presidential Library.
5. Hoover to George Mardikian, February 23, 1963, HP-PPI.
6. Pell to Hoover, March 12, 1963, ibid.
7. Hoover to Pell, March 18, 1963, ibid.
8. *New York Times*, May 24, 1963.
9. Ibid., June 20, 1963.
10. Ibid., June 15, 1963.
11. Ibid., June 21, 1963.
12. Ibid., August 10, 1963.
13. Hoover to Mardikian, September 26, 1963, HP-PPI.
14. Hoover to Mrs. Joseph Kennedy, September 26, 1963, ibid.
15. Mr. and Mrs. William I. Nichols oral history, Hoover Presidential Library.
16. Felix Morley oral history, ibid.
17. Hoover to Kelland, November 6, 1963, Kelland Papers.
18. *New York Times*, November 23, 1963.
19. Ibid., December 9, 1963.
20. Hoover to Hulda McLean, December 10, 1963, Hulda Hoover McLean Papers, Hoover Presidential Library.
21. *New York Times*, December 28, 1963.
22. Wedemeyer to Kelland, February 5, 1963, Kelland Papers.
23. Memorandum in Nixon file, HP-PPI.
24. *New York Times*, February 28, 1964.
25. *Congressional Record*, March 24, 1964, pp. 5942–949.
26. Hoover to Gubser, April 5, 1964, HP-PPI.
27. Hoover to Fellers, April 18, 1964, ibid.

28. Draft letter to Knowland in Goldwater file, ibid.

29. Ibid; see also Ray Henle comments in Jeremiah Milbank, Jr., oral history, Hoover Presidential Library.

30. Jeremiah Milbank, Jr., oral history, Hoover Presidential Library; Goldwater to Hoover, May 28, 1964, HP-PPI.

31. Hoover to Dirksen, June 23, 1964, HP-PPI.

32. Public statements, 1964, Hoover Papers.

33. *New York Times*, July 14, 1964.

34. Note dated July 16, 1964, in Goldwater file, HP-PPI.

35. Hoover to Goldwater, telegram, July 16, 1964, and letter, July 22, 1964, ibid.

36. *New York Times*, August 9, 1964.

37. Bonner Fellers oral history, Hoover Presidential Library.

38. *New York Times*, August 9, 1964.

39. Ibid., August 10, 1964.

40. Ibid., August 17, 1964.

41. See "Nobel Peace Prize" folder, HP-PPS.

42. Ben Moreel oral history, Hoover Presidential Library.

43. Joseph F. Binns oral history, ibid.

44. Neil McNeil oral history, ibid.

45. Goldwater to Hoover, October 3, 1964, HP-PPI.

46. *New York Times*, October 19, 1964.

47. Ibid., October 23, 1964.

48. Ibid., October 24, 1964.

49. Ibid., October 26, 1964.

50. Allan Hoover to the author, May 5, 1980.

Sources

No scholarly biography has yet been written that deals comprehensively with Hoover's postpresidential years. The best biography, David Burner, *Herbert Hoover: A Public Life* (New York, 1979), deals with the period 1933–1964 in a sixteen-page epilogue. Joan Hoff Wilson, *Herbert Hoover: Forgotten Progressive* (Boston, 1975), furnishes a useful introduction to the postpresidential period in some seventy pages. A series of seminars dealing with Hoover's career was sponsored by the Hoover Presidential Library Association during the centennial year of 1974, but the papers for the session dealing with the postpresidential years are disappointing. At the instance of Senator Mark O. Hatfield, approximately thirty essays were written to commemorate the fiftieth anniversary of Hoover's inauguration as president. These appeared first in *Congressional Record* and are now available in *Herbert Hoover Reassessed*, U.S. Senate Document No. 96–63 (Washington, D.C., 1981). Several of these essays deal with the postpresidential years and offer valuable insights. As yet, only a few published articles deal with Hoover's postpresidential years, while general works on the period and biographies of other figures influential during these years are of little use for a study of Hoover. Research for this work, therefore, has relied primarily on manuscript sources, oral histories, and interviews.

MANUSCRIPT COLLECTIONS

Herbert Hoover Presidential Library, West Branch, Iowa

Arthur Ballantine Papers
William R. Castle Papers

Allan Hoover Papers
Clarence B. Kelland Papers

Nathan MacChesney Papers
Raymond Moley Papers
Felix Morley Papers
Edgar Rickard Diary
Edgar Rickard Papers

Harrison Spangler Papers
Charles Teague Papers
William Hallam Tuck Papers
Hugh Wilson Papers
Robert E. Wood Papers

Hoover Institution on War, Revolution and Peace, Stanford, California

George Akerson Papers
Ben S. Allen Papers
Citizens Committee for the Hoover
    Report Papers
Arch Coleman Papers
Famine Emergency Committee Papers
First Aid for Hungary Papers
Perrin C. Galpin Papers
Hugh Gibson Papers
Herbert Hoover Papers

Edward Eyre Hunt Papers
Will Irwin Papers
Julius Klein Papers
May Hoover Leavitt Papers
Hulda Hoover McLean Papers
William Starr Myers Diary
National Committee, Food for the
    Small Democracies Papers
Mark Sullivan Papers
Ray Lyman Wilbur Papers

Kansas Historical Society, Topeka, Kansas

Arthur Capper Papers
Alf M. Landon Papers

Charles Scott Papers

Library of Congress

William Borah Papers
Raymond Clapper Papers
Henry P. Fletcher Papers
Frank Knox Papers
Charles McNary Papers

Ogden Mills Papers
John Callan O'Laughlin Papers
Everett Sanders Papers
Robert A. Taft Papers
William Allen White Papers

Northeast Missouri State University

Glenn Frank Papers

Ohio Historical Center, Columbus, Ohio

John Bricker Papers
Clarence Brown Papers

Walter Brown Papers
John Vorys Papers

Republican National Headquarters, Washington, D.C.

Republican National Committee
    Minutes

University of Vermont

Warren Austin Papers   John Spargo Papers

In addition to manuscript collections, the following unpublished sources were used.

ORAL HISTORIES

Hoover Presidential Library

Richard E. Berlin   Frank E. Mason
Joseph F. Binns   Jeremiah Milbank, Jr.
Herbert Brownell   Ben Moreel
Thomas E. Dewey   William I. Nichols
Bonner Fellers   James P. Selvage
Joseph C. Green   Walter Trohan
John D. M. Hamilton   Albert C. Wedemeyer
Neil McNeil

Columbia University Oral History Collection

Harvey H. Bundy   James W. Wadsworth
H. Alexander Smith

INTERVIEWS

John Bricker   Clare Boothe Luce
Alf M. Landon   Samuel Pryor

CORRESPONDENCE

Allan Hoover   Felix Morley

Published sources that proved useful are cited in the notes.

Index